Tokugawa Ieyasu:
SHOGUN

Tokugawa Ieyasu: SHOGUN

a biography by Conrad Totman

Heian

ISBN #089346-210-1

First Printing 1983
Second Printing 1990
Third Printing 1998

Heian International Inc.
1815 West 205th Street
Suite #301
Torrance, CA. 90501

e-mail: heianemail@heian.com
web site: www.heian.com

Printed in Singapore

DEDICATION

To Al and Tony and my other comrades of
the Iron Triangle and points south.

TABLE OF CONTENTS

MAPS ix

A CHRONOLOGY xiii

PART ONE:
THE FIFTH YEAR OF KEICHŌ (1600) 1

    I. Rumors of War--A Legacy Founders 3
    II. Interlude--A "Brabbling Japon" Meets Some
        "Red-hairs" 14
    III. Voices of War, Old and New 20
    IV. Working Heaven's Will--The Ways of
        Young Men and Old 32
    V. Bedroom Politics--The Thinking Man's Choice 40
    VI. The Art of Military Investment 52
    VII. Deployment for War--Principles, Preparation,
        and Payoff 61
    VIII. Sekigahara--War as Politics 71
    IX. Making Peace--Politics as War 79

PART TWO:
THE SIXTEENTH YEAR OF KEICHŌ (1611) 89

    X. Routines of the New Year 91
    XI. Returns from New Connections 101
    XII. The King-Maker at Work 109
    XIII. Establishing the Way--Utilitarian and Universal 118

PART THREE:
THE NINETEENTH YEAR OF KEICHŌ (1614) 127

    XIV. The Stench of Sedition 129
    XV. Of Children and Courtiers 141
    XVI. The Quest for Eternal Order 146
    XVII. Crisis in the Established Order 151

PART FOUR:
THE FIRST YEAR OF GEN'NA (1615) 159

XVIII.   Rituals and Reckonings of the New Year 161
  XIX.   Hideyori Confronted 164
   XX.   Hideyori Confounded 174
  XXI.   Ordering the Realm 179
 XXII.   Last Flight of the Falcon 182

APPENDICES:
       Ieyasu's Offspring 191
       Ieyasu's Chinese References 192
       Source Citations 193
       Acknowledgments 195
       Map Acknowledgments 197
       Further Reading 199

INDEX 203

MAPS

1. Japan . . . . Inside Cover
2. Hideyoshi in Korea   5
3. Some Notable Daimyo Domains: 1560s to 1590s   9
4. The *Liefde*'s Voyage 15
5. Approaches to Aizu 22
6. The Tōkai Region 24
7. Provinces Mentioned in the Text 43
8. Kantō Locations 53
9. Hidetada's Route West (Gifu Area Inset) 73
10. Sekigahara 76
11. The Izu Vicinity 96
12. East and Southeast Asia 102
13. Kyoto 110
14. Edo 114
15. The Osaka Area 168

INTRODUCTION

An oft-repeated saying in Japan goes like this: When asked what he would do if a cuckoo refused to sing for him, Oda Nobunaga replied, "I would wring its neck." Toyotomi Hideyoshi replied, "I would force it to sing." Tokugawa Ieyasu replied, "I would wait for it to sing."

These three responses are supposed to reveal the differences in character of the three men who dominated Japan's political life between 1570 and 1615. Seizing power one after another, they gradually imposed peace and order on a country that had been torn by recurrent civil war for over a century. Nobunaga faced the most chaotic situation; Ieyasu, the least. Their policies--neck-wringing as against waiting--reflected the differences in their situations.

Building on the harsh triumphs of his two predecessors, Ieyasu founded a dynasty that kept the peace in Japan until 1867. He and his successors exercised dictatorial authority as hereditary shogun to rule one of the largest and most dynamic societies of their day. The values and organizational patterns of those peaceful centuries are still evident in Japan today, and the historic events that produced the peace are recounted in books, on stage, and on movie screens and television sets across the land. This book will introduce Ieyasu, his age, and his society to those who may be curious about the history of Japan.

A note on names: Japanese names are given in the normal Japanese order, family name first: e.g., Toyotomi Hideyori, whom we might refer to as Hideyori of the Toyotomi family.

A note on dates: The dates in this book are according to the Japanese calendar. For the sake of readability I have imposed Western yearly and monthly names on them. Thus, I write January 1, 1600, instead of "the first day of the first month of the fifth year of the Keichō era." In fact, however, the dates of the Gregorian calendar do not coincide with those of the old Japanese calendar: January first in this book is not January first, Gregorian. Depending on the year, it is actually a date between approximately November tenth and December tenth. Since the routines of Ieyasu's life were bound to his calendar, I have adhered to the Japanese dating to keep the logic of his life's rhythms clear.

But enough. Ieyasu believed that the record would speak for itself.

Inokashira, October, 1981

A CHRONOLOGY

About 300 AD	Start of reliable genealogy of Japanese Imperial lineage
604	Prince Shōtoku's 17-article constitution
646	Taika Reform
749	Erection of Great Buddha at Nara
8th century	Kegon and Hossō sects of Buddhism flourish
10th century	Imperial line secure in title; Fujiwara family *(kuge)* preeminent; Shingon and Tendai sects flourish
ca. 1000	*Genji Monogatari* written
12th century	Military families *(buke)* influential
1160s-1170s	Taira Kiyomori powerful
1180s	Minamoto Yoritomo powerful
1192	Yoritomo appointed *seii taishōgun* by Emperor and maintains shogunate in Kamakura
13th century	Hōjō family powerful; *Azuma kagami* written; Zen and Jōdo sects flourish; Lotus sect arises
1330s	Ashikaga shogunate established in Kyoto
1400s	Matsudaira family arises in Mikawa Province; Nō drama develops
1542 Dec. 26	Tokugawa Ieyasu (Matsudaira Takechiyo) born in Okazaki
1543	Portuguese land on Tanegashima
1547	Ieyasu captured by Oda Nobuhide
1549	Ieyasu goes to Sumpu as hostage of Imagawa Yoshimoto
1555	Ieyasu takes the name Motonobu
1557	Ieyasu marries Tsukiyama
1558	Ieyasu goes on his first sortie; takes the name Motoyasu
1560	Imagawa Yoshimoto killed in battle; Ieyasu reclaims Okazaki
1561-62	Ieyasu becomes allied with Oda Nobunaga
1563	Ieyasu changes names from Motonobu to Ieyasu; quells Ikkō sect in Mikawa
1566	Ieyasu titled Governor of Mikawa; named Tokugawa

1570	Ieyasu moves headquarters to Hamamatsu
1571	Oda Nobunaga destroys Mt. Hiei monastery
1572	Takeda Shingen nearly destroys Ieyasu at Mikatagahara
1573	Shogun Ashikaga Yoshiaki driven from Kyoto by Nobunaga; Takeda Shingen dies
1575	Battle of Nagashino
1579	Ieyasu has Tsukiyama murdered and Nobuyasu commit suicide
1580s	Beginning of Spanish challenge to Portuguese monopoly of missionary work in Japan
1581	Ieyasu captures Takatenjin fortress
1582	Ieyasu and Nobunaga seize Takeda domain; Nobunaga murdered and Toyotomi Hideyoshi succeeds him
1582-83	Ieyasu and Odawara Hōjō become allies
1584	Ieyasu and Hideyoshi maneuver; battles of Komaki and Nagakute; Hideyoshi adopts Ieyasu's son, Hideyasu
1585	Hideyoshi appointed *kanpaku*
1586	Ieyasu visits Hideyoshi at Osaka and later marries Asahihime; Ieyasu moves headquarters to Sumpu
1587	Hideyoshi subdues Kyushu; orders Jesuits expelled; builds great Buddha at Hōkōji
1588	Ieyasu swears loyalty to Hideyoshi; Hideyoshi orders Hōjō to submit
1590	Asahihime dies; Hideyoshi destroys Hōjō at Odawara; Ieyasu moves headquarters to Edo
1592	Hideyoshi launches Korean campaign
1593	Truce in Korea; Ieyasu meets Fujiwara Seika in Kyushu; Toyotomi Hideyori born
1596	Fushimi earthquake; Hideyoshi renews war in Korea; Keichō year-period begins; Hideyoshi suppresses some Christian activity
1598	Hideyoshi dies; Korean expedition recalled; Ieyasu has Chinese books published
1599	Ieyasu confines Ishida Mitsunari; moves into Osaka castle; daimyo prepare for war
1600 Jan.	Hideyori and Ieyasu greet daimyo at Osaka Castle
Feb.	Ieyasu orders *Jōgan seiyō* published
Mar.	Ieyasu interrogates *Liefde* officers, including Will Adams
Jun. 6	Ieyasu issues deployment orders against Aizu
16	Ieyasu leaves Osaka for Edo

Jul.	2	Ieyasu reaches Edo
	21	Ieyasu leaves Edo for Aizu investment
Aug.	4	Ieyasu leaves Oyama for Edo
Sep.	1	Ieyasu leaves Edo for Osaka
		Hidetada at Karuizawa
	15	Battle of Sekigahara
		Hidetada in Kiso River valley
	27	Ieyasu and Hidetada enter Osaka Castle
Oct.	10	Ieyasu reduces domain of Mōri family

1601   Ieyasu seeks foreign trade; orders a mint set up
in Fushimi and pack horse system established on
Tōkaidō; transfers Uesugi Kagekatsu to Yonezawa; issues regulations to Mt. Kōya monastery;
fire destroys Edo

1602   Ieyasu orders Nijō Castle built; Odai no Kata
dies; Hideyori commences Hōkōji reconstruction

1603   Ieyasu named *seii taishōgun;* licenses shipping
service on Yodo River; Hideyori marries Senhime; Korean delegation negotiates release of
prisoners of war; Okuni introduces her *kabuki*
to Kyoto

1604   Bakufu establishes rest stops and plants trees
along Tōkaidō; reports circulate of missionary-
daimyo collusion

1605   Hidetada named shogun while in Kyoto with
100,000 men; Ieyasu meets Hayashi Razan; has
Azuma kagami published; orders Edo Castle
greatly expanded; protests missionary activity;
invites Dutch in Malaya to trade with Japan

1606   Ieyasu arranges Sumpu residence

1607   Ieyasu moves to Sumpu to live; prohibits *junshi;*
Korean delegation completes prisoner of war
settlement; Ieyasu's new Sumpu residence burns
down

1608   Ieyasu expels *onna kabuki* from Sumpu; issues
regulations to Mt. Hiei monastery

1609   Ieyasu orders Nagoya Castle built; Shimazu
armies overrun Ryukyus; a Dutch trading vessel
reaches Japan; men of the daimyo Arima clash
with Portuguese

1610   Gangs maraud in Edo; Hideyori and Yodo solicit
support from Maeda; Hideyori resumes construction at Hōkōji

1611   Ieyasu goes to Kyoto with 50,000 men; issues
3-clause code for daimyo; orders Takasegawa
dug; negotiates several foreign trading agree-

	ments; hears lectures on Shingon; indicates Iemitsu to be shogun after Hidetada; has Tokugawa ancestry in Kōzuke Province verified; Emperor Go Mizunoō succeeds Goyōzei
1612	Arima accused of plotting with Christians; Ieyasu prohibits Christian activity in key political centers
1613	Ōkubo Nagayasu dies; his corruption revealed; Ieyasu licenses trade with English ship; issues a 5-clause code for the Court; Ōkubo Tadachika crisis erupts; Ieyasu orders missionaries expelled
1614	About 100 missionaries and their assistants deported; Ieyasu hears lectures on Tendai, Shingon, Zen, Hossō, Kegon
Jul.	Ieyasu criticizes Hideyori's procedures for Hōkō-ji dedication
Aug.	Ieyasu asks why Hideyori is assembling *rōnin*
Oct. 1	Ieyasu orders daimyo to mobilize against Hideyori
11	Ieyasu marches west
Nov. 29	first assault on Osaka Castle
Dec. 22	Ieyasu and Hideyori agree on terms of settlement
1615 Jan. 3	Ieyasu leaves Nijō Castle for Sumpu
Feb. 14	Ieyasu reaches Sumpu
Mar.	Ieyasu orders Razan to publish *Daizō Ichiranshū*
Apr. 4	Ieyasu leaves Sumpu for Nagoya
5	Ieyasu orders daimyo to mobilize again
May 5	Ieyasu leads forces from Kyoto to Osaka
8	Osaka Castle falls; Yodo and Hideyori commit suicide; Senhime saved
summer	Ieyasu hears lectures on Tendai, Shingon, Jōdo
Jul. 7	*Buke shohatto* issued
13	Gen'na year-period begins
17	*Kinchū narabi ni kuge shohatto* issued
Jul-Aug.	Codes for temples and shrines issued
Aug. 4	Ieyasu leaves Kyoto for Sumpu
Aug. 5-8	Ieyasu and Razan discuss *Analects of Confucius*
23	Ieyasu reaches Sumpu
1616 Jan. 19	Ieyasu orders Razan and Ishin Sūden to publish *Gunsho Chiyō*
21	Ieyasu falls ill
Apr. 2	Ieyasu orders Sūden to prepare for his funeral
11	Ieyasu orders Razan to compile *Sumpuki*
17	Ieyasu dies
	Ieyasu named Tōshō Daigongen

PART I

THE FIFTH YEAR OF KEICHŌ (1600)

CHAPTER I:

Rumors of War--A Legacy Founders

The New Year's rituals proceeded properly on the first day of the fifth year of Keichō (1600). Those daimyo, feudal lords, who were in Osaka at the time went first to the main enciente of Osaka castle to extend the season's greetings to their lord, Toyotomi Hideyori. Then they passed through a massive fortified gate and descended a steep slope to the western enciente to call upon Tokugawa Icyasu, acting regent to the six-year-old Hideyori.

The daimyo proceeded in the established manner, riding in palanquins, surrounded by appropriate attendants, and attired in the wing-shouldered dress of classic Court Ceremony. As the lord's retinue reached the entry-way, it halted and the porters set the palanquin down. The lord's sandals were placed at the proper angle beside it. The flap-door was raised and the lord uncoiled himself and stood up. Attendants smoothed his clothes, and the herald announced his presence. Castle attendants bowed him in. He left his sandals at the base of the raised entry-way as he stepped up to a wooden floor that glowed from the ceaseless polishing of soft footwear. Escorts led him along corridors threading the labyrinthine castle residence. While he progressed toward this ceremonial greeting, the attendants moved to a rest area to await his return.

The ritual greetings went well enough: everyone stood, knelt and bowed in the proper manner and uttered the correct phrases. Beyond the world of ritual, however, little was going well. Some lords were preparing for war. Others were expecting it, some with keen anticipation, some with much foreboding.

These men were hardly strangers to war. Yet by 1600, civil war seemed to be a thing of the past. Early in 1591, Toyotomi Hideyoshi, father of Hideyori, had subdued the last stubborn daimyo. For the subsequent nine years Japan had no more civil wars.

Japan was involved in foreign war. In a remarkable departure from the country's tradition of insularity, Hideyoshi, or the Taikō (retired regent), undertook the conquest of Korea and China. He had considered such a venture since at least 1587. At that time he was overwhelming the last of the great lords on Kyushu, Japan's southernmost island. In a letter to his wife, after summing up those accomplishments, he wrote:

I have sent fast ships in order to urge even Korea to pay homage to the Emperor of Japan, stating that, if it does not, I shall conquer it next year. I shall take even China in hand, and have control of it during my lifetime; since [China] has become disdainful [of Japan], the work will be the more exhausting.

The thought of that exhaustion evidently gave him pause, for he added:

After the last battle I feel older than I am; more and more white hairs have grown and I cannot pluck them out. I am very ashamed to be seen by anyone; only you will be tolerant of this, but I still complain.

In 1591, with the end of civil strife in sight, Hideyoshi turned his thoughts to greater things. He ordered the construction of a great ship that would carry him in glory to China. Measuring over 33 meters in length and 11 meters in width, it had two decks above the hull and was propelled by a great cross-sail mounted amidship. Besides this, rows of 60 oarsmen lined each side of the vessel from bow to stern. He christened the ship *Nihonmaru*.

In the following year, after subjugation of all the daimyo, Hideyoshi was able to begin his grand enterprise. He ordered lords in western Japan to mobilize their forces, and during the year they deployed perhaps 150,000 men to Korea. Initially the army surged northward from Pusan, blazing a trail that American soldiers would follow some 260 years later. They drove through southern Korea to Seoul and on to Kaesong. From there, forces under Konishi Yukinaga drove northwestward up to Pyongyang. Others under Katō Kiyomasa headed northeastward past the area known recently to Americans as the Iron Triangle and on over the mountains to north of Wonsan on the east coast. There the advance stalled, and soon the armies retreated southward amidst savage fighting and with heavy losses.

Three factors combined to thwart the venture. First, a Korean admiral, Yi Sunsin, used armored ships and supporting vessels equipped with cannon and incendiary missiles to disrupt Hideyoshi's supply line and create shortages of men and material for the expeditionary force. Second, after their initial reverses, the Koreans effectively resisted by combining guerrilla tactics with set-piece confrontations. Third, Chinese forces intervened in over-

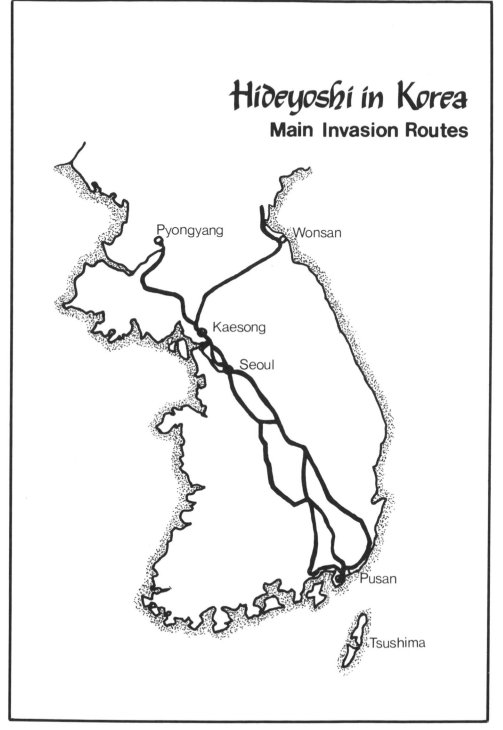

Hideyoshi in Korea
Main Invasion Routes

Pyongyang

Wonsan

Kaesong

Seoul

Pusan

Tsushima

whelming numbers. After a year the Japanese armies withdrew, leaving only a garrison holding a perimeter around Pusan. Konishi and another commander named Ishida Mitsunari escorted Chinese negotiators to the Taikō's camp in western Japan, and a truce was arranged late in 1593.

During the next two years Hideyoshi was occupied with domestic matters, most notably the construction of an immense castle at Fushimi, south of Kyoto. He was also becoming notorious for uncontrollable fits of rage mixed with moments of inexplicable generosity. During 1595, despite the protestations of Ieyasu and other advisors, he slaughtered his adopted heir, Hidetsugu, and Hidetsugu's wife, consorts, and children, a total of thirty people. He did this so that his two-year-old son Hideyori could become his unrivaled heir.

This savage act was the first appalling evidence that the Taikō was losing his judgment and perhaps his sanity. He was also losing his health: By late in the year he was so ill that those around him feared for his life. He recovered, however, as Ieyasu reported in a letter to Natsuka Masaie, an advisor of Hideyoshi, in January 1596:

> *The Taikō is much better, according to notes from his doctor and ladies-in-waiting that I have seen. Truly this is the best news one could want, so I have let you know promptly. We shall talk when we meet.*

Despite this improvement in Hideyoshi's health, the new year brought more evidence that all was not well in the realm. That summer the Kyoto region was rocked by the Great Fushimi Earthquake. The damage was immense, with fires devouring what shocks had failed to ruin. For Hideyoshi, one of the most painful losses was a temple named Hōkōji, a great religious monument in Kyoto. Just ten years earlier he had it built to house a huge sixty foot wooden statue of Buddha. Was its destruction, people wondered, another sign of godly anger or the frowning will of Heaven? Such murmurings multiplied a month later when a typhoon battered central Japan with torrential rains, flooding, and high winds. The months of unnerving aftershocks that followed the Fushimi quake doubtless kept Hideyoshi on edge, lest his fine new castle also be ruined and his precious baby boy killed.

In September of 1596, some forty-five days after the great quake, another Chinese delegation arrived to negotiate a peace treaty. The Taikō had previously spelled out a series of conditions for peace that included the ceding of part of Korea to Japan. The delegates did not know this, and they proceeded on the assumption that he would be pleased to have the Chinese emperor crown him King of Japan. He interpreted their offer as an expression of Chinese disdain and indifference to his earlier proposal. His response was a raging denunciation and an order to renew warfare in Korea, again despite the protests of Ieyasu and others.

Then two and a half months later in yet another gesture of cruel anger, he ordered seven Franciscan missionaries and nineteen converts mutilated, paraded through major cities, and then crucified in Nagasaki. Perhaps he saw his own rages as evidence of his deteriorating faculties, because he decided to have his three-year-old son pronounced an adult. In December, the child received the adult name of Hideyori, a samurai-style haircut, and full ceremonial Court dress. Hoping to perpetuate his family's primacy, Hideyoshi repeatedly compelled the major daimyo to swear allegiance to the child.

His armies returned to Korea where they became bogged down in indecisive and costly fighting. Everything seemed to be going wrong, and at the age of sixty-two Hideyoshi's years were showing. He had taken to wearing a hat to cover his balding head, but the white still showed on his temples. His gaunt face grew ever more emaciated, and the skin stretched tight over his high cheek bones; the wispy beard and mustache did little to conceal the decay. The furrows that lined his brow deepened, and his eyes seemed sunken. In the spring of 1589 he sickened suddenly. Again, he had the lords swear their loyalty to Hideyori. Fearing that death was near, he designated Ieyasu and four other major daimyo as the Five Elders, while five lesser lords were titled the Five Ministers. He died before dawn on August 18, 1598, and with his passing, the fate of the nation lay in the combined hands of the Elders and Ministers.

Hideyoshi's illness and death robbed the realm of its one acknowledged leader. No one else could command the allegiance of the great lords, either those in Japan or those leading armies in Korea. Aware that their authority was tenuous, the new leaders tried to postpone crisis by keeping the Taikō's death a secret. The deception actually began before he died. On July 14, even as Hideyoshi was failing fast, Ieyasu wrote a daimyo named Asano, assuring him that, "Our lord is much improved, which is cause for rejoicing."

After his death the Elders sent out orders from the "ill but recovering" Hideyoshi that recalled the bogged-down armies from Korea. For two months correspondence with commanders in the field maintained the fiction that Hideyoshi was still in control. Despite sharp disagreements over this reversal of foreign policy, the whole plan of conquest was abandoned. Instead, an old question had suddenly been revived: who would rule Japan? The prospect for a peaceful resolution of that question was not enhanced by the return of large armies of frustrated men and battle-hardened officers who were more accustomed to war than peace.

The issue of supremacy quickly pitted the new leaders against one another. From the outset Ieyasu had enjoyed a preeminent position among them. He had been one of Hideyoshi's most trusted and talented lieutenants. On his deathbed the Taikō had singled him out for praise as one deserving to be heeded by others. More to the point, Ieyasu possessed the largest domain and the most powerful army in Japan. His domain covered the vast Kantō Plain, which sprawls along the outer side of the crook where Honshu, the main island, turns northward near modern Tokyo. From that broad agricultural basin, Ieyasu's armies could blockade and intimidate any force to the north. A relatively short march westward could put him in position to menace any baron situated in the central plains around the cities of Kyoto and Osaka. Before a baron to the west could threaten Ieyasu in his Kantō fastness, however, he would first have to pass the mountain barrier at Hakone and the great frontier fortress at Odawara. Or he would have to trek through the tortuous river valleys of the convoluted ranges of central Honshu and break out of the treacherous defiles of Kai and Kōzuke Provinces north of Mt. Fuji, all of which were faced by frontier fortresses under command of Ieyasu's best lieutenants.

Following the Taikō's death, Ieyasu's thinking focused not on these military considerations of march and countermarch but on the civil-political processes of diplomacy and management. He hoped to take Hideyoshi's place with a minimum of fuss. Trying to work with the other lords, he maneuvered as best he could to settle quarrels as they broke out and retain the support of as many daimyo as possible. He stayed in Fushimi for well over a year even though young Hideyori moved to Osaka Castle forty kilometers to the southwest in January, 1599. Ieyasu's old friend and ally, Maeda Toshiie, went there with Hideyori and served as regent while Ieyasu supervised general affairs from Fushimi.

Eschewing the safety of Fushimi Castle, Ieyasu continued to stay at his lightly-guarded mansion, despite growing acrimony and the proliferation of rumors and plots. Even before Hideyoshi died, it had been obvious that his passing might lead to a power struggle. The day after his death, rumors promptly appeared accusing Ishida Mitsunari, one of the Five Ministers, of plotting Ieyasu's assassination. Thereupon Ieyasu dispatched his mature son and heir apparent, Hidetada, back east to his headquarters-castle at Edo. Ieyasu, a prudent man, wanted to be sure that a reliable commander was in charge of his legions of samurai, should they be needed in a hurry. He preferred political maneuvering to armed conflict, however. After all, he was nearly in a dominant position, and there was less risk of losing everything in a game of diplomacy than there

8

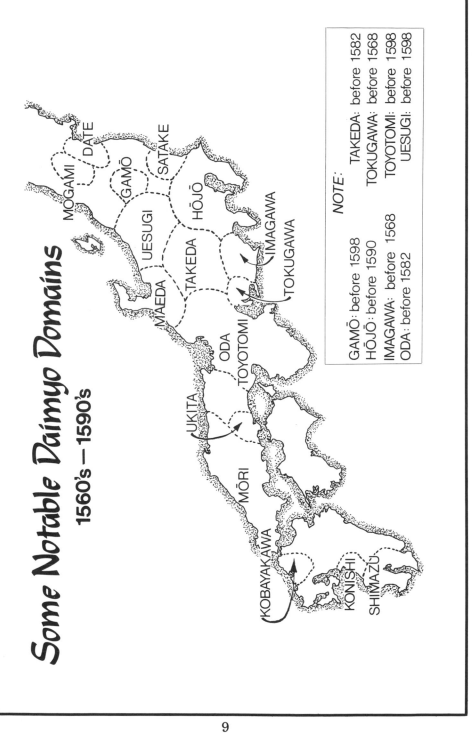

Some Notable Daimyo Domains
1560's — 1590's

MOGAMI
DATE
GAMŌ
SATAKE
UESUGI
HŌJŌ
MAEDA
TAKEDA
IMAGAWA
ODA
TOYOTOMI
TOKUGAWA
UKITA
MŌRI
KOBAYAKAWA
KONISHI
SHIMAZU

NOTE:

GAMŌ: before 1598
HŌJŌ: before 1590
IMAGAWA: before 1568
ODA: before 1582

TAKEDA: before 1582
TOKUGAWA: before 1568
TOYOTOMI: before 1598
UESUGI: before 1598

was in a test of arms.

Versions differ as to how the struggle developed. One version states that within hours of Hideyoshi's death Mitsunari revealed that he was the lord who most resented Ieyasu's favored position. He had been a shrewd intimate of the Taikō, but he was inordinately ambitious and lamentably loose-tongued--an unfortunate combination of traits. He was soon denouncing Ieyasu for alleged power-plays, and when nothing came of that he hatched two plots to have him murdered. An attempt in the early days of 1599 misfired because Ieyasu was not sleeping where the assassin expected him to be. Two months later Mitsunari formulated another plot but failed to carry it through. When some of the most powerful lords learned of Mitsunari's schemes, they set out to seize and kill him. In desperation he fled to Ieyasu for protection, no one else being powerful enough to provide it. Ieyasu, well aware of Mitsunari's machinations, was dismayed by the deteriorating state of affairs. Recalling, perhaps, one of his favorite maxims from Lao Tsu: "Requite malice with kindness," or hoping to reduce the tension while converting this gifted but impetuous man into a useful ally, he gave Ishida the protection he sought. Despite the protests of those who wanted Mitsunari dead, he ordered him escorted safely to house arrest in his modest castle at Sawayama, northeast of Kyoto.

The other version claims that after Hideyoshi's death, Ieyasu wanted to exploit the antagonism that had been growing for years between Ishida and the great lords. Old Maeda Toshiie had restrained him, but with Maeda's death Ieyasu and Ishida allied themselves against the lords. In this version, the reports of Ishida's plots and the lords' move to kill him are later fabrications designed to conceal Ieyasu's ruthless ambition.

One suspects that the truth lies somewhere between these two stories; namely, that Ishida became suspect, that Maeda's death seemed to leave him vulnerable, that he tried to strengthen his position by seeking Ieyasu's goodwill, and that Ieyasu, living up to his reputation as a cunning "old badger," recognized that he could turn these developments to advantage.

Ieyasu may well have assumed that Mitsunari, given his limited military power, had more potential value alive than dead. Ieyasu's willingness, however, to defy respected lords while protecting a man they distrusted disturbed his fellow Elders. It seemed plausible that Ieyasu was hoping Mitsunari would stir up something he could exploit so as to rivet Tokugawa control even more securely on Japan. In any case, there was growing suspicion that the Kantō chieftain was intent on ruling regardless of the advice of others. Ieyasu's decision, nine days after Mitsunari's arrest, to move from his vulnerable mansion into Fushimi Castle, reinforced this suspicion.

Even before that move, when the great lords demanded, politely, that Ieyasu tell them the whereabouts of Ishida, Ieyasu had replied, in an equally polite but decisive manner, "As I instructed, he has come here. If there are any changes, I shall inform you." Four days later he notified them, "I have decided to place Ishida in house arrest at Sawayama. He is to go tomorrow. Last night his son arrived here [to stay as a hostage]." Whatever led Ishida to Fushimi, Ieyasu had manipulated the situation to establish that he was both protector and captor of the Sawayama lord.

Ieyasu's scholarly activities reflected his line of thought. Having developed a considerable respect for Confucian writings on government, he ordered the reproduction of selected Confucian texts during May of 1599. The ones he called for were a set of collected writings about Confucius himself, a trilogy of essays on military strategy, and a group of six essays on civil and military techniques designed to help rulers keep the realm at peace. There were other works devoted to battlefield tactics that he could have studied, had that been his primary concern, but his interest in military matters was secondary to his interest in politics. The military served only as one means to a civil-political end. Seeing himself as charged with keeping the peace, these were the works he wished to have published, especially during those months of escalating tension and preparation for war.

In following months many of the major lords left town with Ieyasu's blessings and returned to their castles. After Maeda Toshiie died, his son, Toshinaga, became daimyo and returned to his castle at Kanazawa. That left Hideyori without a proper regent. So in the fall of 1599, as rumors of war reached his ears and a plot to assassinate him was uncovered, Ieyasu moved with his escort battalions down to Osaka to be near his youthful lord. He stayed at a heavily guarded mansion for several days and then moved into the western enceinte of the immense castle. There he would be safe while he demonstrated his determination to protect Hideyori and make sure that no other daimyo could claim a protector's role or consort with him secretly.

In other ways Ieyasu reinforced the suspicion that he intended to take the Taikō's place. Most notably he began cultivating closer ties with the Imperial Court, sending ceremonial gifts and exchanging ritual visits signifying his benevolent concern for the Emperor and his followers. At that time the Emperor was a twenty-eight-year-old man named Goyōzei. He lived with his attendants in his palace in Kyoto, a few kilometers north of Fushimi. Goyōzei had no armies and no domain. He functioned essentially as a ceremonial figure who awarded daimyo titles that were commensurate with their power. Until Hideyoshi died, Goyōzei had granted the awards he had recommended, and in return the Taikō had assured the courtiers enough income to live comfortably. By cultivating the Court, Ieyasu sought to make it clear that Court officials should consult no one but himself about affairs of state. In return he would see that the Emperor and his friends lived comfortably.

By late 1599 Ieyasu had in fact replaced Hideyoshi. He was running affairs from Osaka while Mitsunari sulked and schemed in Sawayama. The daimyo watched with apprehension mixed with hope as rumors and reports of plots and schemes continued to fly about the country. Among these watchful barons, one of the most covetous of Ieyasu's domain was Uesugi Kagekatsu. A few months before Hideyoshi's death, Kagekatsu had been transferred to a large domain around a castle at Aizu, deep in a mountain valley north of the Kantō plain. There he found his southern flank barricaded by Ieyasu's perimeter fortresses. It was a situation unlikely to foster neighborliness.

At the time of Hideyoshi's death, Kagekatsu was at his castle in Aizu, a consideration that probably crossed Ieyasu's mind when he ordered his son Hidetada posthaste to Edo. Kagekatsu remained calm, however, and went to Kyoto, hoping to carve out a larger role by peaceful means. Ieyasu welcomed him and had him named to the Council of Five Elders. As the months passed, however, Kagekatsu's influence dwindled even as Ieyasu's grew, and in August of 1599 he went home again. Soon thereafter Ieyasu began hearing of the vigor with which Kagekatsu was strengthening his bastion at Aizu and getting his army ready for action.

The news of Kagekatsu's activity did not alarm Ieyasu. It did not come as a surprise, and despite the size and proximity to Edo of the Uesugi domain, Kagekatsu alone was no major threat to the Tokugawa position. The emergence of a hostile coalition could pose a problem, but Kagekatsu in the wilds of Aizu was poorly situated to head a coalition. Instead Mitsunari at Sawayama was the obvious key to such a development. Accordingly, Ieyasu chose to stay in Osaka Castle with Hideyori, to prevent Mitsunari from seizing the boy and claiming to be his protector. At Osaka, moreover, Ieyasu was close to the center of activity, where he could continue cultivating his own alliances and keep himself better informed. Osaka was near enough to Kyoto to discourage Mitsunari from trying to seize that city and ideally situated if a sudden strike at Sawayama seemed necessary.

By the end of 1599, then, the Elders and Ministers were no longer cooperating on behalf of the boy, Hideyori. Four of the Five Elders had packed up and gone home to the security of their own mighty castles, where at least one was preparing to do battle with Ieyasu. Two of the Ministers had ceased to participate in affairs after a third, Ishida, had been escorted into domiciliary confinement in Sawayama, allegedly for plotting Ieyasu's death. At the age of fifty-nine, the Tokugawa lord had emerged as the dominant figure in Japan, to the considerable dissatisfaction of a number of barons.

Due to this chain of events, on New Year's of 1600 Ieyasu was in the western enceinte of Osaka Castle acting as Hideyori's regent and greeting his guests. A few days later he was host to the lords at a Nō theatrical presentation and an elegant banquet.

During the next five weeks, Ieyasu managed a variety of minor matters. He ordered the printing of copies of *Jōgan seiyō*, a famous seventh-century Chinese Confucian text on the art of good government. It is believed to be based on lectures delivered to his retainers by T'ai Tsung, the exceptionally gifted second emperor of the T'ang dynasty, who consolidated the new regime around 600 AD. The printing was executed by Ieyasu's friends, the scholar and Zen monk, Kanshitsu Genkitsu, who had done his publishing work during the preceding summer, and Saishō Shōda, the abbot of the great temple Shōkokuji, headquarters of the Rinzai sect of Zen Buddhism. In his preface to the work Shōda wrote that it was being reprinted at Ieyasu's request to help govern the realm in the way of the ancient sages, to succor the people, honor the memory of the Taikō, and promote loyalty to young Hideyori.

Despite the rumors of war and betrayal that were swirling about, it was a thoroughly civil and refined way to begin the fifth year of Keichō.

CHAPTER II

Interlude--A "Brabbling Japon" Meets Some "Red-hairs"

About the time Ieyasu was putting Genkitsu and Shōda to work, an unusual incident was brought to his attention. He learned that a ship carrying red-haired foreigners had beached in Usuki Bay in Kyushu, far to the west. The lord of that area promptly sent word of the ship's arrival to the Osaka authorities and sought instructions on what to do with the ship and crew. Wishing to learn more about these new foreigners, Ieyasu ordered the ship brought to Osaka Bay and its officers delivered to him for interrogation. The order was carried back to Kyushu, and the ship's captain, mate, and pilot proceeded to Osaka. The captain and mate were Dutch; the pilot, an Englishman. They constituted a species of westerner entirely new to the Japanese.

On March 16, 1600, the three were presented to Ieyasu in Osaka Castle. The pilot, Will Adams, quickly became the key figure because he spoke some Portuguese and could converse with Ieyasu through a Portuguese-speaking Japanese interpreter. Ieyasu had heard that the ship was a pirate vessel laden with weapons and on the hunt for victims. He doubted the veracity of that report, however, and asked Adams to explain who he was and how he came to Japan.

Adams' story was hair-raising. He had hired onto a Dutch vessel, the *Liefde*, part of a five-vessel fleet commissioned to open trade with Japan. At that time the Dutch and Portuguese were mortal enemies both politically and religiously. The objective of the Dutch venture was to consolidate a base in southeast Asia to counter the Portuguese bases at Goa in India and Macao in China. From that base the Dutch intended to drive the Portuguese out of the Japanese trade. The *Liefde* and its four sister ships left Rotterdam in June, 1598. After nearly a year of sporadic encounters with the Portuguese at settlements scattered along the west coast of Africa, the ships headed southwest across the Atlantic toward the Strait of Magellan. They arrived as winter was setting in and laid over, a-waiting better weather. When spring came to the southern hemis-

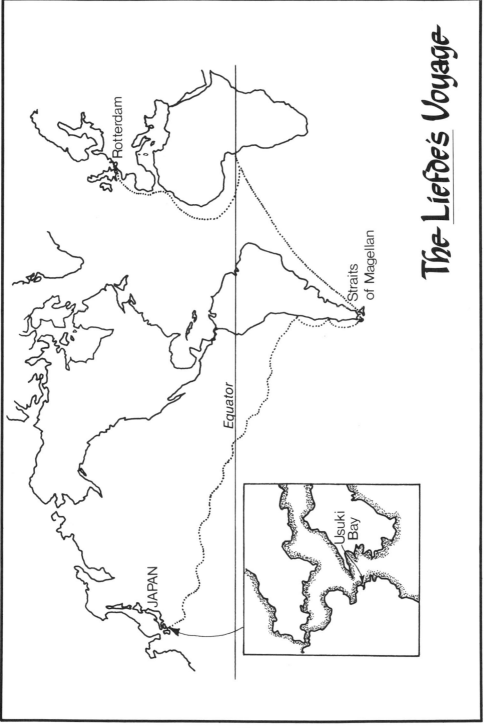

The Liefde's Voyage

Rotterdam

Straits
of Magellan

Equator

JAPAN

Usuki
Bay

phere, in September, 1599, the ships pushed on through the Strait, only to be scattered by storms. The *Liefde* sailed up the west coast of South America. Its original crew of 110 steadily shrank as men fell victim to disease on the high seas and hostile people on shore.

Late in November the *Liefde* headed across the Pacific alone. With each passing week water and food supplies dwindled. Men weakened and died one by one. Four ghastly months later, when the ship reached Japan, only 24 of the original 110 still lived. Of those 24 only 7 had the strength to stand. The others dragged themselves about the deck as best they could to help sail the ship. Although the Japanese gave them aid as soon as they reached land, 6 more died within a few days, too emaciated to recover.

One thin Englishman and 17 lean Dutchmen thus found themselves cast upon the shores of Japan, helpless, captive, and accused of being pirates. The charge of piracy had been made by Portuguese Jesuit missionaries who were summoned to Usuki Bay from Nagasaki to act as interpreters. They evidently hoped their accusations would help crucify these heretics, royal enemies, and potential trade rivals. Their effort was unsuccessful because the Jesuits themselves were not completely trusted by most Japanese daimyo, including Ieyasu.

The Portuguese first reached the southern tip of Japan in 1543, landing on a small island named Tanegashima. Subsequently, they came often, and the Japanese found these visitors an interesting lot. One Japanese observer wrote:

> *I do not know whether they have a proper system of ceremonial etiquette. They eat with their fingers instead of with chopsticks such as we use. They cannot understand the meaning of written characters. They are people who spend their lives roving hither and yon. They have no fixed abode and barter things which they have for those they do not, but withal they are a harmless sort of people.*

The most interesting items the Portuguese introduced were arquebuses, which the Japanese began calling Tanegashima. At the time Japan was torn by civil wars, and some ambitious lords quickly realized that Portuguese firearms had a battlefield potential worth examining. Moreover, the Portuguese wanted to trade, and shrewd daimyo, some of whom already were accustomed to trading with Korea, China and southeast Asia, knew that trade could mean profit.

Besides guns and trade, however, the Portuguese also brought Jesuit missionaries, who presented problems. In the decades that followed, a few daimyo in Kyushu became Christians. Their vassals, if unable to dissuade their lords from that decision, soon realized the prudence of converting themselves and their families or else finding service elsewhere. Most daimyo did not find the Jesuit message persuasive, but rather, viewed with alarm the possibility that the foreign doctrine could subvert the loyalty of their own vassals.

Daimyo were especially sensitive to the political danger inherent in the dogmatism of religious zealots because they already had experience with a comparable Buddhist phenomenon. During the thirteenth and fourteenth centuries popular sects of Buddhism had spread the length and breadth of Japan. Two sects in particular, Ikkō and Lotus, had proven able to mobilize congregations of the faithful in loyal service to their temple leaders. These congregations evolved into armies. Temples grew into fortified bastions. By the mid-sixteenth century temple-led groups of Ikkō Buddhists actually governed a few localities in Japan, and massive fortified temples of the two sects played major roles in the politics of the Kyoto-Osaka region.

Between the 1550s and 1570s, daimyo here and there gradually crushed these sectarian movements, the most savage instance occurring in 1571. That year Oda Nobunaga, who was Hideyoshi's liege lord, decided to rid himself of an obnoxious political rival. Much to Jesuit satisfaction, he deployed an army of some 30,000 around the huge and venerable Buddhist establishment on Mt. Hiei near Kyoto. Oda's men launched their attack, shooting, slashing, and burning, until the entire mountain community--temples, shrines, pagodas, libraries, residences, historic treasures--was a smouldering pyre. They destroyed some 300 buildings and slaughtered 3,000 men, women, and children. Not until American bombers incinerated Japan's cities in World War II would the islands again be visited by such wanton destruction. By the 1580s, daimyo had suppressed most of the religious militants, but they did not forget the zealous commitment and military effectiveness of these religiously motivated groups.

When the Jesuits began to propagate their doctrines, bitterly denouncing Buddhism as the work of the devil while goading their followers into attacking temples, priests, and the Buddhist faithful, the daimyo grew alarmed. Though they might have been glad enough to see Buddhist secular power ravaged, they were not keen to see a familiar threat replaced by an unfamiliar but equally menacing one. To their eye, the "Villanose papisticall rabble at Nangasaque," (as a dogmatic Englishman later called the Jesuits) scarcely seemed the "harmless sort of people" of the earlier Japanese observer.

From the 1580s onward the Jesuits began to encounter increased resistance from Japanese authorities. In 1582 Oda was murdered and Hideyoshi seized control. For the next five years he befriended the Portuguese in return for weapons and trade, but in 1587 he denounced Christian excesses, criticized some daimyo for converting, and ordered the Jesuits to leave the country within twenty days. Trade, he said, could continue. The expulsion edict was not really enforced, however, and the number of faithful kept growing. Consequently, the Jesuits encountered increasing hostility, even though daimyo continued to welcome the Portuguese trade and firearms.

The Jesuits were pressed from other directions. They had become accustomed to their monopoly on missionary work in Japan, a monopoly the Papacy repeatedly affirmed to subjects of the Portuguese crown. Beginning in 1580, however, when Portugal was united with Spain under one monarch, the Spanish church, called by god, gold, and glory, launched its own vigorous missionary ventures into Japan and continental Asia from its colonial bases in Mexico and Manila. Within three years the Jesuits in Japan were mounting arguments against the admission of Spanish missionaries but to no avail. Before the end of the decade Spanish Franciscans began arriving, and sectarian feuding promptly erupted.

Hideyoshi saw in the Spanish a trading alternative to the Portuguese and cultivated their goodwill, much to Jesuit dismay. In 1592, while he was in western Japan supervising the invasion of Korea, a Spanish Dominican monk from Manila visited him and criticized the Portuguese at Nagasaki. A year later a Franciscan group, whom the Taikō received at Kyoto, added fuel to the fire of Christian sectarian squabbling.

It was not really clear, however, that Spaniards were more desirable than the Portuguese. In 1596 the Spanish galleon *San Felipe*, laden with cargo valued at over a million and a half silver pesos, was shipwrecked on the Japanese coast. In the course of settling the disposition of the wreck and its treasure, the Portuguese evidently did their best to vilify the Spanish. Then the Taikō was told that a Spanish officer of the ship had boasted of Spain's vast dominion and had explained that the missionaries were useful forerunners of Spanish conquest--just as Buddhist monks, some of Hideyoshi's advisors, and others had been arguing for years. All of Hideyoshi's latent distrust surged to the fore. He confiscated the ship's treasure, much to his own advantage, and as mentioned earlier, had the Franciscans rounded up and crucified.

No doubt he would have liked to dispose of the Jesuits with similar directness, but they now seemed less a menace than the Spanish sects. He needed trade and especially wished to buy guns for use in Korea and China. After deporting a handful of Jesuits and ordering the dismantling of some 120 of the several hundred churches that dotted southwest Japan during 1596 and 1597, he ceased harassing the Christians.

18

It was against this background that Ieyasu learned in early 1600 that a half-dead, shipwrecked handful of red-haired westerners had been denounced by the Jesuits as pirates. If the Jesuits hated them so much, could these Europeans be so bad? They had guns, which spoke in their favor. They might be interested in trade, and they might present fewer problems of ideology. The Spanish option had not worked, but this one might. An interrogation might prove revealing. So it came about that a nondescript English ship's pilot and two Dutchmen were ushered into the presence of the most powerful man in Japan, a "brabbling Japon" as a frustrated Englishman would label the Japanese a few years later.

Adams' explanation of how the *Liefde* reached Japan did not entirely persuade Ieyasu. The quantities of weapons--reported to be 500 matchlocks, thousands of cannonball and chain shot, thousands of pounds of gunpowder, and hundreds of fire arrows--did raise eyebrows. The *Liefde* hardly sounded like a peaceable merchantman, so Ieyasu pressed his prisoners for information about their countries, whether they engaged in warfare, what their religion was, and what goods they had to trade. As to wars Adams replied, "yea, with the Spaniards and Portugals, beeing in peace with all other nations." This answer may have heartened Ieyasu a bit, but he continued to interrogate Adams well into the night, finally tiring and sending the men back to their place of detention.

Two days later he questioned Adams again, and according to Adams' later recollection, inquired,

> *of the qualities and conditions of our countreys, of warres and peace, of beasts and cattel of all sorts; and of the heavens. It seemed that he was well content with all mine answers unto his demands. Nevertheless, I was commanded to prison againe: but my lodging was bettered in another place.*

Subsequently, Ieyasu ordered the *Liefde* sent east to Edo Bay and his prisoners transferred there also. Domestic affairs were becoming critical and Ieyasu wanted his prizes safely situated in his stronghold. There might come a time when he could learn more and even turn a profit from these red-hairs. In the meantime, he had to turn his attention to the more fundamental business of war and peace.

CHAPTER III

Voices of War, Old and New

Several days after grilling Will Adams, Ieyasu attempted to interrogate a much less cooperative figure. He had learned that Uesugi Kagekatsu was hastily strengthening the fortifications in his domain. Ieyasu, with consent of the Elders and Ministers in Osaka, ordered him to come to Kyoto with an explanation and apology. While awaiting his reply, Ieyasu cultivated political support by guaranteeing influential lords possession of their domains and by developing more connections with the Imperial Court. Expecting that Kagekatsu's reply would prove unacceptable, he began to prepare a punitive expedition against Aizu. Ten days later, on May 3, Kagekatsu's reply arrived. He refused to proceed to Kyoto, and in justifying his military preparation, disparagingly said, "Whereas city *bushi* collect the utensils of the tea ceremony and calligraphy, rural *bushi* gather tools such as lances, firearms, bows and arrows; it is just a difference of custom." A separate letter from one of his vassals ridiculed Ieyasu, and in great anger the Tokugawa chief ordered daimyo to deploy for war.

During the next month and a half Ieyasu directed his attention to three principal tasks. He defended his Aizu policy against critics, issued a variety of orders to daimyo and others, and prepared to deploy his own formidable forces in the Kantō. His mobilization orders called for all forces to be in assault positions encircling the Aizu domain by the latter part of July.

Ieyasu knew his own forces would not be sufficient for the task because he was unwilling to commit them all against Aizu. He wished to have enough reliable troops available to counter whatever moves Ishida Mitsunari might make. Even without the Ishida problem, Aizu was not going to be an easy problem to solve. It was situated in an inland cul-de-sac, surrounded on three sides by precipitous mountains. Long before an attacking army could reach the castle, it would encounter snipers and surprise assaults from forces secreted in wooded hillsides adjoining the road. Kagekatsu could be bottled up easily enough, but to overrun him would re-

20

quire a concerted assault by forces attacking from more overland routes than he could defend simultaneously.

On June 6 Ieyasu assembled the daimyo in Osaka Castle and assigned their assault positions. He and his son, Hidetada, would take up positions at Shirakawa on the main highway south of Aizu. Lord Satake of Mito would be to their east on the mountain road approach. Date Masamune from Sendai would attack from the north. Mogami of Yamagata would strike from Yonezawa, and mighty Maeda Toshinaga of Kanazawa would drive east across the mountains. All exits from the Aizu cul-de-sac would thus be blockaded, and the combined force could advance step by step, crushing the impudent Uesugi in a five-sided vise. None could escape. Uesugi would have good reason to think twice before throwing down any more gauntlets.

The plan required the massive deployment of forces by several major lords. Daimyo domains were measured in terms of their estimated rice production. Each was known as a domain of so many *koku*. A *koku* was a large straw sack holding about five bushels of rice. As a corollary rule of thumb a domain's population was roughly the same as its *koku* figure, and its military potential in terms of army size a fraction thereof, perhaps five to ten percent. In this case Uesugi, with a domain that was said to produce 1,200,000 *koku*, was facing the Tokugawa with some 2,500,000; Satake with 500,000; Date with 600,000; Mogami with 250,000; and Maeda with 800,000, a total of about 4,500,000 *koku* or an army that could number hundreds of thousands of combatants.

The deployment was calculated to leave most of Ieyasu's allies in central Japan free of commitments and ready to move elsewhere. He was not about to forget Mitsunari and his friends, who were actively discussing ways of exploiting the Tokugawa-Uesugi collision.

The Court approved Ieyasu's plan. A number of lords consented to cooperate, and on June 16 Ieyasu and his escort troops strapped on their armor, saddled up, and marched eastward. From Osaka the Tokugawa force headed up the Yodo River to Fushimi, where Ieyasu assigned loyal supporters duties to be carried out during his absence. He left one of his most trusted and experienced men, Torii Mototada, in charge of the Fushimi Castle defense. He bade his old comrade farewell, knowing that if Mitsunari did move, his first task would be the capture of Fushimi Castle. And he knew that Torii would not yield as long as he lived.

Two days later Ieyasu and his escort headed east on the Tōkaidō, stopping at a highway station west of Minakuchi Castle. The lord of Minakuchi, Natsuka Masaie, was one of the Five Ministers, a colleague of Mitsunari. He offered to present Ieyasu with 200 firearms, and proposed to deliver the gift on the following day

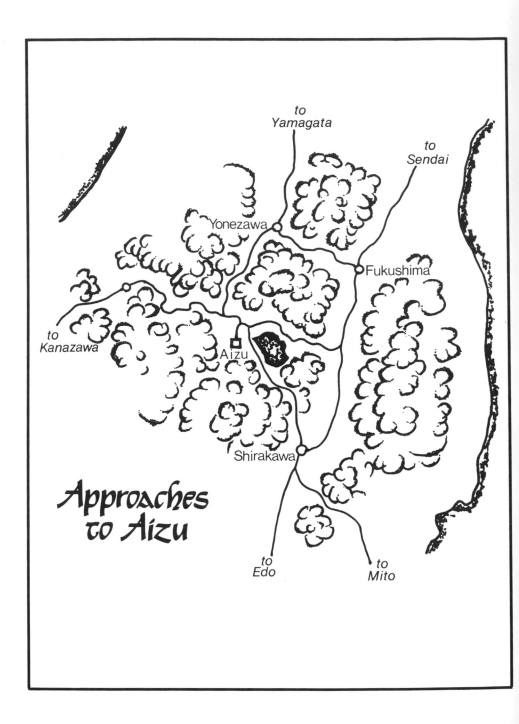

to
Yamagata

to
Sendai

Yonezawa

Fukushima

to
Kanazawa

Aizu

Shirakawa

Approaches
to Aizu

to
Edo

to
Mito

within the castle. Ieyasu seemed to accept the offer and settle down for the night. Around midnight, however, fearing that these firearms would come to him muzzle first, he and his followers abruptly saddled up and dashed eastward through the night, past Minakuchi and on to the border of Ise province at high speed. His alarm proved justified. A few weeks later Masaie revealed himself to be a leader in the coalition trying to destroy him.

After this midnight dash, Ieyasu's force rested at the border and then pushed on to Yokkaichi on Ise Bay. There they boarded ship at sunset on the twentieth and set sail under cover of darkness down the bay and around the tip of Chita Peninsula into Atsumi Bay. After an all-night trip they landed in southwestern Mikawa Province, where Ieyasu was greeted and banqueted by a friendly daimyo who gave him assurances of support against Uesugi.

It was so good to be back in Mikawa! *Mikawa kuni,* "province of the three rivers." Home. Safe again at home, away from the treachery of Masaie. Home to where he and so many of his men were born. Men of Mikawa. Mikawa samurai. Mikawa *bushi* as they would be known even into the day of super-tankers and bullet trains.

How sweet it was, as Ieyasu dined with this lord, to look around and see familiar roads and fields, with place-names so firm in his memory. It was only a few kilometers from there, in the small castle town of Okazaki, that he had been born fifty-seven years before, on December 26, 1542.

To be correct about the date, it was not December 26, 1542 but January 31, 1543. By Japanese reckoning, he was born on the twenty-sixth day of the twelfth month of the eleventh year of Tenmon. For the sake of convenience we are here calling it December 26, 1542, but it happens, in fact, to convert to January 31, 1543 by the Gregorian calendar, which West Europeans were using at the time and which we, and the Japanese, use today.

To complicate matters further, by Japanese calculations Ieyasu was fifty-nine years old in 1600, not fifty-seven. The difference arises because by custom Japanese children were designated "one" on the day of birth (how could a person be "zero"?) and thereafter their age changed at New Year's. Therefore, Ieyasu was considered to be one year of age on the day of his birth, and five days later he became two years of age, which probably makes him the most famous underdeveloped two-year-old in history. Since Japanese historians even today follow this numbering practice in reporting the age of historical figures, there is a persistent difference between the age of Ieyasu as reported in Japanese and English sources.

In any event the new infant was given the name Takechiyo. This raises another problem. Names were not chosen lightly. In Ieyasu's

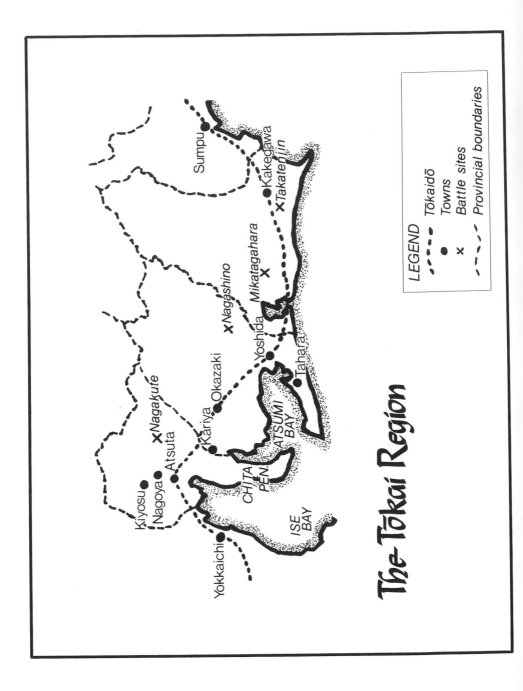

The Tōkai Region

LEGEND
- - - Tōkaidō
● Towns
✗ Battle sites
- - - Provincial boundaries

Sumpu
Kakegawa
✗Takatenjin
Mikatagahara ✗
✗Nagashino
Yoshida
Tahara
Okazaki
Kariya
✗Nagakute
Atsuta
Kiyosu
Nagoya
Yokkaichi
CHITA PEN.
ATSUMI BAY
ISE BAY

day names were regarded as an inseparable part of the indivisible process of being, and names played their role in shaping that process. An appropriate name conduced to the good of all; an inappropriate one only caused trouble. As the times changed and one's situation changed, one's name changed. Ieyasu had been given the auspicious infant name Takechiyo, "bamboo everlasting", in the hope that it would help assure his survival in a world where warriors lived short and bloody lives. At the age of twelve he was pronounced a man and given the adult name Motonobu. *Moto* was in honor of the powerful lord whom he was serving and who supervised the ceremony. *Nobu* was given out of a prudent respect for the powerful lord who was his neighbor to the west. Within three years Ieyasu felt more assertive and began to use names he deemed appropriate to his changing circumstances. In 1562, after his lord had died, he changed his name yet again, this time to Ieyasu. Thereafter, his life proved sufficiently rewarding that he saw no further need to realign his given name and situation.

That, however, lay in the future. At the end of 1542 the infant Takechiyo was born to a local lord named Matsudaira Hirotada and his wife of one year, Odai no Kata. She was the talented, sturdy, and resolute step-daughter of a neighboring lord named Mizuno, an influential family in the Mikawa area. At the time of Ieyasu's birth his father was about sixteen years old, his mother fourteen. Despite her youth she took her maternal duties seriously, and as soon as her infant son was old enough, she carried him to a local Buddhist temple to report his presence and to pray on his behalf to Yakushi Nyorai, the Buddha of healing. A few weeks later she ordered construction of a new temple to house an image of Yakushi, who would guard her son, and a daughter whom she was soon to bear.

Hirotada traced his lineage back through his forceful father, Kiyoyasu, and beyond him through another five generations to the mid-1400s and to a family of warriors living in a locality known as Matsudaira in the foothills north of Okazaki. The men of Matsudaira had gradually imposed their control over neighboring areas and expanded onto the fertile plain of Mikawa Province.

At the time of Ieyasu's birth four families were of great immediate consequence in his life. To the west, at Kiyosu in Owari Province (near modern Nagoya), was the powerful lord Oda Nobuhide, the father of Oda Nobunaga, the man who late in 1571 would slaughter the Buddhists on Mt. Hiei. Some thirty kilometers southeast of Kiyosu was Kariya, the castle town of the Mizuno family. The Mizuno were much weaker than the Oda. About fifteen kilometers farther east were the Matsudaira at Okazaki. They were about equal in strength to the Mizuno. Then much farther east at Sumpu, southwest of Mt. Fuji, was the mighty lord Imagawa Yoshimoto, whose domain was larger than those of the Oda, Mizuno, and Matsudaira combined.

Times were hard, however, and the political facts of one day quickly became the memories of another. From time to time the Matsudaira family was close to annihilation, but repeatedly managed to recoup its fortunes. Kiyoyasu had been a dynamic leader who expanded his domain, fought brilliantly, and made a name for himself in Mikawa and the adjoining provinces. But he was killed by a vassal in a misunderstanding in 1535 when only twenty-four years old. His son and successor, Hirotada, was a boy of nine, quite unable to control his relatives and vassals. For several years the Matsudaira family was torn by internal rivalries and fared poorly in battles with its neighbors.

By 1543 Hirotada was reduced to serving as a vassal of Imagawa, who had come to his aid following a major military defeat. A year later Mizuno, to his west, allied with Imagawa's enemy, Oda. Accordingly, Hirotada broke with Mizuno and sent his wife, Odai no Kata, back to her home at Kariya. Her departure left her two-year-old son motherless at Okazaki and in the care of his aunt, Hirotada's sister. She was available for much the same reason that Odai no Kata was not. Her first husband had been killed in battle, and she had been separated from her second after he broke with the Matsudaira following Kiyoyasu's death in 1535. From the time of Odai no Kata's departure until 1547, she assumed the task of caring for Takechiyo.

That year Hirotada was defeated in battle, this time by Oda. Again he sought Imagawa's aid, and Yoshimoto rose to the occasion--but at further cost. Payment was simple: Takechiyo must come to Sumpu to live as a hostage. Having little choice, Hirotada agreed. In August of 1547 the four-year-old and his samurai escort headed for Sumpu. From Okazaki the boy was taken south, put into a boat, and carried across Atsumi Bay to Tahara. From there he was supposed to travel eastward by highway. Tahara was a rather out-of-the-way place, and his escort was intercepted by the local lord, who was supporting Oda. His men relieved the escort of their charge, transferred the boy to another small boat, and headed westward down Atsumi Bay, around Chita Peninsula, and up Ise Bay to Oda's headquarters at Kiyosu.

Takechiyo surely was at a loss to understand what was happening, but Oda understood at once that he had received a windfall. He promptly wrote Hirotada a short and blunt note: "You had better sever your ties with Imagawa and join me; if you fail to do so, I shall kill Takechiyo." Hirotada was not the ruthless, hard-driving man his father had been, but at the age of twenty-one he was still ready to live recklessly, so he decided to call Oda's bluff. He refused to yield. Oda recognized that a dead Takechiyo would be of no further use to him, while a living one might be, so he let the boy live.

Odai no Kata, the boy's mother, lived in a nearby town. She had not forgotten her son and kept a watchful eye on him. She had revealed her feelings for him when Hirotada had reluctantly sent her back to Kariya. He had assigned about twenty of his vassals to go with her, to serve her at her brother's castle at Kariya. As they approached the castle, she ordered her escort to leave her at that point and return to Okazaki at once. When they protested, saying they could not disobey their lord, she responded:

If you come, my brother will have all of you killed. In that case Takechiyo will hate his uncle forever. Even though we are separated and I live here with my brother, as long as Takechiyo lives, I shall not think of you people at Okazaki as strangers. Especially because Takechiyo and my brother are related, sooner or later the Mizuno and Matsudaira are bound to make peace. However, if my brother now kills you, that peace will be difficult to realize.

Her words prevailed, the men returned to Okazaki, and in later years her interest in Takechiyo survived. Although she was unable to visit him, as far as one can tell, she did send him gifts of clothing and sweets to ease his life as Oda's hostage. But a hostage he remained.

When military fortunes changed again, Oda found his own castle invested by Imagawa Yoshimoto's forces. Imagawa had mounted a fierce offensive into his domain and in the process captured one of Oda's sons. Now each side had something the other wanted. A bargain was struck and again Takechiyo was part of it. His father, Hirotada, had been murdered by a vassal during the fighting, and Matsudaira prospects looked so bad that Oda had little further use for the boy. He agreed to release him to Imagawa in return for the safety of his own son. The exchange was made, and in 1549 Takechiyo headed east toward Sumpu a second time. En route he stopped at Okazaki for a fortnight and planted a small pine tree at his father's freshly-made grave. His filial duty done, his escort hurried him on, and he reached Imagawa's headquarters without further event.

Takechiyo was safe, but his family seemed to be heading for extinction. His father was dead; his mother was gone and would shortly remarry. Many Matsudaira vassals were taking service with other lords. Imagawa Yoshimoto had taken charge of Okazaki Castle. Takechiyo and his handful of samurai loyalists sustained themselves on a small area of land that Imagawa had granted them in support. No one looking at this hapless eight-year-old boy would have seen him as the future ruler of Japan.

His family's troubles notwithstanding, Takechiyo's life acquired a stability hitherto unknown. He stayed at beautiful, comfortable Sumpu for eleven years. Suruga Bay sparkled just beyond the town. Across the bay to the east, Izu Peninsula trailed off southward in a soft haze. To the northeast Mt. Fuji soared above the lush green foothills of Suruga. To the southwest stretched the productive rice plain that paralleled the ocean, running westward through Tōtōmi and Mikawa Provinces to Ise Bay.

As he matured at Sumpu, Takechiyo developed into a short, muscular young man of great endurance and sound health. Vigorous living appealed to him, and he loved to swim in the nearby ocean and go hawking and riding in the fields and hills around Sumpu. Enthusiastic about the martial arts, he worked diligently at archery, swordsmanship, and cavalry techniques. Early on he demonstrated a sharp mind, inherited, some say, from his mother or perhaps his grandfather. He was reputed to be an open, generous, and dependable young man but was evidently capable of unyielding stubbornness. Occasionally he displayed the arrogance that might be expected of someone taught to assume that he would naturally succeed to his father's position and command those who were now teaching and counseling him, waiting on him, and answering his questions.

As with so many heroes of yore, Ieyasu's youth is remembered from scattered and doubtful anecdotes that serve to demonstrate his exceptional perspicacity, talent, and virtue. One apocryphal story, for example, tells us of a time when a group of lords gathered for a ceremonial New Year's dinner at the Imagawa's. One lord turned to his neighbor, asking if the youngster seated nearby was the grandson of Matsudaira Kiyoyasu, a short, sinewy, and sharp-eyed man. The resemblance was very close, but the neighbor was sceptical. While the men speculated, Takechiyo rose and strode over to the sliding door that opened out on a garden. In full view of his elders, he pulled up his gown, flexed his knees, urinated, and returned nonchalantly to his place. The doubter then confessed that on the evidence of such aplomb the boy must indeed be Kiyoyasu's grandson.

Takechiyo was not alone at Sumpu. About seven sons of his father's vassals accompanied him, ranging in age from eight to twenty-seven years. Among them were men to be of great significance in his later life, such as Ishikawa Kazumasa, whose ancestors had served Takechiyo's family for three or four generations, and Torii Mototada, whose father was then serving at Okazaki. He also made friends with a fellow hostage, Hōjō Ujinori, a boy his own age whose father was the lord of Odawara Castle just east of Mt. Fuji. Later in life, Takechiyo would have more and difficult dealings with the relatives of this Hōjō friend of his childhood.

Takechiyo's grandmother, Keyōin, also lived in Sumpu. Her life epitomized the uncertainties of the age. Born in a samurai house, she was adopted by a lord named Ōkōchi and then apparently married to a man by whom she mothered the girl named Odai no Kata. She was betrothed later to Mizuno, who adopted her daughter as his own. Subsequently she married again, this time to Matsudaira Kiyoyasu of Okazaki, who already had a son, Hirotada, by his first wife. In 1541, Keyōin's daughter, Odai no Kata, who had remained at Kariya, became betrothed to Hirotada, her stepson at Okazaki. After Kiyoyasu's death in 1535, the vicissitudes of life led Keyōin to Oda's domain and later to Sumpu, where she finally became a nun in a small hermitage. There she took the Buddhist name by which she is known. She was thus both Takechiyo's maternal grandmother and adoptive paternal grandmother. Keyōin provided an invaluable guiding hand for the lad during his early years at Sumpu, replacing his mother and then the aunt he had abruptly lost so early in life. She started his education, teaching him calligraphy and arranging for a neighborhood priest to educate him further. Keyōin lived until 1562, her grandson having grown up and left Sumpu by then.

Most of Takechiyo's formal education was provided at a local Zen temple, the Rinzaiji, where he continued to write and practice calligraphy. Under the guidance of a distinguished scholar-monk, Takechiyo studied the principles of civil and military arts as expressed in the Confucian rhetoric of the day. Imagawa Yoshimoto had earlier recruited the learned monk, Taigen Sūfu, one of his relatives, from a major Zen temple in Kyoto. Sūfu's reputation as an expert in the principles and practices of warfare attracted Yoshimoto. Sūfu was well-versed in tactics and strategy, his forte being the relationship of warfare to government and administration. Indeed, Yoshimoto's political and military successes are commonly attributed to the excellence of his advice. At Sumpu, Sūfu taught young Takechiyo both military and civil lore.

From the age of ten, Takechiyo began to participate in military duties, initially at noncombatant positions, such as commander of the castle guard. In 1555, he was ceremoniously pronounced a man. He accepted oaths of allegiance from Kazumasa, Mototada, and several other vassals, and assumed the adult name of Motonobu. As the new head of his family, he was allowed to visit Okazaki in the spring of 1556. It was spring planting time when Ieyasu, to call him by his usual name, made the trip. As he neared the castle, he found some of his family's vassals out in the fields transplanting rice. Such work was below their dignity, but having lost much of their land when the Imagawa acquired Okazaki, they eked out a living as best they could, waiting for a revival of

Matsudaira fortunes and avoiding becoming vassals of Yoshimoto.

At the castle Ieyasu was greeted by old Torii Tadayoshi, the father of Mototada. Old Torii had served both his father and grandfather and stayed ·on at Okazaki after Hirotada's death, serving under the command of Imagawa's officials. During the years when Ieyasu was at Sumpu, Torii preserved intact a storeroom of money and equipment for the use of his young lord on the day he would be free of the Imagawa. When Ieyasu reached Okazaki, Torii took him to the storeroom and with great emotion told how he had nurtured the hoard and kept it from the eyes of Imagawa vassals because of his belief that one day his young lord would need those resources to arm and sustain his men as they took the field to regain their lands and rebuild their fortunes. Ieyasu, we are told, was amazed and deeply touched, and he forgot neither the lesson of frugal planning for the future nor the loyalty of Torii. And the Torii would not forget. A half-century later, Mototada would serve Ieyasu even more courageously than had his father, and die in the effort.

While at Okazaki, Ieyasu visited his father's grave again, saw the vigorous young pine tree he had planted there seven years earlier, and then began to exercise his prerogatives as heir to the family position. His first written order related to affairs in the vestigial Matsudaira domain. His continuing affection for his mother, Odai no Kata, was reflected in the order, as it delineated the lands and administrative rights of the temple that his mother had built in 1543 to house the image of Yakushi, the Buddha of healing.

In 1558 Ieyasu went on his first sortie. Some years earlier Oda Nobunaga had succeeded his father, who had died in battle, and fifteen-year-old Ieyasu's first combat assignment was to lead his men in an assault on one of Nobunaga's peripheral fortresses. He destroyed the fort, raided the area, and before withdrawing smashed a pursuit force dispatched by Nobunaga.

This success delighted Ieyasu's men at Okazaki. Hoping to capitalize on these victories, they sent a delegation to Sumpu to ask Yoshimoto to withdraw his men from Okazaki, place Ieyasu in full charge there, and restore Matsudaira lands to the family. Yoshimoto, however, was not ready to release his hostage and end his protectorate. He refused the request but promised to grant it later, after an assault on the main Oda bastion at Kiyosu. Angered that their service and Ieyasu's evident maturity were not properly recognized, the Matsudaira men returned to Okazaki to await another day. Perhaps as a tactful expression of his own displeasure, Ieyasu changed his name again, this time to Motoyasu, the *yasu* being that of his revered grandfather, Kiyoyasu. The *yasu* also, by happy chance, was that of Hōjō Ujiyasu, the powerful lord at Odawara, father of the lad Ujinori who was a hostage at

Sumpu, and a potential ally should Ieyasu try to break with the Imagawa.

For two years Ieyasu continued to serve Yoshimoto from Sumpu, marching here and there as dictated by the ebb and flow of battle. Then, in 1560, Yoshimoto was ready to launch the promised assault on Nobunaga, and in May he led his army of 25,000 westward to overrun Owari Province. His advisor, Taigen Sūfu, had died five years earlier, and it was perhaps for want of sound advice that his army was routed when Nobunaga, himself, commanded a much smaller force in a daring surprise assault mounted during a heavy downpour in the early afternoon. Yoshimoto was killed along with nearly 600 of his samurai and some 2,500 foot soldiers.

In that campaign Ieyasu had led an advance force to a secondary front. On the way he was able to arrange a brief visit with his mother at her home in Owari. They had not seen one another in sixteen years. He also met her three sons by her second husband, lads who later were to serve him as loyal supporters. After this reunion, Ieyasu carried out his orders, overrunning a frontier fortress--only to learn that the main Imagawa force had been smashed. With that dramatic development, seventeen-year-old Ieyasu found his situation again suddenly changed.

This battle, as well as others, demonstrated that Nobunaga, at age twenty-six, was a first-rate tactician and a ruthless and resolute strategist. In contrast, Yoshimoto's heir and successor was incompetent. Ieyasu had no wish to be on the losing side again. Showing the shrewd foresight that would later make him shogun, he decided to go home instead of returning to Sumpu after the battle. Ieyasu left the field promptly and that night, taking advantage of the bright moonlight, made his way across enemy territory, heading directly for Okazaki. He arrived safely, reclaimed the domain for his family, and spent his first night there in the Matsudaira family temple, the Daijūji. After giving the local Imagawa garrison time to pack and leave, he moved into the castle and set about establishing himself as an independent lord. What the Imagawa would not yield gracefully he would take forcefully.

Forty years later, as Ieyasu was heading eastward to punish Uesugi, he could only marvel at how the times had changed; so many triumphs and so many sorrows. Old Torii Tadayoshi had died in 1571, and his son Mototada, now sixty-one years old, was at that very moment at Fushimi, holding the fort with a handful of men. Ieyasu knew that if Ishida Mitsunari decided to move, he would make its capture his first order of business. Four days before, on his last night at Fushimi, when he and Mototada had bid farewell, Mototada had sworn to gain as much time for him as he could. He would hold the fortress as long as possible, then defend its interior enceinte by enceinte, gate by gate, fighting until the last defender lay dead.

CHAPTER IV

Working Heaven's Will--The Ways of Young Men and Old

After banqueting on his first day at Mikawa, Ieyasu returned to his ship and sailed eastward that night along Atsumi Bay to the castle town of Yoshida (Toyohashi). He was received there on June 22 by the daimyo Ikeda Terumasa, husband of his second daughter. Ikeda entertained him and gave him assurances of support in his confrontation with Uesugi.

His arrival at Yoshida placed Ieyasu near the sites of several early victories after his break with the Imagawa forty years before. Actually he had not gotten clear of them as easily as it had appeared. In January of 1557, Yoshimoto had arranged for Ieyasu to marry his niece, Lady Tsukiyama. In March of 1559 she bore him a son -- Takechiyo--and a year later a daughter named Kamehime. Although Ieyasu moved to Okazaki in May of 1560, his wife and children remained at Sumpu as hostages. Moreover, a number of Ieyasu's vassals had relatives living at Sumpu or on lands controlled by Imagawa officials. As long as they lived there, Ieyasu would have to move cautiously lest his relatives and those of his vassals be used for blackmail or even be slaughtered by a vengeful Imagawa.

For about a year Ieyasu tried to build an independent domain at Oda Nobunaga's expense, launching repeated assaults on nearby fortresses held by supporters of the Oda family. He even offered token help to the Imagawa. At the same time he began to negotiate quietly with Nobunaga, working through trusted vassals, such as Ishikawa Kazumasa and his mother's kinsmen, the Mizuno.

Many Matsudaira vassals relished every blow struck against the hated Imagawa, but others strongly opposed the plan to abandon ties with the mighty lord of Sumpu in favor of links with Nobunaga's much smaller organization. Despite that opposition, Ieyasu negotiated an understanding with Oda in the spring of 1561, less than a year after his return to Okazaki. The two agreed, in effect, to press their ambitions at the expense of third parties, not each other. In succeeding months, Ieyasu built up his following, engaged in desultory battles with forces of the Imagawa, and gradually extended his holdings, mostly into Imagawa lands south and east of Okazaki. He granted the acquired lands to loyal vassals and issued regulations for the administration of his growing domain.

In 1562, Ishikawa traveled to Sumpu and successfully negotiated the release of Ieyasu's wife, son, and daughter in exchange for some Imagawa relatives whom Ieyasu had captured. By this time some of the relatives of his vassals had been brutally murdered at Sumpu, but others made good their escape, and so Ieyasu achieved his change of alliances with less cost than his more cautious vassals had feared. A year later, to cement his tie with Oda, Ieyasu agreed that Takechiyo would one day wed Nobunaga's daughter, Tokuhime. The two children were about four years old at the time. They were married five years later.

Clearly the times had changed, so a change in name again seemed appropriate. In July of 1563, Ieyasu, who had been known as Matsudaira Motoyasu for five years, dropped the *moto* that he had received from Imagawa Yoshimoto and changed his name to Ieyasu. The *ie*, which means house or family, was rather rare in names, and signified perhaps that he was beholden to no one and was committed solely to his own family, that of his father Hirotada and his grandfather Kiyoyasu.

Ieyasu had hardly completed the shift from Imagawa to Oda when he found himself facing trouble that threatened his realm from within. Members of the Ikkō and other Buddhist sectarian congregations in Mikawa had resisted the attempts by Ieyasu and his supporters to establish control over their lands. From rice-tax collecting time, in late 1563, they erupted in armed struggle against his spreading control. The congregations, consisting primarily of landed peasants and other commoners, formed local alliances and rapidly won the support of numbers of samurai. Some of the samurai had been overwhelmed by Ieyasu's followers. Some were opportunists seizing a promising chance. And some were vassals of Ieyasu who participated because of personal religious conviction, concern for the complaints of local folks, the prospect of getting ahead, or resentment at his change in alliances.

Ieyasu's quarrel with the Ikkō sectarians was not a religious dispute. The Ikkō were adherents to the Jōdo sect of Buddhism. Jōdo was also the family religion of the Matsudaira, and the Daijūji at Okazaki was a Jōdo temple. The conflict had nothing to do with doctrine and everything to do with politics, concerning who would control or be controlled and how that control would be exercised.

The insurgents organized themselves into units of footsoldiers marching and fighting under elegant battle streamers and flags that invoked the sacred power of Amida on their behalf. Sustained by a sense of shared purpose and faith in Amida's assistance, they succeeded in ousting Matsudaira supporters from a few newly secured fortresses. On two occasions they threatened Okazaki Castle so closely that Ieyasu, himself, took to the field to help repulse them with pike and sword. In a battle in January, 1564, he was twice hit by gunfire, but the two bullets lodged in his armor and he remained unhurt.

After four months of repeated battling and savage guerilla fighting, the sectarians were severely weakened by forces led by Ishikawa, the Toriis, granite-faced Honda Tadakatsu who later became one of Ieyasu's most ferociously devoted lieutenants, and other Matsudaira vassals. These men added another chapter to the story of loyal service to Ieyasu that was to benefit their descendants more richly than they could possibly have imagined in the harrowing days of late 1563.

Fearful of attack from ambitious neighbors, Ieyasu moved to end the strife in Mikawa by conciliating the dissidents. He granted them pardons, lands, tax relief, and other concessions, but at the same time attempted to eradicate the local Ikkō organization and rivet Matsudaira control firmly on central Mikawa by regulating temple activities and placing more trustworthy men in charge of local affairs. In later years he did not forget how sectarian challengers had nearly toppled his nascent regime. The older and more powerful he became, the more cautious he grew in dealing with monks, their messages, and their minions, bribing as many as he could with carefully calibrated generosity, and controlling others with written regulations and severe restrictions.

The preference for manipulation and compromise that Ieyasu showed in quieting the Mikawa insurgents gained him the sobriquet, "the old badger," and stayed with him for life. Years later, when he was retired and his son, Hidetada, was shogun, Ieyasu considered him too serious and upright and wished he showed a keener sense of political shrewdness. One day when they were discussing the adjudication of disputes, Ieyasu said,

> *Adjudication is essential for clarifying right and wrong. However, it is important to handle judgements so that they do not interfere with governance.*

With the Ikkō quelled and his interior secure, Ieyasu turned eastward and began gnawing away at the collapsing Imagawa domain. For over a year he fought and bargained. He captured Yoshida Castle in the summer of 1564, eventually drove all Imagawa supporters from Mikawa, and established control over the entire province.

By late 1565, he was enjoying a respite, thanks to an elaborate

34

set of alliances involving the major daimyo in east-central Japan. Ieyasu was associated with Oda Nobunaga, who in turn was tied to Takeda Shingen, the lord dominating the mountain provinces of Kai and Shinano north of Imagawa's domain. Shingen was at odds with his northern neighbor, Uesugi Kenshin, the father of Kagekatsu. To counter Uesugi, Shingen reached an accommodation with the Imagawa and Hōjō, who faced rivals of their own in the northeast. For the time being, therefore, Ieyasu and the Imagawa were uninterested in fighting one another. Instead, Ieyasu worked at consolidating his control of Mikawa, preparing for whatever the future might have in store.

As part of that preparation, Ieyasu used the years of respite to cultivate influential friends. His oldest surviving personal letter dates from this time, and it reveals how interested he was in becoming part of the broader political scene. The letter, written on February 12, 1566, is addressed to a lord named Isshiki, whose castle was near Kyoto and who was an acquaintance of the current shogun, Ashikaga Yoshiaki. In the letter, Ieyasu asked Isshiki to tell Yoshiaki if he chanced to see him, that he would be warmly welcomed to Mikawa.

Yoshiaki did not come, but Ieyasu's attempts at self-promotion began to bear other fruit. By the end of 1566 his accomplishments had come to the attention of the Emperor in Kyoto, and the Court prepared to award him a title commensurate with his political position. Ieyasu evidently informed the Court that he wished to be named Tokugawa, which presumably had been the original name of his great grandfather's great grandfather's grandfather, Chikauji. The name Tokugawa would distinguish him from all his Matsudaira relatives, some of whom were too ambitious for his comfort. It also might enhance his stature on the broader scene because it supposedly provided him with a shadowy link to the most illustrious warrior family of all, the Minamoto, the lineage of past shogunal lines.

Emperor Ōgimachi pointed out that Ieyasu must be of proper lineage to receive title and rank and that the qualifications of his Tokugawa ancestry were not at all evident. In response Ieyasu promised a considerable bribe to the Court, as was expected. This induced the appropriate Court official to search through promising genealogies. The search finally uncovered an obscure family line called Tokugawa, which could be traced back to Minamoto and subsequently became Fujiwara. Or so, at least, the Court official reported on a fragile piece of tissue paper that he forwarded to the Emperor. (Subsequent scholars never found the lineage again.) Ōgimachi, recognizing that this evidence was the best he could hope for, dutifully made the appointment.

At the New Year's ceremonies that year the twenty-four-year

old Ieyasu was presented, in absentia, with a sword and was granted a name, rank, and title appropriate to his status. The Imperial order announced that, beginning with the new year, Ieyasu was to be known as Lord Tokugawa Ieyasu, Governor of Mikawa Province, a holder of the Lower Fifth Court Rank.

As one may surmise, honors from Kyoto were not terribly significant. The Court itself was powerless and only did as it was advised by others. Actual power lay in the hands of such barons as Shingen, Kenshin, Nobunaga and Hōjō Ujiyasu, who fielded the best armies and struck the best political deals. The new titles were significant only as indicators of relative power. The real value of Ieyasu's new family name, for the time being at least, was that it distinguished him from overly ambitious Matsudaira kinsmen.

These symbolic changes were followed by more substantial developments as the fragile stability of the mid-1560s dissolved. To the west, Ieyasu's ally, Nobunaga, expanded his domain so rapidly that he became the dominant figure in Kyoto. He began to threaten Ieyasu simply by the magnitude of his capacity for warfare and the scope of his ambition: to rule Japan. To the east, Imagawa's domain was collapsing. Ieyasu was nibbling at its western boundary. From Kōfu Castle in the mountains, Takeda Shingen, who was pressed in turn by Uesugi, was overrunning Imagawa land in the northeast. Shingen shortly drove Imagawa out of Sumpu and southward to Kakegawa in Tōtōmi Province. Lest Shingen take over all of Imagawa's domain, Ieyasu sent his legions eastward in December of 1568. He overran Tōtōmi, confronted Shingen's advance forces, and struck a bargain with him. Much as the United States and the Soviet Union divided Germany in 1945, the two men agreed that Shingen should take Suruga while Ieyasu should keep Totomi.

Shortly thereafter, Shingen found the Hōjō and Uesugi allied against him. Lest Ieyasu join them, Shingen withdrew to Kōfu. For nearly two years afterward he was active elsewhere, which gave Ieyasu time to organize his new domain in Tōtōmi. He turned to the task of eliminating the remaining Imagawa holdouts. He ousted the uncooperative and rewarded those who accepted his leadership and who sent hostages to his camp. True to his preference for reconciliation, he exploited old ties to build new bonds of loyalty. Thus in May, 1569, he wrote to an Imagawa vassal who had befriended him during his childhood at Sumpu, mentioning his warm recollection of those past kindnesses, assuring him he bore him no ill will, and telling him that Sakakibara Yasumasa and another of his close advisors would inform the man of his new position.

To consolidate his control of Tōtōmi, Ieyasu moved his headquarters from Okazaki eastward to Hamamatsu in the summer of

1570, leaving the castle that had been his family headquarters for three generations. But he did not abandon the family legacy. Rather, he took the occasion to declare his eleven-year-old son Takechiyo an adult and give him the name Nobuyasu, the *nobu* from Nobunaga and the *yasu* from great grandfather Kiyoyasu (or perhaps Hojo Ujiyasu) via himself. Nobuyasu had been married to Nobunaga's daughter, Tokuhime, in 1567. Ieyasu left the boy and his mother, Lady Tsukiyama, a supervisory staff, and a trusted vassal in charge at Okazaki, as a living link between the allied houses of Oda and Tokugawa and as an enduring symbol of the continuing Tokugawa primacy in Mikawa. The former boy hostage, employing techniques of governance that seemed to work for his powerful neighbors, had become one of the major daimyo in central Japan.

This, however, had occurred some three decades before the fifth year of Keichō (1600). In the summer of 1600 Ieyasu was making his way eastward through those familiar provinces to confront Uesugi Kagekatsu in Aizu. He spent the night at an inn east of Yoshida; the following day, June 23, he and his escort pressed on along the coastal plain that loops south of the central Japanese highlands, moving on to Hamamatsu and another banquet. Hamamatsu was a castle town rich with memories, of chagrin and of amusement, for Ieyasu. Those memories traced back to the early 1570s when he was keeping an eye on Takeda Shingen in Kofu.

After his conquest of Tōtōmi in 1569-1570, Ieyasu deployed his army about central Japan at the behest of Nobunaga to assist him and his gifted general, Hideyoshi, in battles with rival territorial lords northeast of Kyoto. Many of his ablest vassals, such as Ōkubo Tadachika, served in those campaigns. Ishikawa Kazumasa commanded one of his finest assault forces. In conjunction with one such campaign, Ieyasu went to Kyoto for his first formal meeting with the elegant people of the Imperial Court. One suspects that at twenty-seven this ambitious lord felt a mixture of awe and impatience at the finery and polish of the nobles.

Late in the year Ieyasu got himself into a dangerous situation. So many successes so early in his career seemed to have gone to his head. Proud of his military skill, he occasionally referred to himself as "The best bowman on the Tōkaidō." And pleased with his political finesse, he undertook to win an easy victory against a formidable enemy, Takeda Shingen. To immobilize Shingen while he was helping Nobunaga, Ieyasu arranged an alliance with Shingen's eastern enemy, Uesugi Kenshin. In a letter of October 1570 to Kenshin, Ieyasu swore by all the gods he knew, "Benten Taishaku above, the Four Kings below, all the deities of heaven and earth, and in particular the gods manifest (Gongen) in Izu and Hakone, the Daimyōjin of Mishima, Hachiman Daibosatsu, and the independent god of Tenman," that he would faithfully cooperate with Kenshin against Shingen and that he would attempt to break up Nobunaga's marriage alliance with the Takeda so as to draw Nobunaga and Kenshin together.

Shingen learned of the ploy and was furious. Round-faced and bald-headed, he was a big bear of a man, sporting a mustache and a fine set of sideburns. A celebrated military leader, he was, at fifty, intolerant of obstreperous *arriviste* youngsters such as Ieyasu. He resolved to teach him a lesson. He began forming a broad coalition that eventually included the Hōjō of Odawara, some of Nobunaga's enemies to the northeast of Kyoto, and a number of fortified temples, including the huge establishment on Mt. Hiei, and the Ishiyama Honganji, the great Ikkō bastion at Osaka. In early 1571, before his coalition was complete, he launched a punitive sortie into Mikawa and Tōtōmi. Tokugawa forces under fiery Honda Tadakatsu repelled his first assault, but other Takeda units succeeded in overrunning a few bastions held by others of Ieyasu's lieutenants. With his path cleared, Shingen assembled a main force of 23,000 men that swept southward and trapped Ieyasu with 2,000 soldiers in his castle at Yoshida. Shingen's men overran the outer defenses and prepared for the kill. Then, lest he get bogged down in a siege, only to be hit from behind by Kenshin, or lest Nobunaga feel forced to come to Ieyasu's aid despite his marriage ties to Shingen, Takeda decided to halt. He plundered the district and withdrew, hoping the upstart Ieyasu had learned not to toy with his powerful northern neighbor.

Ieyasu apparently did not learn quickly enough. A year later, Shingen had his system of alliances much more solidly in place, despite Nobunaga's destruction of Mt. Hiei. In the autumn of 1572, he led a force that included units of Hōjō men from Odawara southwest from Kōfu toward Hamamatsu. On December 22 he deployed his 27,000 men at Mikatagahara on the open plain some 10 kilometers north of Hamamatsu Castle. Uesugi Kenshin sent Ieyasu no help, but Nobunaga deployed commanders with some 3,000 supporting troops to assist him. Ieyasu was able to field 7,000 of his own solders.

Late in the afternoon, as snow settled over the plain, fighting erupted and Shingen's massive force soon routed Nobunaga's men and pummeled Ieyasu, forcing him to retreat to his castle at dusk. Knowing that his decimated garrison could never survive an onslaught, Ieyasu tried a ruse. He ordered the front gate left open and huge bonfires built inside and out. He hoped they would guide his scattered warriors home and perplex Shingen's commanders. After Shingen's forces had amassed, one of Ieyasu's senior commanders opened the gate wide, ascended a watch tower, and commenced pounding a large drum, as though to signal a combined attack by forces secreted both inside and outside the castle. Remarkably enough, the ruse worked: Shingen's generals withdrew to avoid entrapment, and after some nocturnal skirmishes, the attacking army headed home. It had been a sanguine battle, Shingen losing over 400 men, Ieyasu near 1,200. In a life of risks and narrow escapes, the battle of Mikatagahara was one of the narrowest, and of his several military defeats, it was clearly the worst.

Twenty-eight years later, as he was entering Hamamatsu, Ieyasu could only wonder at that bizarre battle. All his advisors had urged him to avoid the fight. Shingen probably would have been content to hold him in his castle while pressing on to his real foe, Nobunaga at Kiyosu. But Ieyasu, bursting with an excess of youthful self-assurance and choosing to fight, brazenly sallied forth and was trounced. He nearly lost everything and muddled through only by the sheerest luck and daring.

Afterward, it is said, he retired to take a long hot bath and devour three heaping bowls of rice. Later he would view his actions as reckless and unwarranted, but at the time he shrugged it off with the comment, "As Heaven wills it." He was then only twenty-nine years old, and the comment stemmed from the brashness of youth, not from profundity of religious insight. No fatalism, neither that of Hindu *karma* nor the Christian fatalism of "God's Will," was really to his taste. In the summer of 1600, as he progressed eastward along the Tōkaidō, obtaining promises of support from daimyo on his route, he was a wiser fifty-seven, and was very intent on helping Heaven work its will favorably toward himself.

CHAPTER V:

Bedroom Politics--The Thinking Man's Choice

Ieyasu could have moved eastward much more rapidly had he so wished, and he had reason to hurry. His enemies were plotting feverishly. They might yet steal a march on him. Specifically, on June 20, the day Ieyasu reached Ise Bay after bypassing Minakuchi, Ishida Mitsunari rushed a message to Uesugi Kagekatsu at Aizu, advising him of Ieyasu's movements and proposing joint military action. He then contacted a vassal of Kagekatsu and began to discuss the proposal.

Ieyasu did not know of Ishida's initiative, and other factors determined his rate of advance. A hurried trip to Edo would have hinted at panic. More importantly, political bonds needed strengthening en route because the commanders of the castles along the Tōkaidō might soon be of critical importance to him. He knew the value of personal and family connections. Adoption and marriage was a booming business. Indeed, as he headed east for a showdown with Uesugi, he adopted the daughter of one minor lord and presented her as wife to another; that maneuver consolidated his links with two families.

Ieyasu understood the system well. He was born of a political marriage, lost his mother at two years of age due to political turmoil, became a hostage and in 1557 received a wife for political reasons.

One particular practice expedited marriage politics. In Ieyasu's day vigorous political leaders made a point of befriending a number of women who would bear them children. This practice helped assure competent successors and facilitated the forging of alliances. Ieyasu's first son and daughter, Nobuyasu and Kamehime, had been born of his wife, Lady Tsukiyama, who was Imagawa's niece. In 1565, he had a second daughter, Tokuhime, born of a woman named Udono, whose family he visited on his eastward journey in 1600. In 1574, he had a son, Hideyasu, of a woman named Nagai, who was the daughter of a Shintō priest and who served as a maid in his household until she became pregnant. During 1579-1580 he had two more sons born of a Saijō, and a third daughter of an Akiyama, both women residing at Hamamatsu. In 1583 Akiyama gave him yet another son.

The children were valuable, as were three half-sisters by his father. His one half-brother was a cripple from the age of thirteen and unable to play an active political role, but by 1582 he had two of the sisters married to favored vassals. He had also given his eldest daughter to another vassal and his fourth son to yet another as an adopted heir. That left his second son, Hideyasu (whom he had been slow to claim lest it anger Tsukiyama), to be placed at an advantageous location when opportune. A third more legitimate son was being reared as his own successor.

Yes, Hidetada, his third son, would be his successor, not Nobuyasu, his first. Therein lay the most terrible tragedy of his personal life. When he had moved to Hamamatsu in 1570, he left Lady Tsukiyama and her son at Okazaki. Nobuyasu had previously married Nobunaga's daughter, Tokuhime, and the couple produced two children. Around 1576, Nobuyasu began leading military forces and fought fiercely. He was a violent, unpredictable young man, who abused his wife and embittered many of Ieyasu's vassals by treating them badly. Then he became entangled in an anti-Oda political intrigue. Lady Tsukiyama, who got along poorly with her daughter-in-law, and who probably had never forgiven Ieyasu for throwing over her relatives in favor of Nobunaga, was centrally involved. Nobunaga learned of the intrigue in July, 1579, when his daughter wrote him a letter denouncing her husband and mother-in-law on twelve counts of anti-Oda plotting and abuse. He was enraged and demanded that Ieyasu have the young man commit suicide.

Ieyasu was thunderstruck. His wife of twenty-two years was sabotaging his alliance with Nobunaga. His son was accused of plotting against the family ally and his own father-in-law. It put Ieyasu in a terrible dilemma. On the one hand he could not afford to anger Nobunaga. On the other, Nobuyasu, for all his lack of self-control, was a bold warrior. In the past three years they had begun to march together, and the twenty-year-old had performed fearlessly. Moreover, he was heir to the Tokugawa house. If he must now die, that would leave as potential successors to Ieyasu one son five years old, and a four-month-old infant boy. Either might die. Neither was anywhere near maturity. Both might prove incompetent. The Matsudaira family experience was replete with evidence that child-heirs were family disasters.

It was a hideous predicament for Ieyasu, and worse yet for Nobuyasu and his mother. On receiving Oda's demand, Ieyasu rushed with a small escort force down the Tōkaidō from Hamamatsu to Okazaki. He had Nobuyasu put in custody and then procrastinated for nearly a month and a half, trying to find a way out of his dilemma. He finally sent a vassal named Okamoto to assassinate the boy's mother, whom he held responsible for the mess and whose value to him had ended with Imagawa's collapse. He still refused to kill Nobuyasu, but in the end he could find no way out, having obtained no great help from his vassals, some of whom were relieved to be done with the young man. On September 15, 1579, at Ieyasu's order, his eldest son disemboweled himself.

In later years, scenes that reminded him of that terrible time could still bring tears to his eyes. By 1600, the hurt was buried deeply, surviving as one of those quiet, unending regrets that a person carries to the grave. The four-month-old infant had grown into a responsible young man, Hidetada, and so the practical issue of concern had long been resolved.

On June 23, 1600, Ieyasu had no time to dwell on such matters. The scheming and intentions of Ishida Mitsunari was much on his mind. During his stay at Hamamatsu, the castle lord pledged his support. Ieyasu then instructed him to have his father, whose castle was in Echizen Province, north of Sawayama, return home promptly to keep an eye on Mitsunari.

Ieyasu waged these politics of family management and diplomatic maneuver not because of an inability to wage war but because he had had his fill of it. He knew the satisfaction of winning. And to the end of his life he knew the exhilaration of casting doubt aside, abandoning the tension and tedium of political management, and deciding to reach a decision by sword. For example, when he made his last great decision for war at the age of seventy-one, his closest advisor described him as "feeling very spirited about it" and "enjoying the process" of issuing deployment orders. But Ieyasu also knew from hard experience that such elation was transient and that war was a costly, risky, painful, destructive, and inefficient way to gain his ends. His narrow escape from Takeda Shingen at Mikatagahara in 1572 and his forced destruction of Nobuyasu in 1579 had been but moments in a decade of incessant and devastating warfare.

Ieyasu had fought then because he was engaged in a life and death struggle with the Takeda for control of the rich coastal plain running from Mt. Fuji westward to Ise Bay. In 1573, Shingen died of an illness, but Ieyasu and Nobunaga were soon at war with his son and successor. For much of the next decade the fires of war flickered and flared along the borderlands of Suruga and Tōtōmi Provinces as Takeda and Tokugawa hammered away at one another, mounting forays and counter-forays, burning and pillaging, and seizing and abandoning frontier castles.

One of the most significant battles of that decade occurred near Nagashino, a frontier fortress of Ieyasu. It stood at the confluence

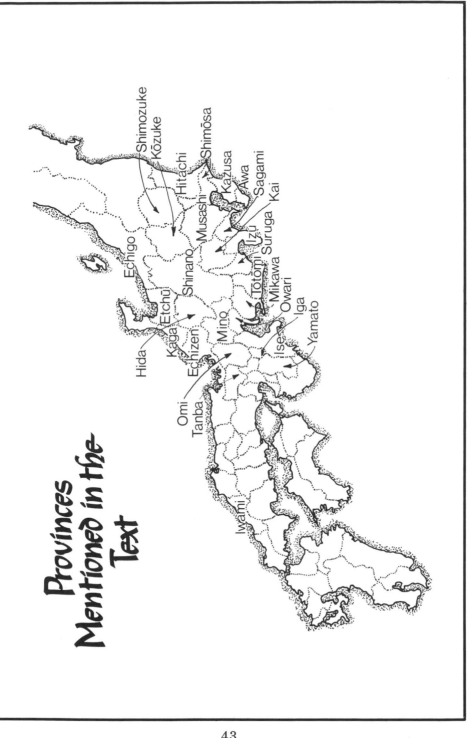

Provinces Mentioned in the Text

Shimozuke
Kōzuke
Hitachi
Shimōsa
Musashi
Kazusa
Awa
Sagami
Kai
Echigo
Izu
Suruga
Totomi
Mikawa
Etchū
Shinano
Owari
Kaga
Mino
Iga
Hida
Echizen
Yamato
Omi
Tanba
Ise
Iwami

43

of two river valleys northeast of Yoshida and blocked the Takeda advance south into Mikawa. In 1575, Takeda armies invested it in preparation for driving southward. Ieyasu and Nobunaga agreed on a strategy to stop them. They selected an open battle site facing a nearby stream that Takeda must cross. Ieyasu ordered Sakakibara Yasumasa and Torii Mototada to erect a running palisade before the stream, and behind that Oda deployed ranks of gunners bearing Portuguese-style firearms. On May 21 the battle was fought. One after another Takeda units advanced, and from behind the palisades, Oda's men mowed them down. It was a bloody battle, forcing Takeda back out of Mikawa, and demonstrating that when properly employed, the new weapons were fearsomely effective. As Ieyasu summed it up in a characteristically cryptic letter to a monk in Kyoto, "I wish to report that in Mikawa the other day the Takeda advanced in force but Nobunaga rode forth and instantly defeated them. I could not be more delighted."

Other battles, most notably Ieyasu's destruction of the Takeda bastion at Takatenjin in 1580, gradually weakened the Takeda army. Not until 1582, however, did Nobunaga and Ieyasu finally mount a successful pincer drive from west and east, pushing the last of the Takeda back to their castle in the mountains and destroying them root and branch. In the settlement that followed, Nobunaga gave mountain areas to his own men and accepted Ieyasu's claim to Suruga. This gain made the Tokugawa chief more powerful than ever and transformed him into a direct neighbor of the Hōjō at Odawara.

The Takeda defeat marked the end of endemic warfare in the Tokugawa area and initiated a period of extraordinarily complex political maneuvering that lasted until 1588. These maneuvers involved Ieyasu, his Hōjō neighbors on the east, and, initially, Nobunaga on the west. For Ieyasu, it constituted an extended lesson in the art of civil politics that was as valuable as his earlier lessons in military politics.

During Ieyasu's ten-year struggle with the Takeda, the Hōjō had vacillated from side to side, but in 1582 they happened to be allied with Nobunaga and him against the mountain lord. When the Takeda empire collapsed, therefore, there were three major lords situated side by side along the coast from the Osaka area to the Kantō, all in one political alliance. The situation was transparently unstable. Two of the three could be expected to combine against the third, and being in the middle Ieyasu was obviously most vulnerable. For the moment, however, he was safe because he was a true and tested ally of Nobunaga, while the Hōjō had not really established their reliability. The Hōjō, it appeared, were the most likely to be eliminated from this *ménage-a-trois*.

Within months of the Takeda collapse, Ieyasu's situation suddenly became precarious. In the summer of 1582, Nobunaga was murdered by a senior vassal named Akechi Mitsuhide. Nobunaga's son and heir died in the fracas and so all of central Japan was again disputable territory. Hideyoshi quickly avenged his deceased lord and set about taking control of Nobunaga's domain, accepting the allegiance of those who would follow him, attacking those who would not. Ieyasu's relationship with Hideyoshi was not clearly defined. The two men had cooperated more or less as peers in Nobunaga's wars, but they were not close. Hideyoshi had spent much of his time battling to the north and west some distance from Ieyasu. Hideyoshi was also clearly a subordinate of Oda, a gifted vassal it is true, but a vassal nonetheless, while Ieyasu was an ally, not a vassal of Oda. Was he now to subordinate himself to the subordinate of his former ally? Who then would lead whom? Would Hideyoshi inherit Oda's mantle and try to live with--or overwhelm--Ieyasu? Who would turn the Hōjō alliance to advantage against whom?

Ieyasu did not wait to find out. He heard of Nobunaga's death as he and a neighboring lord were en route to Oda's headquarters where he hoped to bring the neighbor and Oda into alliance--another of Ieyasu's ventures in diplomacy. Upon learning of Oda's death, Ieyasu's party recognized at once that a struggle for power would erupt. They headed home as directly as possible, avoiding the main highway lest they be seized by an enterprising lord. Leaving the main road, they dashed east through dangerous bandit-infested territory in a trek that is popularly known rather like "Washington Crossing the Delaware" as "The Dangerous Flight through Iga." Ieyasu made it to Okazaki safely, but his neighbor was slain before reaching his castle in southern Kai.

Losing no time, Ieyasu moved to absorb his dead neighbor's domain. Two days after reaching Okazaki, he sent this notice to a vassal named Okabe: "You are now to move to Shimoyama. Investigate defensive sites there and erect your castle. Sakon Saemon will give you the details." Okabe did as ordered, giving Ieyasu a stronghold well into the southern edge of Kai Province due west of Mt. Fuji. Okabe, incidentally, was the vassal of Imagawa who had been kind to Ieyasu during his youth in Sumpu, and to whom Ieyasu had written in 1569, assuring him of his goodwill and welcoming his services. Okabe had accepted the invitation and served loyally for the next thirteen years, as his assignment to Shimoyama testifies.

When disorder erupted in the mountains of Kai, less than a month after Nobunaga's death, Ieyasu was ready to exploit it. He led an army northward to seize as much of the old Takeda domain as he could before Hideyoshi could consolidate his position or before the Hōjō could move in. In response, the Hōjō deployed troops to rout him. The Hōjō army of 43,000 was many times larger than Ieyasu's so he minimized contact with it. Forces under such stalwarts as Torii Mototada slowed the Hōjō advance, giving Ieyasu time to quiet the province, to form ties with local warriors, and to keep moving on ahead of his pursuers. After three months of cat-and-mouse, winter began to close in on the two armies, and Ieyasu and the Hōjō agreed to settle their differences. They decided to let Hōjō take over old Takeda lands in Kōzuke Province while Ieyasu would receive Kai and southern Shinano. To seal the bargain, Ieyasu agreed late in 1582 to send his seventeen-year-old daughter Tokuhime to be the wife of Hōjō Ujinao. He was heir to the domain and nephew of the former hostage and friend of Ieyasu, Ujinori, who had played a key role in negotiating the settlement. Marriage negotiations proceeded, and in April of 1583 Tokuhime went to Odawara.

Meanwhile, Ieyasu was corresponding with Hideyoshi and cultivating his goodwill. His shrewdly calculating style is nicely illustrated by a letter of April 22, 1583, that he sent Hideyoshi at his camp headquarters. Hideyoshi had just defeated his arch-rival Shibata Katuie in a major battle at Shizugatake in the north of Ōmi Province, and Ieyasu wrote to congratulate him. He said:

When Shibata advanced to the southern border of Echizen, you rode north to Nagahara. Your situation worried me so I sent a messenger. It is now clear the enemy strategy was unsound. Shibata advanced to seize Kyūtarō's fortress [at Shizugatake] and fighting erupted. I am delighted to hear that his forces were crushed and large numbers slain by your incomparable performance. I am very gratified to hear the details of these developments. Here I have thoroughly quieted Shinano and when I have a respite shall unsaddle my horses, so please feel at ease.

Hideyoshi's triumph had occurred just the day before, and in this letter Ieyasu appears to have been letting him know how well he was informed and thus the effectiveness of his system of communication by carrier pigeon. He also indicated that he was well-disposed to Hideyoshi's victory, that he was pursuing his own activities successfully, that he would soon halt his operations, and that Hideyoshi should feel pleased by this.

In succeeding months Ieyasu continued to seek Hideyoshi's goodwill. At one point he sent old Ishikawa Kazumasa to deliver a flower vase and congratulate him on his battlefield exploits. At that time, Hideyoshi was busy consolidating his position in the Osaka area, which he had chosen as his base of operations and where he was in the process of constructing a huge castle. Knowing of Ieyasu's success in expanding his domain and improving his ties to Hōjō, Hideyoshi welcomed the Tokugawa gestures of goodwill. In response, he sent gifts and kind words, trying to entice Ieyasu into an even more cooperative relationship. A few days before Tokuhime rode to Odawara, for example, Hideyoshi responded to the vase by sending Ieyasu a fine sword. Two months later, he sent him a falcon, knowing that hawking was Ieyasu's favorite pastime.

Despite these attempts at political courtship, Ieyasu and Hideyoshi slid into opposing camps during the following months. Ieyasu was unwilling to subordinate himself to his former ally's vassal; but Hideyoshi, the peasant's son, wanted absolute proof that the more aristocratic Ieyasu did not view him with condescension, lest surviving members of the Oda family persuade Ieyasu to support them in challenging him.

The growing tension did not lead to full scale war because neither man wished it. As in his dealings with the Hōjō, Ieyasu preferred to feint and maneuver. Doing so gave "the old badger" time to deepen and broaden his political alliances and consolidate control of his domain.

The Taikō, to use the informal title by which Hideyoshi was known after 1586, was no more eager for war than was Ieyasu. He also preferred diplomacy and maneuver, so during 1584, the two moved their armies about, lashed out at one another's frontier fortresses, and at one point deployed their armies face to face but then backed off from a major test of strength. The main skirmishes, fought during April of 1584, are known as the battles of Komaki and Nagakute. Even though the two leaders never committed their forces in a major showdown, casualties in these battles were still substantial, numbering over 3,000 by one account.

Ieyasu and Hideyoshi were bargaining for control of the rich and pivotal province of Owari while working out the nature of their future relationship. Each knew the other to be a first class general, and neither wished to lose all in a single roll of the dice. The forty-one-year-old Ieyasu of 1584 was not the brash young man who, twelve years earlier at Mikatagahara, had defied his advisors and faced a horde he could not defeat. In lieu of direct military confrontation, he waged war with his writing brush, aggressively cultivating allies throughout central Japan and encouraging others to resist Hideyoshi.

By November the two were ready to settle peacefully. A fifth son, Nobuyoshi, had been born to Ieyasu. The boy was over a year old, and in him Ieyasu had a reserve heir and so agreed that the Taikō could adopt his second son, ten-year-old Hideyasu. In December, the boy went with great ceremony to Hideyoshi's bastion in Osaka. Accompanying him were many gifts, a son of old Ishikawa Kazumasa, and other attendants. Owari was left with a member of the Oda family whom Ieyasu had supported and who had finally agreed to accept the Taikō's leadership in return for retention of his domain. The precise nature of the Ieyasu-Hideyoshi relationship was still unclear. However, Ieyasu's acts implied his acceptance of Hideyoshi's new status as the dominant figure in central Japan, and the two men seemed to agree that they were not at war.

With the danger of war to the west averted, and with the Taikō's preeminence in central Japan acknowledged, Ieyasu again turned his attention to the mountainous northeast, devoting much of 1585 to consolidating his control there. Although he had made concessions to his powerful western neighbor, Ieyasu was unwilling to move fully into his camp. In his military operations that year, he again came into conflict with forces supporting the Taikō. This led to one completely unexpected outcome: one of Ieyasu's closest vassals abandoned him for Hideyoshi.

Several of his retainers, and most especially Ishikawa Kazumasa, were alarmed by both Ieyasu's insistence on playing the dangerous balancing game between the Taikō and the Hōjō and his willingness to provoke the former's anger. Kazumasa, a wily old diplomat who had handled delicate negotiations with the Imagawa, Oda, and Hōjō, as well as with Hideyoshi, concluded that the Taikō was the most able among them. Hideyoshi's stature was further enhanced when he received in July of 1585, the high Court office of *kanpaku* or Regent to the Emperor. So impressed was Kazumasa with Hideyoshi that he labored for some time to achieve a Toyotomi-Tokugawa reconciliation. He felt Ieyasu was unnecessarily stiff-necked in his dealings with his western neighbor, that he was foolishly provoking trouble, and that his behavior suggested he no longer valued his old vassal's advice and service. After concluding he could not reconcile the two, Kazumasa secretly moved his family beyond Ieyasu's reach and in November 1585 defected to Hideyoshi at Osaka. He took with him a lifetime's knowledge of Ieyasu's way of thinking, his military organization, and his defense arrangements. Consequently, Ieyasu had to reorganize his defenses, restructure his military forces, and be ever more vigilant against a potential enemy who now had inside information about his strategic thinking and tactical behavior.

Meanwhile the Taikō continued to urge Ieyasu to come to Kyoto as a formal gesture of submission. Hōjō leaders strove equally hard to offset those blandishments by repeatedly assuring the Tokugawa of their loyal support. Ieyasu did his best to keep both sides humored. Hideyoshi kept pressing, and in early 1586 the Tokugawa lord reluctantly agreed to closer ties with Hideyoshi. Most notably, he agreed to marry the Taikō's half-sister,

Asahihime. She was a year younger than he, already married, and thoroughly dismayed by the prospect of changing partners.

Despite the marriage agreement, Ieyasu felt closer to the Hōjō than to Hideyoshi. They were far less dangerous. His ties with them were older; the Hōjō and Tokugawa were allied but independent baronies. The Taikō, by contrast, had no intention of treating Ieyasu as an independent figure if he could help it, and Ieyasu was not about to submit to him. Accordingly, he decided to move his headquarters toward the east again, from Hamamatsu to Sumpu. The move would place him nearer the Hōjō and would put another seventy-five kilometers and two more broad, unbridged rivers between himself and his mighty brother-in-law.

The Tokugawa-Toyotomi marriage agreement stirred the Hōjō to renewed displays of interest in Ieyasu. In March of 1586, while the negotiations for Asahihime's marriage proceeded, the Hōjō met him at Mishima on their mutual border for a lavish ceremonial visit designed to deepen their friendship. As a parting gesture of goodwill, Ieyasu had men tear down the outer defenses of his recently-erected frontier fortress at nearby Numazu. He then returned to Hamamatsu. Two months later, Asahihime travelled east to Ieyasu's domain for the formal wedding ceremony. She and her ladies travelled in a caravan of twelve palanquins; fifteen more accommodated her possessions and wealth.

Ieyasu's visit to Mishima in March was a testing of the waters, and the warmth of the Hōjō reception encouraged him to proceed with his move to Sumpu. He felt, however, that it would be politic to humor Hideyoshi a bit more before doing so, lest the Taikō be persuaded that the Tokugawa were making common cause with the Hōjō, leaving him out of the triumvirate. Accordingly, he accepted Hideyoshi's next proposal, an ingenious one. On September 26, 1586, Hideyoshi offered to send his mother to Okazaki, nominally to visit her daughter, Asahihime, but actually to stay there as a hostage. Meanwhile, Ieyasu would make a ceremonial visit to the Taikō's camp, nominally to visit his son Hideyasu, but actually to make a gesture of respect and discuss affairs with Hideyoshi.

The Court gave the two lords identical titles for the occasion, and on October 13 Hideyoshi's mother left Kyoto for Okazaki, where Asahihime lived. With his honor fortified and his safety assured, on the following day, Ieyasu left Hamamatsu for the west. He proceeded at a snail's pace and did not reach Okazaki until the eighteenth, just after his mother-in-law had arrived. He greeted her, thereby assuring himself that it was indeed she who had come and not a surrogate, and then he headed west, accompanied by Honda Tadakatsu, Sakakibara Yasumasa, and other close retainers. Stopping at Kyoto for a few days, he made security arrangements in case of betrayal, and then went on to Osaka. Hideyoshi entertained him royally there, and to the Taikō's great delight, Ieyasu responded by making an open display of respect before the assembled daimyo. Ieyasu then went back to Kyoto where, in his turn, he entertained his host. On November 5 the two were given yet higher but still equal Court ranks, and three days later the ceremonies were completed and Ieyasu departed for home.

When Ieyasu reached Okazaki, he sent Hideyoshi's mother ceremoniously on her way west to Osaka. Then he sent Asahihime east to Hamamatsu. Shortly after this he went to Hamamatsu himself. He stayed long enough to pack his equipment and on December 4 moved on to his new home at Sumpu. He left his wife at Hamamatsu. It was politically judicious to do so and seemed the best way to start a marriage that was filled with unhappiness from its first moment.

A few days later Ieyasu learned that Hideyoshi had been promoted again, this time from *kanpaku* to *dajō daijin*, the highest Court title below that of Emperor. Ieyasu was not promoted. Ritual equality proved elusive. But Ieyasu was not upset. He had never been one to confuse appearances with substance, and it was already clear that Hideyoshi was the more powerful of the two. The Tokugawa leader was content to let the symbols reflect this reality. He and the Taikō had resolved their differences, at least for the time being, and he had peace on his western border.

Those peaceful borders made the tedious and complex process of bedroom politics--marriage alliances and adoption arrangements--worth all the trouble. In contrast to war, the process left a residue of goodwill that helped sustain peace. While Hideyoshi turned his attention to the west, subduing the great lords of Kyushu during 1587, Ieyasu's life was free of trouble. Once again, as during his childhood, Sumpu seemed to be a haven of tranquility. The months passed in the routine of administration, with frequent pauses to go hawking here and there on his lands. Ieyasu found time to strengthen and embellish Sumpu castle and consolidate his domain. He promoted mining, quarrying, metal forging, and other crafts. He surveyed his realm, fostered agricultural production, and improved transportation by setting up regular post stations linking Sumpu, Hamamatsu, and Okazaki. He even found time to visit Hideyoshi in Kyoto and mediate between him and some lords in the northeast, notably Mogami of Yamagata. He also received more Imperial honors and met the new Emperor, sixteen-year-old Goyōzei.

Having consolidated his realm and feeling secure in his *de facto* autonomy, Ieyasu joined other lords in swearing loyalty to the Taikō in 1588. He had reached, at his own pace, the political position Ishikawa felt was best for him. Hōjō, on the other hand, was apparently the odd-man-out of the *ménage a trois*.

In the decade of political maneuvering between the Hōjō and Hideyoshi, Ieyasu became a master of artful deliberation. He learned the value of patience and civil connections. As he headed east to discipline Uesugi Kagekatsu in June of 1600, he moved slowly, mending fences and strengthening political-personal ties as he went. There might come a moment when boldness and savage speed would be needed, but in June they were not.

CHAPTER VI:

The Art of Military Investment

In the fifth year of Keichō, Ieyasu did not travel east for pleasure. Two days of banqueting in Mikawa had cheered him, but he remembered that Natsuka Masaie had seemed as friendly as his hosts in Mikawa. He was unwilling to have his small escort force surrounded at night. After dashing past Minakuchi, he spent two nights aboard ship in Ise and Atsumi Bays. On the night of June 22, he stayed at a small highway station after leaving Yoshida. The following day he reached Hamamatsu, where he banqueted and moved on to sleep at another way-station a few kilometers down the road. He repeated the pattern the next night, and the night of the twenty-fifth he stayed at a temple, the Seikenji in Okitsu, after passing through the castle town of Sumpu. The following night he reached Mishima at the foot of the Hakone Mountains.

Almost every town on the road held memories for him. Mishima, a small town that was famous because of its large Shintō shrine, with its deity, the Daimyōjin, called to mind the splendid banquet the Hōjō had laid out for him there in the spring of 1586. But as he looked ahead at the Tōkaidō winding its way up the ridge to Hakone, other more sobering memories recalled the ruination of the Hōjō four years after that spring banquet.

Ieyasu recalled such memories because he was headed east to subdue Uesugi Kagekatsu, and he intended to invest Aizu and give him the same two basic choices that Hideyoshi had presented the Hōjō in 1590. Kagakatsu could choose to sally forth, fight and see his army defeated in blood and fury, or he could remain secluded in his mighty bastion and see his forces disintegrate from hunger and desperation.

Ieyasu knew the art of investment well, having learned it from two experts, Nobunaga and Hideyoshi. In 1574, when he and Nobunaga had been at war with the Takeda and assorted others, including Ikkō Buddhist congregations, Nobunaga decided to suppress a powerful Ikkō group situated in two adjacent bastions on Ise Bay north of Yokkaichi. By successive attacks, Nobunaga

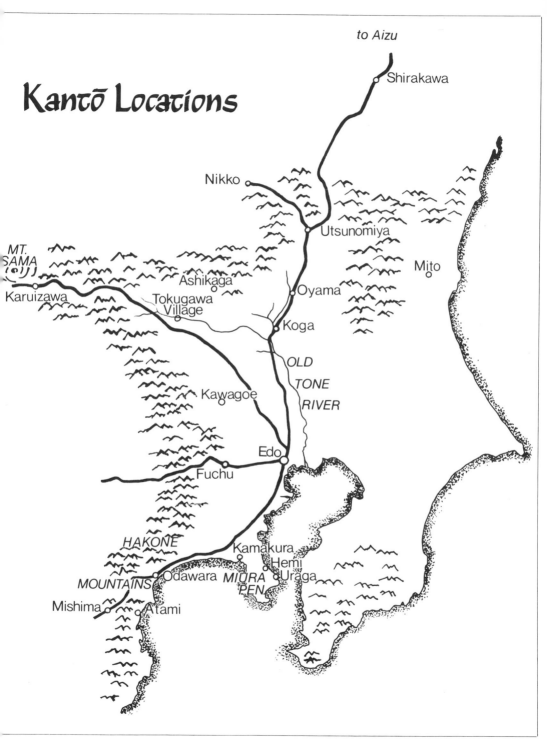

Kantō Locations

to Aizu

Shirakawa

Nikko

Utsunomiya

Mito

MT.
SAMA

Karuizawa

Ashikaga

Oyama

Tokugawa
Village

Koga

OLD

TONE

Kawagoe

RIVER

Edo

Fuchu

HAKONE

Kamakura
Hemi

MOUNTAINS Odawara *MIURA* Uraga
PEN.

Mishima Atami

drove the 20,000 defenders deeper into their citadel, where he held them until they began to starve. When they were sufficiently weakened, he ignited their stockades, burning them to death.

Six years later, Ieyasu invested Takatenjin fortress in Tōtōmi. Takeda forces held it, and in Ieyasu's view that placed them too close to his home castle at Hamamatsu. An initial attack failed, so he tried again. His attempt at burning the fort was unsuccessful, so he barricaded it. Takeda failed to push a relief column through, and by the spring of 1581, the castle defenders were sufficiently desperate to attempt an escape. This enabled Ieyasu's besiegers to hunt them down, and Takatenjin fell, paving the way for Takeda's final defeat in 1582.

In 1590, Ieyasu participated in the most elaborate investment of all, that of the great Hōjō fortress at Odawara. The story began in 1588 after Hideyoshi had completed the subjugation of western Japan and Ieyasu had joined other daimyo in swearing allegiance to the Taikō. That left only two major lords who still had not accepted his suzerainty. One was Date Masamune in Sendai far to the north; the other was Ieyasu's neighbor, Hōjō of Odawara. In May of 1588 Hideyoshi sent messengers to Odawara calling upon the Hōjō to submit. Ieyasu, wishing not to be caught in the middle, wrote the Hōjō himself, fervently urging the ex-daimyo Ujimasa and his obedient son, the daimyo Ujinao, to submit peacefully. While protesting the purity of his motives, he warned that if they defied the Taikō by not visiting Kyoto, he would insist that Ujinao divorce his daughter Tokuhime and return her to Sumpu, calling upon all the gods to punish them should they fail to obey.

Nevertheless Ujimasa and his son refused to submit, even at the risk of turning their Tokugawa neighbor into an enemy. Ieyasu still hoped for a peaceful solution and wrote again two months later, urging them to yield. He was at Kyoto at the time, having hurried there to call on Hideyoshi after learning that the Taikō's mother was ill--another instance of the shrewd personal touch in his political style--and he offered the Hōjō his good offices. His letter to a senior Hōjō advisor said:

> *In delaying his trip to Kyoto, your lord is absolutely going too far. He must come at once; it is essential. I am at Kyoto now, and it will be best if he comes while I am here. If he delays, I shall have returned home. I await a full reply from you.*

Ieyasu's efforts were to no avail. His boyhood friend Hōjō Ujinori did journey to Kyoto to plead his family's case, accompanied by one of Ieyasu's closest vassals, Sakakibara Yasumasa, but Ujimasa and Ujinao tried to bargain rather than submit, seeking concessions in a long-standing dispute over a castle in Kai. In November, Ieyasu wrote again, warning them of the perils ahead. In early 1589, Hideyoshi handed down a judgment in the castle dispute case, and when it was dispatched, he again ordered them to come to Kyoto. Ujinao did not come, and the castle settlement also fell through when the Hōjō mounted an assault on an adjacent one. Ieyasu wrote to Odawara yet again, urging Ujinao to come to Kyoto to salvage the matter, but again he refused to yield. In November of 1589, Hideyoshi denounced them. He announced his decision to punish them and ordered the lords to make preparations.

The Hōjō remained defiant, and Ieyasu was quickly enmeshed in the Taikō's plans, becoming the vanguard of his army. During the first days of 1590, he began to make preparations for war against neighbors, relatives, and supporters of a few years earlier. In February, Ieyasu marched eastward from Sumpu to the border. Two months later, Hideyoshi and his huge army moved down the Tōkaidō to Suruga. Ieyasu greeted his lord and together they rode along the shore road between shimmering Suruga Bay to the south and the towering snow-topped hulk of the silent volcano to the north. At Mishima they crossed into Izu Province and headed across the Hakone mountains to oversee the investment of Odawara Castle.

Hideyoshi was the mastermind of this operation. Even before his army of some 150,000 appeared at their border, the Hōjō had decided to pull back into their well-stocked bastion. They were confident that Hideyoshi would be unable to sustain such an immense deployment, given the difficulty of transporting essential goods over the Hakone barrier. Learning of their withdrawal, the Taikō overran their frontier fortresses. This proved an easy task, and his armies ringed Odawara Castle. To overcome the problem of hauling materials over Hakone, he had enough ships assembled to carry supplies and ammunition around the Izu Peninsula by sea. The same fleet prevented the Hōjō from escaping or replenishing their resources in the same manner.

Hideyoshi initially attempted to burn the castle down, but the tactic failed, and so he prepared for a long siege. As he explained in a letter sent to reassure his wife, Kōdaiin, "We have surrounded Odawara with two or three rings and have constructed a pair of moats and walls, and we do not intend to let a single enemy out." He arranged varieties of entertainment to sustain the morale of his troops, built himself a comfortable house, decorated it with his favorite consort, Lady Yodo, and settled back to let time do its work for him:

Since I am applying moxa and taking care of my own

55

health [his letter continued], you ought not to worry. I
have ordered everyone here, especially the daimyo, to sum-
mon their concubines and allow them to stay at Odawara,
thus keeping a long encampment, and so for this reason I
would like to summon Lady Yodo. To this end you, too,
must write to her and tell her to be ready to make detailed
arrangements. If Lady Yodo knows that you are commu-
nicating this matter to her, she will take great care to be
ready to make me happy. So please send a messenger say-
ing that I am asking for her with tender feelings.

Fortunately for Hideyoshi, his wife understood her calling as
manager of a household. She arranged for Yodo to join him, and
her cooperation helped him to complete successfully the investment of Odawara Castle. As one author has described the siege:

The various commanders built themselves quite handsome
residences with . . . . reception rooms and tea rooms sur-
rounded by landscape gardens, while the men laid out
vegetable patches, where they grew melons and eggplants
and varieties of beans, while tradespeople from the western
province towns came and set up shops, not only for every-
day commodities, but for curios and European imported
articles as well. And these were followed by the keepers of
inns and restaurants, while, of course, strumpets were in
proportion to the rest of these nonproducers.

On Hideyoshi's orders, Ieyasu deployed forces under Honda
Tadakatsu, Torii Mototada, and others to mop up some remaining
Hōjō garrisons around the Kantō. Meanwhile, the defenders in
Odawara felt their hopes fade and watched dissension grow within
their ranks. After three months they capitulated. On July 10,
Ieyasu was sent into the castle to accept the surrender and deliver
the Taikō's judgements. The Hōjō leaders were required to disembowel themselves. But Ieyasu's old friend Ujinori and his son-in-
law, the twenty-eight-year-old daimyo Ujinao--who had offered to
commit suicide if the others were spared--were pardoned. The former was assigned a minor fief, the latter sent to a temple, and both
ordered to mind their manners.

Ten years later Ieyasu was again winding his way down from the
heights of Hakone to Odawara by the sea. This time, however, he
traveled peacefully with his small escort, and on June 27 he
emerged on the western edge of his home territory, the Kantō
Plain. From Odawara he pushed on, detouring to Kamakura, a
sleepy fishing village containing a large Hachiman shrine associated
with many historic battles. He stopped and prayed at the shrine,

invoking the godly powers toward his interests in the impending confrontation. Certainly a little godly intercession would not hurt his attempts to nudge the Will of Heaven in a favorable direction.

He returned to the high road and on July 2 met his son and heir, Hidetada, on the outskirts of Edo. They rode together through the bustling castle town and into the welcoming gate of his own bastion, Chiyoda Castle. The castle survives in modern Tokyo as the Imperial Palace, home of the Emperor, and the name lives on in Chiyoda-ku, Chiyoda Ward, the political heart of the city and the nation. Okazaki had been Ieyasu's family home; Sumpu, the warm home of his childhood; but Edo, the eastern terminus of the Tōkaidō, was the home of Ieyasu, the preeminent man of Japan.

He rested in his castle residence for a few days and then turned to the task at hand. A month earlier, before leaving Kyoto, he had outlined a plan to invest Aizu by throwing the combined weight of the Tokugawa, Satake, Date, Mogami, and Maeda armies at Uesugi in his mountain fastness. He had good reason to feel confident about his prospects for success. Precedents suggested that one way or another Kagakatsu's great bastion at Aizu would fall. But precedents also indicated that capturing castles was a demanding task, requiring time, the commitment of massive resources, and a secure environment. In short, the investment of Aizu would succeed only if events in the west did not disrupt the enterprise.

At Kyoto, Ieyasu had ordered the armies deployed for assault by the latter part of July. On July 7 he set the date more precisely: the twenty-first. He issued tactical orders to Mogami and the others. His order to Mogami illustrates the genre:

> *It is now definite. The deployment before Aizu is set for the coming twenty-first. The deployment will be a shared effort and you must be there. As indicated in earlier plans, you are to cooperate with forces from the north, hitting Aizu from the northern approach. [My vassals] Tsugane and Nakagawa will fill you in.*

On the following day Sakakibara Yasumasa, one of his best commanders and a key figure at Nagakute in 1584, set out for Aizu with an advance force. Eleven days later, Hidetada led the main force northward, accompanied by two of his brothers, and assisted by more of Ieyasu's top commanders, including Honda Tadakatsu. Linking up with Gamō (whose wife was a daughter of Ieyasu) and another daimyo, Hidetada had a force of 37,000 poised to strike. Pressing in from north, east, and west were thousands more under Mogami, Maeda, Date, and about a dozen lesser lords. Two days later, on the twenty-first, Ieyasu followed with his own reserve force of 32,000. Uesugi Kagekatsu appeared to be in a tight spot.

Ieyasu had already learned, however, that developments in the west threatened to disrupt the Aizu campaign. Ishida Mitsunari's plans appeared to be well advanced. Some days earlier, on July 17, he and a number of his collaborators, notably Natsuka Masaie, had issued a denunciation of Ieyasu and sent it to those whom they hoped to rally to their cause. They began mobilizing their forces and ordered Torii Mototada to surrender Fushimi Castle. They tried to arrange their own political relationships, but without much success, because while Mitsunari wished to lead, few really cared to follow. Ieyasu took pains to keep informed, to cultivate as many lords as possible, and to get as clear a sense as he could of who were implacable enemies and who could be bought off at opportune moments.

While waiting for the picture in Kyoto to become clear, Ieyasu pushed cautiously on toward Aizu. He let the twenty-first, the day of attack, come and go, and two days later instructed Mogami to halt his advance on Aizu and await further deployment orders. His reason was that, "Ishida and Ōtani have a plan and are circulating a statement and making vulgar assertions." He himself took four days to reach a place called Oyama even though it was only sixty-five kilometers, one good day's ride, north of Chiyoda Castle. On the day of his arrival, a messenger sent by Torii reported the contents of Ishida's summons to the daimyo. Ieyasu's caution had been warranted.

On the twenty-fourth, he also learned that to the east Satake was refusing to deploy against Uesugi. More reports poured in from the west, meanwhile, and these revealed that Mitsunari's plans were developing very rapidly. Important and strategically placed lords were throwing their support to him. Danger existed of a mass defection that might leave Ieyasu exposed and without sufficient support. Ieyasu, however, also learned that Ikeda Terumasa and several other daimyo in the Mikawa-Tōtōmi-Suruga area were giving their support to him. Evidently his political fence-mending en route east was paying off. Or it may be that these minor lords realized how well Ieyasu knew the area and could likely crush any resistance they might offer.

On the twenty-fifth, a council of war was held at Oyama. With his lords and commanders Ieyasu worked out plans to confront the menace in the west, and during the next few days he began to implement them. He wrote letters to important lords, announcing his intention to march west soon and promising generous rewards when they seemed likely to help. These moves seemed to halt most of the defection and to rally men in the Kyoto area who may have feared that Ieyasu had been outmaneuvered by Mitsunari.

On August 4, Ieyasu left Oyama for Edo by boat, swiftly and comfortably navigated the old Tone River, and arrived at Chiyoda

Castle the following day. There he commenced to mobilize his allies and deploy his forces to the west. He left part of his army at Utsunomiya with Hidetada and soon ordered him to launch an all-out assault on Satake. This was done and Satake ceased to be a threat. He had Maeda pull back to Kanazawa in the west and prepare for deployment elsewhere. He wrote Date Masamune that the Aizu assault had been postponed and ordered Mogami and him to keep Uesugi penned up in his castle. For the rest of the month he devoted his attention to a seemingly endless stream of messengers who brought news and carried away messages of congratulations and gratitude, promises, and rewards. He issued an equally profuse flow of deployment orders that kept pace with changes wrought by a series of advance battles being fought in central Japan by the gathering eastern and western coalitions as they jockeyed for position.

Most of these messages and orders were drafted by Ieyasu's official scribes and affixed with his seal, but one was written in cursive script by Ieyasu himself. This was a letter he sent to a retainer of Hōshuin, the mother of Maeda Toshinaga and wife of the deceased Toshiie. She was at Edo, staying as a hostage, and Ieyasu wished to put her at ease, presumably so that her family in Kaga would be the more favorably disposed toward him. Hence the special personal touch:

> I have not written a letter in a long time, but I am so pleased at the news that I shall write in my own hand. Recently I learned of Toshinaga's exploits [in crushing anti-Tokugawa forces] at the Taishūji temple in Kaga. He is being very faithful to me. I am much pleased by this news. Moreover, once we have broken up the northland, I shall reward him with it. Be sure to inform Hōshuin of all this. And thank you, too, for your long dutiful service. Finally, I am looking forward to meeting Hōshuin after the Kyoto area is brought under control.

During August, Ieyasu's attention was not completely focused on the west. He consoled those lords who were displeased to have been deployed against Aizu, only to have their orders reversed. He instructed a few more minor lords in the Kantō and northeast areas to stay home, keep an eye on Uesugi, and repulse him if he should venture forth. He devoted most of his time, however, to preparing for war with Ishida's alliance.

In some of his letters Ieyasu reported that he would head west on August 26. When that day arrived, however, he was still unsure of the loyalty of certain key lords, so he stayed put. Finally, on the last day of August he learned that Ikeda and the other lords in his old domain had proved their commitment by attacking and capturing Gifu Castle, which lay astride the Nakasendō, one of the two main highways to Kyoto. The eastward advance of the western army had been halted. His own way to the west was clear.

Meanwhile Hidetada received more orders. After drubbing Satake, he wheeled his army about and took it westward across the northern rim of the Kantō to where the Nakasendō encounters the Kantō Range below the towering crater of Mt. Asama. On September 1, his 38,000 ascended the narrow defile to Karuizawa in the highlands on the eastern edge of Shinano Province, where they halted to regroup and await further orders. On the same day Ieyasu headed west via the Tōkaidō. He and Hidetada were to meet at Gifu, and then, 70,000 strong, they would surge on into Kyoto and Osaka and restore order to the realm.

The investment of Aizu had not come to pass. Bigger things had intervened. Over fourteen years would elapse before Ieyasu could make political capital out of military investment.

CHAPTER VII:

Deployment for War--Principles, Preparation, and Payoff

On September 1, 1600, the great gates creaked open and Ieyasu rode out of Chiyoda Castle. He knew he was heading for the decisive confrontation of his life and so did not ride alone. In fact, he was accompanied by 32,700 good friends and well-wishers, all armed to the teeth.

Two days later, the Tōkaidō took him near Kamakura, but this time he did not detour to solicit Hachiman's help. As matters were developing, it was not the powers of Hachiman that were the most noteworthy legacy of Kamakura. Rather, it was the legacy of the Minamoto family; they had governed Japan from Kamakura as the shogunal family some four hundred years before.

In 1566, as we noted before, the Court designated Ieyasu Governor of Mikawa and assigned him the family name Tokugawa on the flimsiest of genealogical evidence. That shadowy Tokugawa family had later taken the name Fujiwara, it was reported, and for a few years during the 1580s Ieyasu had used the name Fujiwara. Later, however, he returned to using the name Tokugawa, which reportedly had been adopted by a family previously named Minamoto. Ieyasu claimed that his distant ancestor Matsudaira Chikauji originally hailed from the Kantō and a family named Tokugawa that traced its lineage back by way of a family named Nitta to the Minamoto. Whatever the merits of the case, by 1600 Ieyasu had a long-established claim to Tokugawa-Nitta-Minamoto ancestry and hence a nominal right to the shogunal title, should opportunity permit him to exercise the right.

The linkage of family to title was by 1600 a well-entrenched Japanese practice. The Japanese Imperial family has an ancestry that traces back quite reliably to about 300 AD or so. From there the lineage slides effortlessly into myth and legend that eventually carries it to the Plain of High Heaven, the Sun Goddess Amaterasu, and the other founding gods and goddesses of the universe. By the tenth century, rivals for power in Japan had accepted the practice that only members of that Imperial line could take the title of

Emperor. Consequently, the line never needed or acquired a family name, there being no need to distinguish a Japanese Tudor from a Japanese Stuart or a Ming from a Ch'ing.

For that matter, if we may digress a bit, Japanese emperors do not have functional first names. At birth they are given names, but when they become heir to the throne they cease to be known by their names and are known as Kōtaishi, the "Crown Prince." Later, when they succeed to the throne, they are known as Tennō Heika, the "Reigning Emperor." Thus the child Hirohito was born in 1901, became Kōtaishi in 1916, and Tennō Heika in December of 1926. The years of his reign are known as the Shōwa era (1980 was Shōwa 55), and after his death Tennō Heika will be known as the Shōwa Tennō or Shōwa Emperor. Then his heir, the present Kōtaishi, *ne* Akihito, will become the Tennō Heika of an era yet to be designated. Happily for us foreigners, the Japanese forgive us our limitations and bear up cheerfully while we continue to call their Reigning Emperor by his childhood name.

To return to our story, during the tenth century the powerful Fujiwara family came to overshadow the Imperial family. Its members, however, were content to establish new titles, most notably that of *kanpaku* or Regent to the Emperor, using the office of Regent to control all orders issued from the Emperor's hand. When Hideyoshi, that shrewd old farmer's son, aspired to rule the country, he asked the recently-ousted Ashikaga shogun, Yoshiaki, to adopt him so that he could claim a legitimate right to the shogunal title. Yoshiaki was unwilling to accept such a peon as his peer and refused, so Hideyoshi tried another ploy. Hoping to exploit the tenth-century political tradition of regency, he concocted an egregiously unpersuasive claim to Fujiwara ancestry that enabled him to take the title of Regent. No one, after all, was prepared to call him a fraud to his face.

For Ieyasu there were problems with the *kanpaku* title. He could claim a sort of Fujiwara ancestry because that shadowy Tokugawa family of noble lineage had subsequently taken the name Fujiwara, but it was hardly a promising claim. And he lacked Hideyoshi's *chutzpah*. More importantly, the title *kanpaku* was associated with officialdom in the Imperial Court at Kyoto, and Ieyasu's real base of power lay in the Kantō. Furthermore, the title of *kanpaku* was not only associated with the Fujiwara family, specifically, but with the whole pattern of government by civil aristocrats of the classical period, from about the ninth to the twelfth centuries. These civil aristocats, or *kuge*, were socially distinct from the samurai or military families, called *buke*. Ieyasu, unlike Hideyoshi, was indisputably of a *buke* family, and there were certain advantages to claiming *buke* status despite the peculiar origins of that status.

When Imperial family leaders initially spread their rule over central Japan in the seventh century, they established a regulation to prevent the proliferation of legal claimants to the throne. It stipulated that after six generations of descent from an Emperor, branch families would lose their status as members of the Imperial family and become independent families bearing the name Taira or Minamoto. As the centuries passed, Taira and Minamoto family members proliferated. Many of them found employment as local administrators, police officers and military leaders who managed the rural estates of the *kuge* who lived in the capital at Kyoto. These Taira and Minamoto became known as military families or *buke* and were treated by the *kuge* as servants and social inferiors. By the twelfth century some had in fact acquired substantial power as the military arm of the *kuge*, and they began to assert their strength in factional rivalries at Court.

During the 1160s and 1170s a leader of the Taira family by the name of Kiyomori emerged as the dominant political figure in Kyoto, only to be overthrown amidst widespread warfare during the 1180s by forces under the command of Minamoto Yoritomo. Yoritomo had his headquarters at Kamakura, and the Kantō was his base of power. Kiyomori had lived and ruled from Kyoto, but Yoritomo preferred to rule through the simple military administration located at his own headquarters. He was accorded some Imperial titles, but the customary title that best fit his position as head of a government in a distant province was that of *seii taishōgun*, "barbarian-subduing-generalissimo." This title had formerly been assigned on a temporary basis to military commanders whom the Court had dispatched to lead expeditions against insurgents or independent tribal groups on the borders of the Imperial realm.

In 1192 Yoritomo was designated shogun. What distinguished this shogunal appointment from previous ones was that it sanctioned what became a permanent government known as a *bakufu*, "tent government." As matters worked out, Yoritomo's sons were assassinated and a vassal family took charge of their shogunate. This family, the Hōjō (whose name was used much later by another family, the Hōjō of Odawara) was not of Minamoto descent and its leaders served as *shikken*, "regents" to successive shogun much as the Fujiwara served as *kanpaku*, "Regents to Emperors." They arranged to have malleable people from Kyoto designated shogun, never claiming the title for themselves.

During the 1330s, Hōjō rule was threatened by open rebellion, and a new shogunate emerged from the resulting disorder, that of Ashikaga Takauji. He was able to show direct descent from the Minamoto and purported to be restoring a Minamoto rule that the Hōjō had usurped. Takauji and his successors, however, located their shogunate within Kyoto rather than Kamakura. By skillful maneuvering among powerful regional lords, the line continued until the 1570s even though the Ashikaga directly controlled only a small and dwindling area in the vicinity of Kyoto. The shogun Ashikaga Yoshiaki made the grievous mistake of aligning himself with Takeda Shingen and other rivals of Oda Nobunaga. Nobunaga did not take kindly to that choice and in 1573 unceremoniously drove Yoshiaki out of Kyoto. Because Nobunaga was not subsequently defeated, Yoshiaki did not return to Kyoto and the Ashikaga shogunate ceased to be. Not very many people noticed its passing.

By 1600, *kuge* or civil aristocratic government had been defunct for centuries. The aristocratic families still lived in Kyoto, and the rituals of Imperial government were still acted out, as when Emperor Goyōzei granted titles and received people in state. But the *kuge* in fact were almost powerless, and in the eyes of military men they were sycophants incapable of governing the realm. By then, however, the Japanese political tradition also included a hereditary high office appropriate to members of any military family with Minamoto antecedents that wished to govern the country. They had precedents for ruling from either Kyoto or the Kantō, doing so through a governing organization that was separate from the Imperial Court, nominally appointed by the Emperor, but in fact in control of the Court. The office, that of "barbarian-subduing-generalissimo," was vacant. It fit Ieyasu's circumstances, and he satisfied most of its requirements. In principle he could qualify for the title of shogun. The only requirement he had yet to demonstrate was the actual capacity to beat his challengers into submission. On the afternoon of September 1, 1600, as he passed Kamakura with all its echoes of the past, he was intent on satisfying that last critical requirement.

The next night he rested at Odawara. The investment of that castle ten years earlier and the resultant collapse of the Hōjō domain had opened the way to a massive increase in Ieyasu's power. That increase in power had been essential preparation for his emergence as the preeminent figure in Japan and a real pretender to the title of shogun.

Even before the investment of Odawara, Hideyoshi evidently had decided that he wanted Ieyasu to move out of the Mikawa-Tōtōmi-Suruga area into the Kantō. Perhaps his main objective was to put weaker, more pliable lords in his place. Or it was hope that a cooperative Ieyasu would be able to keep peace in the Kantō where five generations of stubbornly independent Hōjō had established deep roots.

Hideyoshi may very well have calculated that the move eastward would weaken Ieyasu, making him a less dangerous subordinate. Some of Ieyasu's vassals might choose to remain in their home area. The move would force Ieyasu to construct an entirely new administrative system. More importantly, it would remove him from his homeland and put him among strangers. Some would surely be militantly pro-Hōjō, others determined to run their own affairs, and many unlikely to welcome his presence. Perhaps they could resist him effectively and thus serve the Taikō's interests.

While the investment of Odawara was still in progress, as the story is told, the two men were standing on a hill overlooking the scene when Hideyoshi offered Ieyasu the Kantō provinces and he accepted them. The two men then stood side by side and urinated to seal the bargain. On June 28 the Taikō instructed him to make Edo rather than Odawara his castle town, and that too proved acceptable. Not that Ieyasu really had much choice in the matter, as another lord discovered a few days later when he carelessly declined a "suggested" move by the Taikō. That lord soon found a monk's habit to his liking. Six days later, on July 6, Odawara Castle fell. Ieyasu entered the castle on the tenth to accept the Hōjō surrender and admitted the leaders to his own encampment to execute the required disembowelment.

Both Hideyoshi and Ieyasu realized that the fall of the Hōjō had changed the political basis of their relationship. With the Hōjō gone, Hideyoshi did not need to be quite so solicitous of Tokugawa goodwill as in the past, and he decided to put social as well as geographical distance between himself and Ieyasu. He had earlier adopted Ieyasu's son Hideyasu as his own and given his sister Asahihime to Ieyasu as wife. She had become ill, however, and in 1588 returned to Kyoto to live. Her illness worsened, and she died in January of 1590. Then in July, after assigning Ieyasu to the Kantō, the Taikō gave Hideyasu to the Yūki family as heir, assigning him a fief of 50,000 *koku*.

Presumably Hideyoshi gave the sixteen-year-old away because in May 1589 Lady Yodo had borne him a son, Tsurumatsu, and he wished to eliminate a potential rival to the infant's succession. Hideyasu provided the Taikō with an excuse to do so when, in a fit of impetuous rage, he killed one of his favorite footmen for an alleged discourtesy. The Yūki lord accepted Hideyoshi's inescapable gift, promptly retired, passed his titles to the young man, and arranged for a daughter of Ieyasu's precedessor at Edo to become his new son's wife. By this maneuver Hideyoshi distanced himself from Ieyasu and set up Hideyasu—with a wife whose family had reason to resent the Tokugawa—as a potential rival for Ieyasu, should the Kantō transfer overwhelm him. The ploy backfired, however, because in 1591 Tsurumatsu died, forcing the grief-stricken Taikō to adopt his 23-year-old nephew Hidetsugu to be his heir, and that, as we noted earlier, led to a later tragedy.

For Ieyasu 1590 marked an even sharper break in his life. Two days after accepting the Hōjō surrender, he turned his attention to the future. Hearing vassals voicing dismay at the transfer to the Kantō, he commented, "Well, now, even though it is a move out into the back country, it amounts to a 1,000,000 *koku* increase in land. With that we can pacify the realm." Sustained by that glowing vision of the future, he and his vassals set to work. He sent an advance party to Edo to check the water and food situation, in particular the water supply in the Inokashira pond due west from Edo. The following day, July 13, Hideyoshi formally executed his transfer offer. It included the six Kantō provinces of Izu, Sagami, Musashi, Kōzuke, Kazusa, and Shimōsa, plus 110,000 *koku* of land in Ōmi and Ise Provinces not far from Kyoto. It was a huge increase over Ieyasu's old domain west of Hakone, and to get it Ieyasu readily abandoned the area that had been his family's homeland for two centuries.

On the day after formally receiving the Hōjō domain, Ieyasu began a campaign to win former Hōjō followers to his side. He notified two of Hideyoshi's commanders that the families of certain vanquished Hōjō supporters were to be protected from harm and allowed to live where they chose. In following days other letters to other people continued this policy of reconciliation. The Taikō might be hoping that Ieyasu would bungle the move east, but the Tokugawa lord had no such intention. A few days later he rode off to take charge of his domain, reaching Edo on August first.

What Ieyasu found when he reached Edo was enough to make a strong man cry. Edo consisted of some scattered fishermen's huts and a few small peasant villages. The castle site was partially a swamp. There were no outer stone parapets at all, merely an encircling grassy embankment. Within this peripheral ridge were a few dilapidated wooden buildings with rotten roofs through which rain leaked on soggy, mildewed *tatami*, sedge mats. The front entrance had an earthen floor, and the raised inner floor was made out of the coarse wood commonly used for ship's planking. Had he traded the handsome castles at Okazaki, Hamamatsu, and Sumpu for this? Clearly, much work would be required to convert this rustic hovel into a respectable, militarily significant bastion.

In his tumbledown little headquarters at Edo, Ieyasu quickly set about cultivating friends and consolidating his power. He distributed rice to the local people, appointed some merchants to administer nearby villages under a trusted official, and started construction of bridges and canals to facilitate movement about the castle. He assigned some forty reliable vassals to take charge of designated sections of the Kantō for the purpose of keeping the peace and supervising the resettlement of their followers. These forty included such stalwarts as Sakakibara Yasumasa, Ōkubo

Tadachika, Torii Mototada, Honda Tadakatsu, and Ii Naomasa, a man from Tōtōmi who had joined Ieyasu in 1575.

During the next year and a half Ieyasu spent as much time as possible organizing his new domain. Occasionally, however, his attention was diverted. At one point his energies were directed to negotiating an accommodation between the Taikō and the last daimyo holdout, Date Masamune of Sendai. Another time he deployed forces under Honda, Sakakibara, Ii, and other chief vassals to help quell unrest in northeast Japan. And he was always careful to maintain his diplomatic correspondence with powerful lords and those close to the center of power in Kyoto. He found considerable pleasure in the company of some of these influential figures. For example, near the end of 1591 Gamō Ujisato, the lord of Aizu, stopped to visit at Edo while returning home from Kyoto. It was a pleasurable visit for Ieyasu, and he found it too short. He sent this letter to Gamō a few days later:

> The other day went by too quickly. Much was left undone. It offends my sensibilities that I could not treat you to more than a simple meal. Did you arrive at Aizu uneventfully despite the snow? Do let me know. Some mandarin oranges and fresh sea urchin are accompanying this letter. Please accept them with my best wishes. I have heard that Sanshō [Shiba Yoshikane, the heir to a distinguished old family that had lost its domain] has wandered into Aizu as a rōnin. That is such a pity. No doubt you feel the same way. I am expecting you to visit again before too long.

By early 1592 Ieyasu had successfully negotiated his move to the Kantō. With the essential tasks of his transfer complete, he at last turned his attention to the rickety castle. He requisitioned an adjoining piece of land where villagers had found yūraku, "racy entertainment," an area adjacent to Yūrakuchō in modern Tokyo. During a year of work he deepened part of the brakish swamp to the east to form an encircling moat. He steepened the embankments and topped them with stone, erected some sturdy gates and buildings, and made the area the center of his castle. In later years, as Chiyoda Castle grew, this section was designated the nishimaru, "western enceinte," and today it contains the residence of the Emperor.

Ensconced in a sturdy new castle, and in control of a well-managed domain, Ieyasu was stronger, more secure against Hideyoshi, and on better terms with his neighbors than ever before. He had started a new era, and later generations of Tokugawa leaders never forgot the significance of his successful transfer to the east. August first became an annual ceremonial day of thanksgiving at shogunal headquarters in memory of Ieyasu's entry into Edo on that day in 1590.

It was the beginning of a golden decade for Ieyasu, and of a tragic one for Hideyoshi. The latter, as we noted at the outset, mismanaged his own succession, dragged the armies of his supporters into disastrous adventures in Korea, and deteriorated personally into a brutal, frantic wreck of a man who died a pitiful, whimpering death in 1598.

Ieyasu blossomed. He deployed a back-up force of some 15,000 west to Kyushu, but managed to avoid all involvement with combat operations in Korea. Nevertheless he emerged as Hideyoshi's most powerful and trusted advisor, one who served him well as mediator with the many daimyo who disapproved of the whole Korean venture or who became victims of the Taikō's increasingly uncontrollable rages. Ieyasu consolidated his domain and turned Edo into a boom town. He saw his son Hidetada grow into a responsible successor who, ably supervised at first by such men as Sakakibara and Ii, substituted for his father at Edo when Ieyasu was away advising the Taikō.

As Ieyasu emerged the second man of importance in the realm, he associated with such lords as Date, Uesugi, and Satake, acquired more allies and friends, and received more honors at Court. With status came prestige: he attended--and even participated in--Nō dramas and tea ceremonies hosted by Hideyoshi. Observant lords such as Ishida Mitsunari and Katō Kiyomasa recognized the purpose behind Ieyasu's humoring of Hideyoshi. One of them observed once that Nobunaga's successor was a fool because he engaged in Nō for the pleasure of it. "Of what use is dancing to a *bushi*? But of course that old badger, Ieyasu, acts the fool and pleases the Taikō. He's a formidable fellow." Hideyoshi also had taken Ieyasu's measure. After dismissing Nobunaga's successor as an inconsequential playboy, he noted,

> *"By way of contrast, Ieyasu may not be very refined, and he lacks musical skills, but he can govern a realm, is an astute judge of men, and is expert at arms. He is an impressive man by any standard."*

For the first time since his years as a child hostage at Sumpu, Ieyasu had time to devote to learning. While stationed in Kyushu with Hideyoshi in 1593, with time hanging heavy on his hands, he was introduced to a bright and rising Zen monk and scholar by the name of Fujiwara Seika. Seika was the son of a poet and a descendant of the Fujiwara of the classical age. At the time he was thirty-two years old and was serving as a tutor to Hideyoshi's adopted son and heir, Hidetsugu. Seika was well versed in Confucian thought, even preferring it to Zen doctrine, and his reputation was such that Ieyasu invited him to lecture to him from a text on government attributed to one of China's greatest rulers. The text was *Jōgan seiyō* or *The Essentials of Governance During the Founding Years of the T'ang dynasty*. (This was the work he would reproduce seven years later, in the spring of 1600.)

After returning to Kyoto, Ieyasu continued his scholarly pursuits, learning from both Chinese and Japanese sources, preferably works dealing with the art of government. He shared some of his own volumes with friends and returned a valuable work to a long-established library located in the northwest Kantō at the town of Ashikaga, a library originally established by Ashikaga rulers and later preserved and enlarged by ancestors of Uesugi Kagekatsu.

One thing Ieyasu never seems to have done well was maintain a personal correspondence. One looks in vain for revealing private letters of the sort that Hideyoshi wrote to his women from time to time. Ieyasu's personal life was rich, but the few letters that survive reveal a man unable or unwilling to engage in idle correspondence. The letter, just cited, that he sent to Gamō Ujisato in 1591 contained more inessential banter than almost any other he ever wrote. When deep concern for his children would finally prompt Ieyasu to write, as we note much later, he could do little more than say again and again how much he cared for them.

Ieyasu's inarticulateness notwithstanding, during the 1590s his family life reflected his newfound tranquility. In contrast to the hectic and nearly barren eighties, he enjoyed a newly prolific home life until the turmoil of the late nineties distracted him again. His second wife Asahihime had died after four years of wedded unhappiness. His two consorts, the ladies Saijō and Akiyama, the mothers of his last four children, also died. So he started new friendships. During a trip to Kyoto in 1591 to negotiate a settlement between Hideyoshi and Date of Sendai, the forty eight-year-old Ieyasu evidently engaged in a dalliance en route at his old home of Hamamatsu. The fruit of that interlude was his sixth son, Tadateru, born in January of 1592 to a woman named Kawamura (or perhaps Yamada). Later that year Ieyasu lost another consort in childbirth, but in two years the lady Kawamura gave him a second son. The following year his eighth son was born of a woman named Shimizu and his fourth daughter of a woman named Mamiya. Shortly thereafter Hidetada joined the enterprise. He married the sister of Hideyoshi's consort, Yodo, in 1595, and by 1599 he had begotten two daughters by her.

As Ieyasu's offspring grew up, he placed them with other families, turning them to maximum political advantage. In 1590 he betrothed two of his granddaughters, the children of his dead Nobuyasu, to lords of two major vassal families. His daughter Tokuhime, who had returned from Hōjō Ujinao after his death from illness in 1591, was remarried to Ikeda Terumasa, the lord at Yoshida in Mikawa. His third daughter Furuhime was married to mighty Gamō Hideyuki, Ujisato's successor at Aizu. Ieyasu adopted a son of Lord Hoshina and served as go-between to arrange any number of other useful connections.

As Ieyasu surveyed his realm from the heights of Hakone in the fall of 1600, the 1590s stood out in memory as a time of pleasurable profit, a decade that left him well prepared for the dogfight he was about to enter. In the fifth year of Keichō, however, as he headed west to call Ishida Mitsunari to account, he had no time to luxuriate in past triumphs. On September fourth he traversed the Hakone mountains and during the next few days moved briskly along the Tōkaidō. He spent one night at Mishima and another at the Seikenji. He passed through Sumpu and Hamamatsu, resting at inns on the way and sleeping one night at Okazaki. He proceeded from there to Atsuta in Owari and then to Kiyosu, where he rested two days to shake off a cold. Then he cut north and on the thirteenth reached the great castle at Gifu on the Nakasendō. As he advanced, he maintained his correspondence, receiving bits of good news and sending more deployment instructions. He learned of more lords joining his side, some of them confessing to having initially made a wrong choice, which they were speedily rectifying. As Ieyasu and his 32,700 hardy comrades neared the day of reckoning, matters were looking better and better. With a bit of luck his careful planning would be rewarded, disorder would be foreshortened, and a new era of tranquility would ensue.

CHAPTER VIII:

Sekigahara--War as Politics

Before sunrise, September 14, 1600, Ieyasu and his troops were up and in motion. They moved out of Gifu, crossed the Nagara River on a pontoon bridge, and proceeded westward through the villages of Gōdo and Ikejiri to the town of Akasaka, where his advance units had been deployed atop a hill earlier in the night. This placed them under the very nose of the enemy, about five kilometers northeast of Ōgaki Castle, where Mitsunari, his major allies, and their forces were gathered.

By noon Ieyasu had pitched camp. As the army's battle streamers fluttered in the breeze, he conducted a council of war with allied daimyo and his principal vassal commanders. The group discussed two propositions. Ii Naomasa and others proposed to attack Mitsunari and his friends at Ōgaki Castle, while Honda Tadakatsu and his supporters advised Ieyasu to march directly to Osaka and establish control there. After hearing the views of his advisors, Ieyasu decided to deploy sufficient forces to immobilize the enemy within Ōgaki Castle. The main force would push westward to overrun Sawayama Castle, then drive south to seize Osaka. This operation was to be launched the next morning.

The strategy was designed to strike directly at the heart of the enemy coalition, the key weakness of which was its leadership. The initial thrust was to be at Sawayama because it was the home castle of Mitsunari, who at forty years of age was the driving force behind the coalition. The thrust at Osaka was intended to reestablish Tokugawa control over both Hideyori and the Emperor by dislodging Mōri Terumoto, the worst political threat of all.

Terumoto was one of the Five Elders appointed in 1598 by the dying Hideyoshi. In the prime of his life at forty-seven, he ruled the second largest domain in Japan. From his castle at Hiroshima he controlled over one million *koku* of productive resources in western Honshū. He commanded one of the largest armies and emerged as the most distinguished figure in the anti-Ieyasu coalition. Although he had a reputation for being both manipulative and manipulated, he was not known for prowess as a military commander. After Ieyasu went east to punish Uesugi earlier in the year, Terumoto returned to Osaka at Mitsunari's behest. On July 17 he joined Mitsunari and others in publicly denouncing Ieyasu. Then he ousted the castellan Ieyasu had posted at Osaka before his departure and established himself in the castle as protector of the young Hideyori and as presumptive guardian of the Toyotomi family, its followers, and its pretensions to national leadership. He seized relatives of several pro-Tokugawa lords as hostages, deployed his own forces against Tokugawa supporters in the Osaka vicinity, and assumed responsibility for ordering about other daimyo.

Under the semicoordinated leadership of Mitsunari and Terumoto, the western forces overran Fushimi Castle as Ieyasu had expected. But Torii Mototada was as good as his word, mounting a defense-to-the-death that tied down important elements of Ishida's army for over ten days, and complicated attempts to concentrate a main battle force for use against Ieyasu. Western forces also overran a number of other castles held by Ieyasu's supporters, consolidating their grip on Ise Province and gaining control of the western end of the Tōkaidō. They also sent forces to capture Ōgaki Castle and win the support of the lord holding Gifu Castle, thereby dominating Mino Province and securing the Nakasendō approach to Kyoto.

During the summer as mentioned earlier, news of these developments had caused Ieyasu to delay and then abandon his plans to destroy Uesugi Kagekatsu. Instead he sent advance forces out to capture Gifu. The seizure of Gifu by Ikeda Terumasa and others on August 23 gave Ieyasu a strong forward staging position that was accessible by both the Nakasendō and Tōkaidō. Ikeda and his colleagues then pushed westward about twenty kilometers to take up a forward field position at Akasaka. Their deployment immobilized the enemy force holding Ōgaki and twenty days later provided a site for Ieyasu to pitch his camp when he arrived from Edo.

Ieyasu's political activity was as important as these military preparations. His summer letter-writing campaign proved to be prodigious and productive. According to one count, he wrote 180 letters to daimyo during his summer stay in the Kantō, sending them to 108 of the 214 lords. Of these 108 lords, 99 threw in their lot with him. By that count each letter was worth about a thousand men, with all their armor, weapons, horses and logistical support.

Ieyasu had sound reason for preparing so carefully. Much was at stake because the country was rapidly slipping into armed strife that pitted neighbor against neighbor. Regional and local barons guessed and gambled on who would win. Some lords in Kyushu

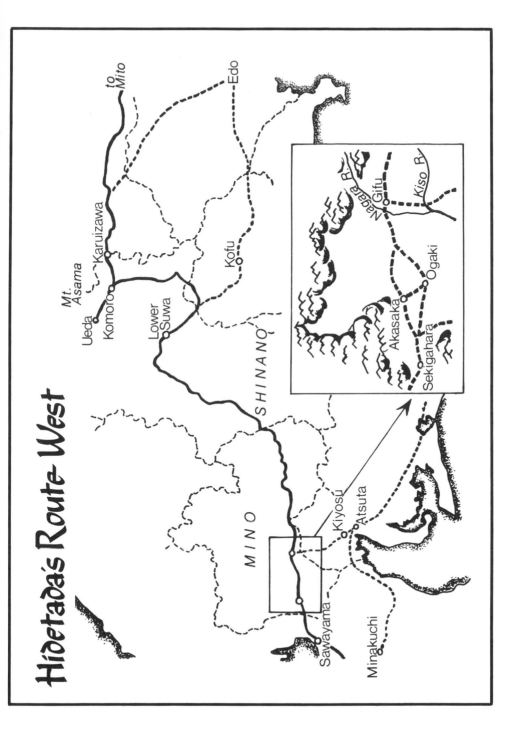

Hidetada's Route West

to Mito

Edo

Karuizawa

Mt. Asama

Ueda

Komoro

Lower Suwa

Kofu

S H I N A N O

M I N O

Kiyosu

Atsuta

Sawayama

Minakuchi

Nagara R.

Gifu

Kiso R.

Ogaki

Akasaka

Sekigahara

threw in their lot with Mitsunari; others bet on Ieyasu. In the east Uesugi battled his neighbors. So, too, did Maeda north of Kyoto. A decisive outcome in a direct confrontation between Ieyasu and Mitsunari would likely lead to rapid pacification elsewhere. An inconclusive confrontation would exacerbate local warfare everywhere.

Ieyasu had deployed his force so that when he learned of Gifu's capture, he was in a position to dispatch Hidetada along the Nakasendō while he proceeded down the Tōkaidō. The two forces were supposed to converge at Akasaka and use their combined strength to overwhelm the westerners.

At that juncture the carefully constructed plan began to fall apart. Hidetada's progress was slowed by heavy rains, and more time was lost when he besieged a castle en route. His army, which was at Karuizawa on September 1, reached Komoro, 25 kilometers distant, on the third and then bogged down in a siege of nearby Ueda Castle. He did not head south from Komoro until the ninth, after a messenger from Ieyasu told him of the Tōkaidō army's advance. An alarmed young Hidetada then hurried along, reaching Lower Suwa, some fifty kilometers away, four days later. On the morning of September 14, as Ieyasu and his commanders made their battle plans at Akasaka, Hidetada and his army were still slogging over the rugged passes and through the tortuous valleys of Shinano Province some 200 kilometers to the northeast of their destination.

Ieyasu thus found himself with half of his main force out of reach. Fortunately, he had been so careful in his preparation that he was able to proceed with one hand tied down. His forces at Akasaka were well organized and ably led. As news spread among the gathered battalions of the eastern army that Ieyasu, himself, had arrived and had defiantly established his headquarters under the very noses of the enemy, spirits soared.

In contrast the enemy was demoralized. The westerners were riddled with doubt and lacked cohesion. Even Mitsunari was discouraged. He had badly underestimated the numbers of lords who would support Ieyasu. He was disturbed by his army's lack of preparation and frustrated by his inability to anticipate Ieyasu's maneuvers. Ieyasu was supposed to be in the Kantō, tied down by Uesugi and Satake, not here below the very walls of his own headquarters! His ally, Terumoto, was procrastinating in Osaka, keeping his 30,000 troops out of the fray despite Mitsunari's requests for help. The powerful Shimazu of Kyushu were not fully committed and had few troops in the area. Some lords had already changed sides, and others were behaving suspiciously.

When scouts reported to Mitsunari and his allies in Ōgaki that Ieyasu himself was within view to their north and well placed to cut off an escape to the west, consternation raced through the castle. With Mōri Terumoto refusing to advance further than Osaka, it was another of Hideyoshi's Five Elders, the young and inexperienced Ukita Hideie, who emerged as the central military figure. He discussed the situation with Mitsunari and others, notably Konishi Yukinaga, who had returned to Japan in 1598 after years of combat duty in the Korean campaign. Not far away were Natsuka Masaie and several other lords, including another Mōri and a relative of the Mōri named Kikkawa.

During the day while the Ōgaki leaders debated strategy, Ieyasu kept up his political activity. As his army prepared for the morrow, he made contact with several of Mitsunari's key supporters, most notably Kikkawa, a major lord named Kobayakawa Hideaki, and several lesser daimyo. No final understanding was reached with Kikkawa, but Kobayakawa and the others agreed to betray Mitsunari at the opportune moment.

The support of these men had a price, needless to say, but the old badger preferred buying the men to defeating them; it was much easier to do and far more helpful to his overall objective of ruling a peaceful realm. To snare Kobayakawa, for example, Ieyasu sent Honda Tadakatsu and Ii Naomasa to talk with his senior advisors. They were to assure Kobayakawa that Ieyasu bore him no ill will and to promise him that if he served Ieyasu loyally, he would be granted a domain embracing two provinces. When Hideaki was informed, he found the price right and agreed to fight for Ieyasu.

That night word spread through Mitsunari's army that Ieyasu planned to bottle them up and move on westward. When the leaders in Ōgaki, notably Mitsunari, Konishi, and Ukita, realized what was developing, they were aghast. To avoid being trapped, they assembled their forces at once and headed west through a torrential downpour. Although harassed by elements of Ieyasu's army, they reached the vicinity of Sekigahara village sometime after midnight. The commanders deployed their forces west of the village to form a barrier across the two roads that cut westward through the hills toward Sawayama and Kyoto. At the center were the battalions of Ukita and Konishi, with Mitsunari prudently situated on the north flank and to the rear, where he could run home to Sawayama if necessary. Kobayakawa and other incipient turncoats held the south flank.

Between the downpour, the noise of the enemy's movements, and the attempts at hot pursuit, Ieyasu's army spent a sleepless night. Ieyasu was sufficiently aroused that at about two in the morning he had his horse saddled and rode out to reconnoiter. He headed west along the highway some five kilometers and then moved his forces forward. The advance units took positions direct-

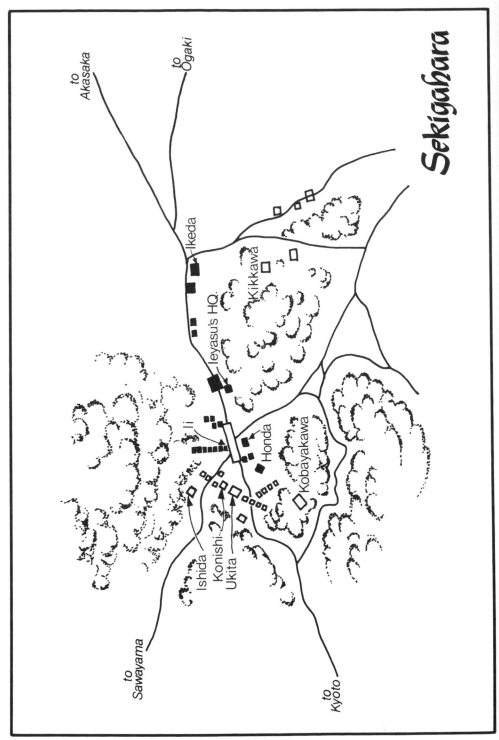

Sekigahara

to Akasaka

to Ogaki

Ikeda

Ieyasu's HQ

Kikkawa

Ii

Honda

Kobayakawa

Ishida
Konishi
Ukita

to Sawayama

to Kyoto

ly facing the enemy at Sekigahara. About two kilometers from the front Ieyasu set up his command post on a low bluff, Momokuri-yama, overlooking the village and battle field. Amassing a large reserve striking force there, he deployed a series of units along the road to his rear. They were to protect his flank from attack by enemy forces reportedly numbering some 30,000 that were spread out along a side road to the south. Those units, particularly some led by Kikkawa and also those of Natsuka Masaie, had no real stomach for the contest. From the previous day's communication with Kikkawa, Ieyasu realized that they were unlikely to consti-tute a real threat, and in the flanking deployment he wished only to sustain their doubts until the main force at Sekigahara had been routed.

When the sky brightened, Ieyasu rode down from his command post to survey the front. Satisfied that all was ready--troops well deployed; men, horses, and weapons ready; defectors prepared to defect--he returned to his post. A decisive moment for his family was at hand. Where, he wondered in irritation, was Hidetada? And perhaps that thought led to the next, a recollection of his first-born, whom he had ordered to commit suicide on that same day twenty-one years earlier. He was heard to murmur, "Well, I'm get-ting old and this leaves me bone-tired. If only Nobuyasu were here."

At about eight in the morning on September 15 the battle be-gan. In mud, noise, and sweat the forces struggled indecisively throughout the morning. To Ieyasu's growing consternation Koba-yakawa and the other turncoats did not turn. Evidently they were waiting to see whether it would be wise to throw in their lot with Ieyasu or with their nominal allies. Prodded by Ieyasu, who had a few warning shots fired his way, Kobayakawa finally sent his force of 8,000 hurtling at the flank of his allies. Seeing this, Ieyasu un-leashed his reserves and signalled a general attack in all sectors. Like a great swarm of screaming, steel-tipped hornets his men flew into the midst of the enemy, and in one massive two-hour brawl routed them. The forces of Ukita and Konishi were crushed. Mi-tsunari was defeated and fell back. The contingents of Shimazu extricated themselves and in a series of running skirmishes made good their escape to the south. Those enemy forces on the sep-arate southern flank, which had managed to sit the battle out, were subsequently scattered. The casualties of Ieyasu's army are unknown; his opponents reportedly suffered about 4,000 to 5,000 killed or, by another account, 8,000 dead and wounded.

Ever mindful of the larger picture, after the battle Ieyasu dashed off a note to Date Masamune, who was back east keeping an eye on Uesugi Kagekatsu, "Around noon today, the fifteenth, in the hills of Mino, we fought and routed Ukita, Shimazu, Konishi, and

Ishida. Finally the punishments and other matters can be attended to." Once that information circulated, Ieyasu knew that no one in the east would make the mistake of challenging him.

With victory, the west lay open to him. The great contest was settled. The months of careful planning were rewarded. It did not really matter where Hidetada and his 38,000 were, at least not for the moment.

CHAPTER IX:

Making Peace--Politics as War

Much had happened and quickly. On June 16 Ieyasu had left Osaka to march east and punish Uesugi Kagekatsu. He moved carefully, nourishing alliances all the way. Cautiously, he flung his noose around Aizu. For a month he followed reports closely and on August 4 made the critical decision. Throwing caution to the winds, he rushed from Oyama back to Edo and poured all his energies into preparing and deploying forces for a final confrontation with Mitsunari and his supporters. After twenty-five of the busiest days of his life, he headed west on September 1 and fifteen days later crushed his challengers at Sekigahara.

During the evening of the fifteenth, after rewarding the heroes and examining heads of the vanquished, Ieyasu set about the task that would consume him for weeks to come, that of consolidating peace by consolidating his advantage.

Those who recently became allies-of-convenience received an opportunity to prove their loyalty. Ieyasu put Kobayakawa and the other turncoats under the command of Ii Naomasa and ordered them to march on and capture Sawayama. They marched as ordered, and after a two-day siege the castle fell. Mitsunari's father, older brother, and nephew ordered their own families killed and then committed suicide. Mitsunari himself was not there, having fled from Sekigahara into the mountains. A few days later he was captured, as was Konishi. On October 1, they were placarded as rebels, paraded about Osaka and Sakai, and then taken to Kyoto and publicly beheaded. Their heads were displayed at the Sanjō bridge for the edification of everyone.

Natsuka Masaie, the peddler of guns who sat out the battle, returned briefly to his castle at Minakuchi and then moved into house arrest. There he received from Ieyasu an invitation to disembowel himself; after reflecting on the alternatives, he did so. His head was taken to Kyoto where it joined those of Mitsunari and Konishi. A few more egregious trouble-makers were disposed of with equal finality. Most, however, were managed more gently.

Ukita, for example, was ordered to return home to Kyushu to live there quietly. Later reports indicated that he was conniving with the Shimazu; so he was exiled to Hachijō Island, where he died in 1655 at the ripe old age of eighty-two.

As Ieyasu settled the more immediate scores, his forces fanned out to consolidate their hold on the Kyoto vicinity, mopping up pockets of resistance and assuring control of fortresses here and there. Ieyasu opened negotiations with Mōri Terumoto in Osaka, seeking a peaceful surrender of the castle and the return of Hideyori. To reassure the general populace and implant his control in central Japan, he promptly issued administrative orders for Kyoto and its environs. He assigned commanders to run the affairs of the city and the Imperial Court as evidence that he was again in charge.

Five days after Sekigahara, Ieyasu set up headquarters in Ōtsu, at the southern tip of Lake Biwa and just about twelve kilometers east of Kyoto. By then the Court recognized the new political realities. An Imperial emissary came to his camp to express heartfelt thanks for Ieyasu's service in quelling the rebels and restoring peace to the realm. Indubitably Ieyasu understood and appreciated the Court's practiced adaptability.

At that juncture a small but potentially disastrous family drama unfolded. While Ieyasu was at Ōtsu, Hidetada finally caught up with him. Five days earlier, as Ieyasu's army was demolishing the westerners at Sekigahara, Hidetada and his army were working their way down the narrow valley of the Kiso River some 150-200 kilometers to the east of the battle field. Two days later, as he was reaching the border of Mino province, still some 120 kilometers to the east, Hidetada learned that the battle had already been fought and won. He was grateful for the outcome but aghast at the news. He knew that his tardiness was sufficient cause for the most stringent punishment. He ordered a forced march, and in one day he and a select escort covered the 100 kilometers to Akasaka. Two days later, on September 20, he reached Ōtsu, another 90 kilometers to the west. Despite this belated display of celerity, Ieyasu was still furious that in this most critical of operations Hidetada had allowed himself to be delayed in Shinano and therefore to be of no help at Sekigahara. He had jeopardized the peace of the realm and a lifetime of effort. In his anger Ieyasu refused to meet his son.

The situation alarmed Ieyasu's advisors. This was no minor spat and its implications were fearsome. They knew very well the story of the Minamoto founder, Yoritomo, who was so distrustful of his relatives that he slaughtered most of them to eliminate rivals and ended with only two possible heirs, neither of whom proved able to perpetuate his family. Within two decades of Yoritomo's death his shogunate at Kamakura had fallen into the hands of the Hōjō family. Thereafter, at Hōjō behest, a succession of puppets took the place of the Minamoto until the regime collapsed a century later.

Ieyasu's advisors could remember how in their own lifetime Hideyoshi had destroyed the family of his adopted son Hidetsugu to assure the succession for his infant son Hideyori. Where were the Toyotomi now, with Hideyori seven years old and Ieyasu supreme? How ironic it would be if at this moment of sublime triumph a Tokugawa family quarrel should undermine the entire accomplishment! This was no time for Ieyasu to break with Hidetada, a tested and true young man who, after all, had been guilty of only one error of judgement in attempting to capture a castle he was supposed to have bypassed.

To prevent the break, Sakakibara Yasumasa and Honda Masazumi, one of Ieyasu's younger advisors at the age of thirty-five, launched a vigorous campaign of reasoning and cajoling. After three days they persuaded their lord to forgive his son and get on with the business at hand. On the night of the twenty-third Ieyasu and Hidetada met, apologies were offered and accepted, and a few days later Hidetada was again actively participating in political deliberations. One of the greatest threats to political stability--quarrels at high levels of legitimate leadership--was avoided.

Meanwhile intensive lobbying by Honda Tadakatsu, Ii Naomasa, and some major daimyo had persuaded Mōri Terumoto to turn Osaka Castle over to Ieyasu. On September 22 he notified Ieyasu that he would vacate the castle and serve him loyally henceforth. Tokugawa advance units moved in on the twenty-fifth, and two days later Ieyasu and Hidetada entered the fortress. They greeted young Hideyori and then settled in. Ieyasu again held the most powerful bastion in the country, the citadel from which he had marched in June to crush Uesugi Kagekatsu. It had been exactly one hundred days, portal to portal.

It was a fine moment, but soon, back to business: Ieyasu ordered six of his senior officials, including Ii, Honda, Sakakibara, and Ōkubo Tadachika, to assess the lands seized in the Kinai region and to prepare rewards for allied daimyo and Tokugawa vassals. He ordered Hidetada to lead forces westward to suppress holdouts and extract oaths of submission from the recalcitrant Shimazu. Just as Kobayakawa had been in the forefront of the assault on Sawayama, so Terumoto was honored with command of the vanguard sent against Shimazu.

Other fence-sitters threw in their lot with the winners, and with his hand rapidly being strengthened, Ieyasu seems to have lived up to his reputation for guile. Previously Honda and Ii allegedly had assured Terumoto that his domain would not be touched if he served Ieyasu loyally, and on that understanding Terumoto withdrew from Osaka. With Hideyori securely in hand, the old badger supposedly changed his mind. On the ground that he had learned more about Terumoto's misdeeds while cooperating with Mitsunari, on October 10 Ieyasu ordered the Mōri chief to surrender his 1,005,000 *koku* seven-province domain that sprawled across most of western Honshu and take in its place 369,000 *koku* in the two economically backward provinces that lay at the western tip of the island. Ieyasu put it this way in his formal notice to Terumoto and his son:

> *ITEM: you are awarded the provinces of Suo and Nagato.*
> *ITEM: no one is to harm either of you, father or son.*
> *ITEM: any rumors or loose comments about these matters*
> *are to be fully investigated.*
> *If there be any deception in these conditions, may I be punished by Benten Taishaku, the Four Kings, the gods great and small of sixty provinces of Japan, and in particular the Gongen of Izu and Hakone, the Daimyōjin of Mishima, Hachiman Daibosatsu and the independent god to Tenman.*

Even the most reassuring phrasing could not conceal the magnitude of the Mōri loss. Having indecisively thrown in his lot with the wrong side in the first place and then belatedly jumped to the winner's side, Terumoto had been rewarded with a massive reduction of his family possessions. It was better than having one's head posted in Kyoto, of course, and better than being shipped to Hachijō Island, but it was no cause for rejoicing. Knowing at last the price of poor judgement, Terumoto took the tonsure and became a Buddhist monk. This gave him time to reflect on the transience of glory, and the Mōri did not trouble the Tokugawa again for over 250 years.

So the autumn passed. Courtiers assiduously cultivated the new ruler, and Ieyasu showered gifts on the Court. Depending on how they assessed their prospects, a few daimyo committed suicide, went into hiding, or retired. But far more curried favor, and Ieyasu received them in both formal audiences and informal meetings. He shifted lords about, eliminated or trimmed the domains of the less worthy, and elevated and rewarded the more deserving. His officials strengthened their control of those lands he kept for himself in the Kinai region by issuing regulations, deploying administrators, posting police forces, collecting taxes, surveying lands and villages, and assigning small fiefs to deserving minor vassals.

Ieyasu found time to address the Aizu question again. On October 15 he wrote Date Masamune, who was still keeping an eye on

Uesugi. He reported on his current situation, informed Masamune that in the following spring he would return to the interrupted task of destroying the Aizu lord, and instructed him to help suppress a vassal of Uesugi's, who was pillaging the countryside. A few days later he wrote to Mogami as well, ordering him to prepare for an assault on Aizu.

Ieyasu did not forget Maeda, his other great ally of the aborted Aizu campaign. While he was at Ōtsu, even before meeting Hidetada, he rewarded Maeda and promised him that in the fullness of time Hidetada's daughter Tamahime would be wed to Maeda's adopted son.

Life was returning to normal. On November 9 Ieyasu found time to attend a Nō performance, which he praised and rewarded. Nineteen days later the fifty-seven-year-old man learned that Lady Shimizu at Fushimi had borne him his ninth son, Yoshinao.

It did not matter much that on New Year's Day of 1601 Ieyasu was sick in bed with a slight cold. He simply postponed his season's greeting to everyone. Who, after all, would tell him what to do? A few days later, when he was well again, the daimyo came to pay their respects. Courtiers also came to visit, and Hideyori honored him and Hidetada with a fine banquet. Meanwhile salutations poured in from all over the land. He replied by presenting assurances, honors, lands, and other rewards to vassals, allies, temples, shrines, and the Court.

By March of 1601 much of this happy activity had been completed. Ieyasu cancelled the campaign against the Shimazu family because their leaders agreed to submit. All seemed well, so he left Hideyori at Osaka and moved back up to Fushimi. He sent Hidetada back to Edo to take charge there. Ieyasu himself found time in May to assign lands to the Emperor and the Court nobility, and to visit the Court and accept new titles and honors. These, however, did not yet include the title of shogun. He concentrated on the minutia of rewarding vassals, assigning land, settling disputes of myriad sorts, issuing administrative regulations for temples, villages, towns, daimyo, and Court nobles, and meeting an endless stream of visitors.

An illustration of his administrative technique was his order of October 9 that called for the measurement of all residences in Kyoto. Block by block mapping of the city would serve three purposes. Identification of the holders of all dwellings would enable Ieyasu to know whom to arrest when criminals or political enemies were found hiding in any house or other structure. It would establish which land belonged to whom so that if fire swept a neighborhood and consumed the wooden structures, it would be possible to delineate again the boundaries of everyone's property. This would eliminate a potential source of endless litigation. Measurement would determine the amount of land and buildings one held, suggesting the general magnitude of one's wealth and hence the level of impost one could be asked to pay the government.

For similar reasons Ieyasu ordered land surveys conducted and ledgers prepared in which the productive potential of an increasing number of villages was fully recorded. Enduring government involved elaborate record-keeping, a game of numbers. He who had access to the right numbers could rule; he who did not, could not.

As order and regularity were imposed on the land, Ieyasu fell ill near the end of June. This time it was no mere head cold. A worried Court ordered temples and shrines about the land to pray on his behalf, and seven days later, as his illness dragged on, the Court sent him medicinal potions and wishes for a prompt recovery. But he did not recover. While he lay ill, political decision-making slowed to a crawl and the country watched with hushed breath. Would he die? Would war resume? Would the realm again dissolve into violence and bloodshed? The oppressive summer days dragged by in Fushimi. Fetid heat, mosquitoes, and uncertainty about the future poisoned the atmosphere. After a month-and-a-half the fever finally subsided, Ieyasu revived, and the business of securing the peace was resumed.

With illness behind him, Ieyasu returned his attention to Uesugi. The delayed spring campaign was cancelled because Uesugi realized how things stood and expressed a newfound readiness to submit. On August 8 Ieyasu's eldest surviving son, Yūki Hideyasu, escorted Uesugi to Fushimi. Sixteen days later, Ieyasu graciously allowed him to transfer from his mountain-rimmed, insular, 1,200,000 *koku* fief of Aizu to the even more insular, even more mountain-rimmed, 300,000 *koku* domain of Yonezawa to the north. In Kagekatsu's place at Aizu, Ieyasu reassigned his old ally, friend, and son-in-law, Gamō Hideyuki, with 600,000 *koku* of land. The shift put a reliable man on his northern border and left him with 600,000 *koku* to distribute to others. This transaction was carried out without having to field a single soldier. Nobody died. No one became a hero. No new obligations were incurred. He had 600,000 *koku* of land to spend as he pleased. Good politics was demonstrably a profitable way to wage war.

By September of 1601 Ieyasu again had time to think of cultural matters. He ordered a temple school and library built and opened in Fushimi, naming it Enkōji. He placed in it the printing press that his scholar-friend Kanshitsu Genkitsu and the Zen abbot Saishō Shōda had used in producing books for him before Sekigahara. Then he appointed Genkitsu master of the Enkōji. Before taking service in Kyoto, Genkitsu had served as head of the Ashikaga library, founded by a shogun of the Ashikaga family. One suspects that in making that appointment Ieyasu was consciously laying another foundation stone for a Tokugawa shogunate.

A month later Ieyasu found time and reason to think again of those exotic creatures from afar, the foreigners from Europe. Hideyoshi had crucified some Franciscan missionaries and their followers in 1596 in an apparent attempt to prevent Spanish encroachment on Japan. A few months later, when in a less rancorous spirit, he backed off, and a few Franciscans remained in Japan while others later returned surreptitiously. During October of 1601 Ieyasu granted an audience to one of these returnees, Jeronimo de Jesus. De Jesus wished to establish a good working relationship with the new ruler, and Ieyasu agreed to send a message to his superior in Manila, expressing goodwill and a desire for more commercial ties.

Then there were the English pilot, Will Adams, and his Dutch companions, who had crossed the Pacific under harrowing circumstances only two years earlier. They had been sent eastward to Edo after the interview in Osaka Castle in early 1600. The particulars of their situation in Edo in following months are unknown except that they were billeted somewhere in the Kantō during the months before and after Sekigahara. They sought to leave Japan, but Ieyasu refused permission, evidently hoping they would prove useful in promoting trade with Holland and England. They had no choice but to make do for the time being on the monies left over from their ship's treasury plus such modest support as Ieyasu assigned to them.

By the autumn of 1601 the realm seemed in order. On October 12 Ieyasu departed Fushimi for Edo, taking time to hawk en route. He stayed two and a half months in Edo, hawking now and again, and then returned to Fushimi shortly after New Year's of 1602. He occupied most of his hours with the myriad affairs of state but found some time for family matters. Early in 1602 his tenth son, Yorinobu, was born. A few days before, his old mother, Odai no Kata, came up to Kyoto to visit him, bringing along two of her sons by her second marriage.

Odai no Kata's life had been busy. After being taken from her first husband and her baby boy by the exigencies of war in 1544, she married a man named Hisamatsu and bore him three sons and four daughters. Yet she never forgot her first-born, Ieyasu. When he was brought to Owari, as a child hostage in 1547, she sent him gifts and tried to ease his life. When he was transferred to Sumpu, she sent servants to check on his condition. He visited her in 1560 just before breaking with the Imagawa. As his fortunes improved, she continued to keep in touch from her home in Owari. Late in 1601, as he was heading east for his brief visit to Edo, he stopped to invite her to pay a formal visit to Court after his return. And she came.

Ieyasu was delighted to see his mother and welcomed his half-brothers, whose children later proved useful in his marriage politics. Odai no Kata surely had reason to marvel at the ways of the world. Her first-born, separated from her when he was two years old, taken hostage and kidnapped at the age of four, now was the ruler of Japan. His Court rank was the highest in the land, surpassing even that of Hideyori. He entertained her lavishly, and two months later she had an audience with Emperor Goyōzei; it was a time of extraordinary triumph in her life.

Three months later, however, she fell ill. Despite vigorous Imperial prayers at temples and shrines, after a month's illness she died at Fushimi on August 28, 1602. The Fushimi summer, which nearly killed Ieyasu the year before, had claimed his mother. Her ashes were removed to Edo and placed in the Dentsūin temple in the Koishikawa district of the city. Dentsūin, as she was posthumously called, was 74 years old.

Shortly after his mother's death, Ieyasu made a short trip to Edo, as he did in late 1601, leaving Fushimi early in October and returning by New Year's. He ran through the usual New Year's greetings with Imperial princes, lesser courtiers, religious leaders, and daimyo, and then he turned his attention to more dramatic affairs.

A year earlier, on February 20, 1602, the Court had discreetly suggested that it was prepared to designate Ieyasu "Head of the Minamoto" (Genji no chōja), a title that was direct prelude to appointment as shogun. Perhaps because he was busy entertaining his mother at the time, or more likely because his relationship with Shimazu and Satake was not yet settled, he declined the offer. By early 1603 his mother was gone, the Shimazu had formally submitted, and Satake was relocated to a more modest and very cold domain at Akita in northern Japan.

With affairs thus ordered, Ieyasu evidently felt it was time to accept the shogunal title. To set the process in motion, he notified the Court that his ancestry traced back to the Minamoto by way of a family named Nitta. According to the later official Tokugawa version, his distant ancestor Chikauji had originated in a family named Tokugawa (but written with a slightly different character from Ieyasu's) residing in the village of Tokugawa adjacent to Nitta town in the northwest Kantō. That Tokugawa family was a branch of the Nitta family, which was, in turn, descended from the Minamoto. Chikauji, it was asserted, had gone to Mikawa, been adopted by the Matsudaira, and founded the line that led through five generations to Kiyoyasu, Hirotada, and Ieyasu.

In historical fact Ieyasu's genealogy is obscure. The most plausible set of records indicates that the Matsudaira line is firm back to

Chikauji's son Yasuchika. The record for Chikauji is vague, which gave Ieyasu's genealogists their opportunity for invention. It appears that about Chikauji's time an itinerant priest-entertainer came from the Kantō and was adopted into either the Matsudaira family or another family in the same vicinity. There he sired an heir. No harm was done to the record to say that he was the Chikauji in question and that his ancestors were named Tokugawa and were from that Kantō village called Tokugawa near where, years earlier, there had indeed lived a family named Nitta, which was indeed derived from the Minamoto. It was a modest improvement on the record, and it might be true.

In January of 1603 those finer points were still to be clarified, but presumably because the proper signals had been given and received, an official Court delegate informed Ieyasu on the twenty-first that the Emperor intended to designate him shogun. Ieyasu acquiesced to the Imperial wish, the elaborate planning went ahead, and on February 12 the titles were conferred. The day began rainy and unpromising, but it cleared by mid-morning before the official Court delegation bearing Emperor Goyōzei's appointments reached Fushimi for their formal presentation. On arrival, the heralds of the delegation advanced through the garden to the front entry of Ieyasu's mansion. Standing there in their formal flowing Court robes, they twice sang out, "A promotion in rank." Then they and their escorts were admitted up onto the veranda where they sat in two rows to form a pathway leading into the mansion. The senior delegate stepped up onto the veranda, advanced between the sitting escorts, and presented a box containing one of the formal patents of appointment to Ieyasu's ceremonial receptionist. The receptionist accepted the box, pivoted about, and carried it to Ieyasu, who received it sitting on his dais. He opened the box, took out the patent, and had his receptionist carry the box to another room. There a sack of gold dust was placed in it and the receptionist carried it back to the Court delegate, who took it back out to the veranda. The process was repeated until each of Ieyasu's new titles had been conferred, whereupon a considerably enriched Imperial delegation returned to Kyoto.

The appointments themselves followed precedents of the Ashikaga shogunate. They were spare, single-line notices written in formal Chinese. They stated matter-of-factly that the message of the delegate, Lord Fujiwara so-and-so, designated Ieyasu (identified by his current Court title as Minister of the Center and Imperial Retainer, Lower First Class Minamoto) as shogun (*seii taishō-gun*), Head of the Minamoto (*Genji no chōja*), Minister of the Right (*udaijin*), or whatever the particular new title of that appointment was.

Ieyasu responded by writing a prayer beseeching the gods of Taishan, the sacred Chinese mountain, to help him properly discharge his great new duties: namely, to preserve the public tranquility, keep the armies stilled, assure generations of prosperity, govern consistently, bring good fortune and health, and eradicate malign spirits and sworn enemies.

During the following weeks Ieyasu sent gifts to the Court, and on March 21 the new shogun moved from Fushimi to Kyoto to receive Imperial congratulations on his new appointment. Four days later he went to Court for an elaborate celebration, and then he entered nearby Nijō Castle, which he had ordered to be constructed only a few months earlier in the summer of 1602. Nijō was a new castle for a new shogunal dynasty.

Two days later Imperial princes and Court officials went to Nijō to offer gifts and conduct more rituals of entitlement. Ieyasu's relatives called to pay their respects. Visitors and messages poured in. For three days in early April, Ieyasu sponsored banquets and had Nō dramas performed on the stage in Nijō for the entertainment of courtiers and lords. After nearly a month of such entertainment and ritual, he returned to Fushimi.

Everything had gone well. Titles of office were in order. Symbols conformed to reality. The realm conformed to "the Way," as Taigen Sūfu had propounded it years earlier, as Hayashi Razan taught it to any who would listen, and as it was explained in such Confucian works as *Jōgan Seiyō*. The arts of war and the arts of peace had been employed properly, and in consequence an age of war had ended and an age of peace had begun.

PART II

THE SIXTEENTH YEAR OF KEICHŌ (1611)

CHAPTER X:

Routines of the New Year

Ieyasu probably felt that if he'd seen one New Year's, he'd seen them all. Before him on the first day of the first month of the sixteenth year of Keichō was the usual greeting from Hidetada at Edo. Beside it was the usual message from Toyotomi Hideyori at Osaka. There were greetings from the Court, from the daimyo, from monks, from vassals, from family members, and in all likelihood, somewhere in the pile one from the household of Will Adams. It was routine, but pleasant. It was clearly preferable to certain obvious alternatives.

On the first day of 1611, Ieyasu was in good health and reasonably good spirits for a sixty-eight-year-old man with quite enough to disturb his mind. Time had taken its toll. The tough old muscles had slowly softened, and his short stocky body had rounded out. The wrinkles of his weather-beaten old face had deepened, but his eyes still twinkled from a pudgy visage suggesting more and more the mellow spirit of a loving grandfather who was harvesting the fruits of a life devoted to honest and satisfying labor. At that time he was living in Sumpu, where he had been in nominal retirement for nearly four years, after two years of even more nominal retirement at Edo and Fushimi.

In 1605, only two years after taking the title of shogun, he had passed it on to Hidetada. He did so to establish that Tokugawa succession to the title of *seii taishōgun* was a matter of routine, involving none but the Tokugawa family and the Imperial Court. He was able to establish this principle because the country had been so remarkably tranquil during the five years since Sekigahara that there was no need for Ieyasu to retain the shogunal title himself.

The tranquility of Japan was fairly palpable. The biggest excitement in Ieyasu's two years as shogun had been the investiture of Hidetada as his successor. Planning for this succession had begun in 1604, and on February 14, 1605, Hidetada left Edo for the ceremony. He went to Kyoto, not with a small retinue, however, but with an army of 100,000, claiming that he was following Kamakura precedents. His army was divided into three segments: a vanguard, a main force, and a rear guard. It included 40 accompanying daimyo with their retinues. It required 16 days of continual passage by men and horses for the entire army to pass any single spot on its route. Crowds came from far and near to watch the great train as it advanced. After watching day after day of passing military clout, no one could doubt that Hidetada was the most powerful person in the land. That, of course, was the point of it all.

On reaching the Kyoto-Fushimi area on March 21, Hidetada saw to it that his men were billeted; then the process of formal investiture began. In a series of elaborate ceremonial steps Ieyasu and Hidetada formally greeted the Court delegates who welcomed them to Fushimi. On April 7 Ieyasu dispatched a delegate to Court to petition that he be allowed to step down and have Hidetada succeed him as shogun. During the next several days Ieyasu travelled to Nijō Castle in Kyoto, went to Court in formal attire to exchange expressions of goodwill with the Emperor, and returned to Nijō to receive a variety of lordly visitors. On the fifteenth he returned to Fushimi, and on the following day the Court conveyed the Emperor's appointment to Hidetada, who then moved into Nijō, the shogun's castle. After another ten days of ceremonial exchanges, Hidetada also returned to Fushimi. There the new shogun entertained his daimyo and the Court nobility for several days and distributed gifts lavishly. A fortnight later the ceremonies were complete. On May 15, after his army had assembled its gear and paid its bills, he started east to his Kantō bastion.

Ieyasu accomplished two things in transferring the shogunal title to Hidetada. First, he established the principle that the shogunal title was the hereditary possession of the Tokugawa family, meaning expressly the descendants of one Matsudaira Takechiyo, a.k.a. Motonobu, a.k.a. Motoyasu, a.k.a. Ieyasu, a.k.a. Tokugawa Ieyasu. Second, he shifted a host of tedious administrative and judgemental matters onto Hidetada's shoulders. For example, some days after the transfer of title, a daimyo came to Ieyasu in Fushimi to lodge a complaint against another daimyo concerning a territorial dispute. Ieyasu seized the opportunity to indicate what the transfer of authority meant. He told the daimyo to take his problem to the shogun.

Ieyasu did not, however, intend to surrender his ruling power. He was still truly in charge. It was no accident that he retained for himself the title *Genji no chōja*, Head of the Minamoto. His power derived from the horde of Tokugawa vassals who followed his orders, including those whom he had assigned to Hidetada. As long as he was head of the family, he was lord of the horde.

Ieyasu's dominance resulted in the continuing routine of commuting that he had followed since 1601. This routine took him back and forth along the Tōkaidō between Edo and Fushimi two times each year. The commute began late in 1601 when he returned to visit Edo for about two months at year's end. Then again, late in 1602, he went east for another brief visit.

The following spring he took the title of shogun, which presented a problem. As shogun he headed a government, a *bakufu*, "tent government." But where was his bakufu to be located? In Edo or Fushimi? Since his triumph at Sekigahara he had spent most of his time in Fushimi and governed from there. Perhaps he should continue to do so. Hideyoshi, and Oda Nobunaga before him, had governed from the Kyoto area. The Ashikaga bakufu had been situated in Kyoto. Being at Fushimi placed him close enough to both the Emperor and Hideyori to assure that no rivals could steal a march on him. It placed him centrally among the daimyo and in the middle of the most economically developed part of Japan. Besides, the splendid castle at Fushimi made his little fortress at Edo look like a rustic hovel.

His own domain, however, was in the east, where he and his vassals were firmly entrenched. Moreover, one could hardly point to Hideyoshi or Oda as a model to emulate. Nor, for that matter, did the Ashikaga have a record that could stand up to close scrutiny if real governance and a tranquil realm were what one had in mind. There was, finally, the basic source book on shogunal government, the *Azuma kagami* or *Mirror of the East*, the history of Minamoto Yoritomo and the Kamakura regime's early years. Ieyasu claimed Yoritomo as an ancestor and studied his life for the lessons he might learn. Yoritomo had specifically ordered his vassals to stay away from the debilitating influences of the Court and to stay on their land and remain simple and hardy fighting men. Ieyasu could appreciate that attitude. The Kamakura shogunate, a *buke* or samurai regime, had been situated in the east, clearly separated from the *kuge*, the nobility of Kyoto.

The idea appealed mightily to Ieyasu. He preferred a simple, straightforward, no-nonsense life, a *bushi* life free of *kuge* clutter. He found it in hawking. He found it in history with its practical lessons, as contrasted to poetry, which bored him with its clever pointlessness. He decided to abide by the Kamakura model and make Edo his headquarters. If Chiyoda Castle were a rustic hovel, no matter: he knew how to make it larger.

Deciding that Edo should be home for the bakufu or shogunate was not difficult, but making it function as such was another matter. Many of the bakufu's tasks involved people and matters far from Edo. Both the Court and Hideyori had to be watched. There were foreigners to deal with, to say nothing of great daimyo in the west. Ieyasu ended by trying to operate two shogunates, one in Edo and one in Fushimi. He kept commuting, as in 1601 and 1602, simply spending more time in Edo than he had before becoming shogun. He would travel west during the spring, spend the summer at Kyoto and Fushimi, then return to Edo in the fall, spend the winter there, and again head westward. He made four such round trips between the spring of 1603 and the autumn of 1606.

While in Edo during the winter, Ieyasu would receive daimyo in formal audience as they began practicing that pattern of periodic visitation which later became a compulsory routine called *sankin kōtai*, or "alternate attendance" on the shogun. They also began bringing their wives or heirs to Edo as tokens of loyalty to Ieyasu, housing them in substantial mansions built near the castle on large lots assigned by the shogunate. Before Ieyasu died, most major daimyo had erected mansions in Edo and had family members living there. This practice was later standardized as a compulsory hostage system for daimyo.

At Edo, Ieyasu and Hidetada discussed matters in general and dealt with affairs relating to the Tokugawa domain. One chronic problem of the domain, for example, was that district administrators extorted excessive taxes from the populace under their jurisdiction. Given the absolute character of shogunal authority, it was easy for such appointees to demand more and get it. Such exactions periodically led farmers to protest or even flee, abandoning their lands and homes in search of less oppressive conditions. Ieyasu wished to prevent such abscondings and protests for two reasons: they interfered with productive work and took arable land out of production, thus reducing the tax base. Moreover, they were but the tip of an iceberg of public discontent: for every farm family desperate enough to flee, there was a score that was unhappy. Seeking a stable and tranquil society for his descendants to govern for generations to come, he repeatedly punished exploitative administrators, tightened up administrative regulations to restrict their authority, and set up mechanisms of inspection to audit their performance. Eventually these efforts bore fruit, and in later generations farmers on daimyo lands would flee into the Tokugawa domain to escape high taxes and harsh rule.

During his summers at Fushimi, Ieyasu's attention was usually directed to other affairs. He received some daimyo in formal audiences and informal visits. He dealt with the Court, addressed matters relating to temples and shrines, issued licenses for foreign trade, and met occasional foreigners. A lingering problem was reconciliation with Korea. Understandably neither Korean nor Chinese authorities responded to the first peace overtures of the post-Hideyoshi regime. Finally in 1603 the Koreans suggested that if Ieyasu wished to renew contacts, the first step would be to repatriate prisoners of war. The daimyo of Tsushima, who wished to restore a lucrative trade with Korea, urged Ieyasu to pursue the Korean reconciliation. When negotiations between Ieyasu and Korea broke down, he stepped in adroitly and arranged an exchange of some 1700 prisoners. A year later trade was resumed between Pusan and Tsushima.

Those developments encouraged Ieyasu to invite a Korean delegation to visit him in Fushimi. They came, met him in early March of 1605, negotiated a peace settlement, arranged the release of 3,000 more prisoners of war, and resolved other differences left over from Hideyoshi's invasion. In 1606, negotiations collapsed again, the Tsushima lord again stepped in to heal the breach, and in May, 1607, Ieyasu met another Korean delegation at Sumpu to arrange the return of the last few prisoners of war. With the Tsushima lord again playing an astute role as sly intermediary, formal statements of diplomatic recognition were exchanged. The basis for over two centuries of trade and amity had been successfully laid.

Japanese-Ryukyuan relations worked out very differently. For years the Shimazu family of southern Kyushu had retained an ambiguous but lucrative trading relationship with the rulers of the Ryukyus. During the years of disorder in Japan, the Shimazu were unable to maintain their influence in the islands, but in the early 1600s they felt encouraged to reassert their role.

In 1603, after Ieyasu assured them possession of their domain, the Shimazu finally acknowledged Tokugawa supremacy, and in 1604 they tried to turn their subordination to profit. In February they sent a letter to the Ryukyuan ruler at his headquarters on Okinawa, reporting that Ieyasu had recently repatriated some Ryukyuan shipwreck survivors with generous assistance. The letter complained that the ruler had not made any particular expression of gratitude and advised him to do so during the coming summer or fall. An acceptable response was not forthcoming, however, and trade did not develop. In 1606, having further consolidated his ties to Ieyasu in the previous year, the Shimazu lord seized on the Okinawan's supposed insult as an excuse to launch a punitive attack on the Ryukyuan regime, and he requested Ieyasu's authorization to do so. Ieyasu, who wished to establish a China trade through Okinawa, saw this so-called punishment as a means to do so and approved. In September the Shimazu lord sent another delegate to the Ryukyuan headquarters to inform the ruler that he had better submit because Ieyasu had subdued all the daimyo and unified all Japan. He also sent a message to Chinese authorities requesting permission to conduct trade with China through Okinawa. Neither the Chinese nor the Okinawans agreed, and a further Shimazu re-

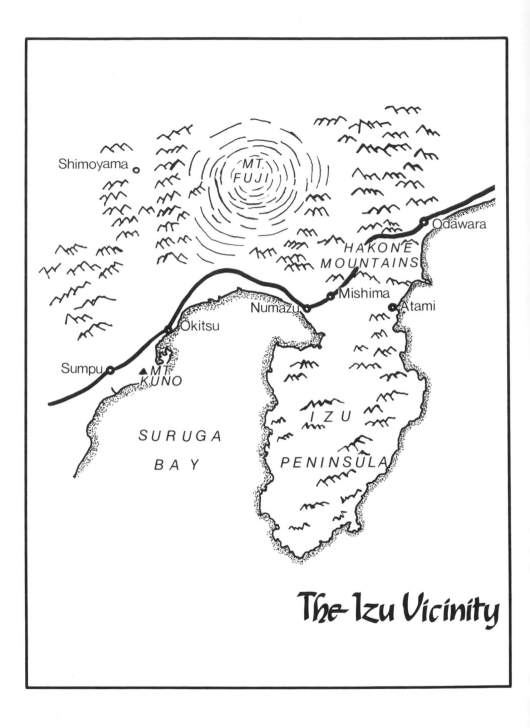

The Izu Vicinity

96

quest for trading rights in 1608 received no reply. So in the spring of 1609 Shimazu sent a force of 1500 armed men island-hopping south to Okinawa, where they overran the ruler's castle. When Ieyasu heard in July that the islands had been subdued, he granted them to Shimazu as part of the family's domain. The following year the Ryukyuan ruler journeyed to Sumpu and Edo and paid a formal visit to the Tokugawa, the lords of his lord. Even today some Ryukyuans, like Basques, Bretons, and supporters of Shays' Rebellion, wish history had worked out differently.

During his years as commuter, Ieyasu succeeded in mixing pleasure with his work. On one trip westward, for example, he stopped at a hot springs resort at Atami, just south of Odawara on the Izu Peninsula. He spent six days there, soaking in hot baths, being massaged, enjoying the scenery, talking, and eating royally. On another trip he sponsored a gala dance at Nijō to show members of the Court aristocracy the vigor and cheerfulness with which the common folk celebrated the festivals of life. On other occasions he found time to visit temples, to see famous sights, to go hawking, to engage scholars in conversation, and to promote scholarly publications, such as a new edition of *Azuma kagami*, his handbook on shogunal governance.

Nevertheless, the continual travelling punished him. Even transferring the shogunal title did not make much difference for nearly two years. It is true that when he went back east in 1605 after the investiture ceremony, he poked along, visiting several lords en route, hawking at every opportunity, and thoroughly enjoying his forty-three-day retirement-vacation trip. The next spring he headed west again on schedule, but did one thing differently. He stopped at Sumpu for four days, decided to make it his home as *ōgosho*, "retired shogun," and left orders for some castle remodeling and expansion. Then he went on to his summer's work in Fushimi and the usual round of meetings with Court people and lords.

In the autumn of 1606 he left Kyoto for his last commuter-trip east. On the way back he stopped again at Sumpu and spent twenty days there, inspecting construction work, arranging for some changes to make the castle more comfortable, and hawking as much as time permitted. He went on to Edo to stay the winter while the work was completed. He planned to move back permanently in the spring.

The winter of 1606-1607 was a watershed in Ieyasu's life. It marked the end of his years as a regular denizen of the Tōkaidō and the start of a new, more relaxed phase of life. Even the intimacies of his private life seem to have changed. Shortly after New Year's the sixty-four-year-old Ieyasu became a father for the last time, when Lady Ōta of his chamber, who was rearing his youngest son, gave birth to his fifth daughter, Ichihime.

In the winter of 1606 Ieyasu had ample reason to stop producing offspring. Not only had he plenty of children of his own, but his successor, Hidetada also had two healthy sons, as well as daughters. His own youngest sons had been assigned large domains, which his most trusted vassals administered in their names. Others of his children and grandchildren, as well as a number of adopted children and grandchildren, had been granted in marriage here and there, steadily expanding the network of family ties that would bind powerful men to Ieyasu and his descendants.

During the winter Ieyasu went hawking about the Kantō. A month after Ichihime's birth he provided a farewell party, inviting daimyo and wealthy Edo townsfolk to a Nō performance in Chiyoda Castle. Never one to entertain purposelessly, however, Ieyasu used the performance to raise support for his favorite local temples.

Then, having entertained the people and delighted the prelates in Edo, on February 29 he left for Sumpu, which became his permanent home. As with every move he had made for nearly a decade, it was accompanied by elaborate ceremonies, and after his settlement a stream of messengers brought gifts and congratulatory announcements from the Court, from Hideyori at Osaka, and from the daimyo all over Japan.

For nearly a decade thereafter the bakufu had a physically bifurcated leadership. Fortunately for many people Hidetada was a hard-working, dutiful son, and the fact that he was shogun in Edo while his forceful father continued to exercise real decision-making power in Sumpu did not lead to severe rifts and political disorder. Instead, the realm prospered under a consistent and generally benign governance.

Ieyasu and Hidetada worked hard at getting along. Each would visit the other periodically. Occasionally they went hawking together. They discussed affairs directly with one another, and they entertained one another frequently. They both enjoyed the tea ceremony. Sometimes they would sit together to be served by a tea master who would perform the graceful preparation. At other times they would serve one another. They would attend Nō productions together, would organize them for one another, and on occasion, would perform for one another on stage.

Normally Ieyasu was reasonably careful to see that shogunal edicts came from Edo before, or at the same time, that he issued his own notices at Sumpu. And when he did act unilaterally, Hidetada consistently followed his lead. For example, on June 20, 1607, Ieyasu issued a brief order establishing the position of promoter and supervisor of shipping along the rivers of Shinano Province. He named to that position a merchant, Suminokura Ryōi, who already operated an extensive domestic and overseas shipping business. On July 11 Hidetada issued a shogunal order to the same effect.

To give a more dramatic example, shortly after Ieyasu's move to Sumpu, two of his mature sons died suddenly. They were Tadayoshi and Hideyasu, both of whom were daimyo holding strategically important domains. In both cases a few close vassals of the two followed the hallowed practice of *junshi*, "following their lord in death," disemboweling themselves as a last act of supreme loyal service (or perhaps as a way to avoid blame for their lord's death or as a means of escaping other recriminations once their lord and protector was out of the way). Whatever the reason for their action, Ieyasu disapproved of the practice and Hidetada evidently concurred. To prevent the establishment of precedents, Ieyasu sent a notice to Hideyasu's senior advisors stating that reports indicated some vassals had committed suicide following their lord's death. The practice was not to be condoned, he wrote, because the domain of Echizen was very important and those who were loyal to Hideyasu should devote their services to governing Echizen. Then in a letter dated eight days earlier--but logically following Ieyasu's--Hidetada reiterated that "as directed in the order" (from Ieyasu), men should loyally serve Hideyasu's successor, Tadanao.

Over the years, moreover, Ieyasu carefully treated Hidetada with appropriate respect. His letters of state to the shogun were informal but polite. For example, following the death of Tadayoshi of Kiyosu in March, 1607, Hidetada sought his father's opinion of the posthumous punishment he had in mind for a Kiyosu vassal who had committed *junshi*. In a letter in his own hand, Ieyasu approved Hidetada's proposal in this way:

> *I agree with you. It is correct to inquire about the fief of Izumi [the dead vassal] and to confiscate it. I have read your letter. On the Izumi matter, you are right. It will be proper to examine his fief situation carefully and send a confiscation order. Implement the punishment without making any changes at Kiyosu. Warmest regards.*
> *To: Shogun*   *From: Ieyasu*
> *1607/3/11*

Surely Hidetada's character was important to the success of the dual regime. He has been described as upright, serious, cautious, and accommodating. One day Ieyasu complained to an advisor about him, saying, "Hidetada is too upright; it's not wise to be so virtuous all the time." The advisor reported the comment to Hidetada, adding, "On occasion it would do if you lie a bit." Hidetada, true to his ingenuous self, responded with a smile, "When a man such as father tells a lie, people will believe him. But when someone like myself, who has no particular attainments, tries to lie, there are no takers." Guileless by nature, he would not try to emulate his father. Instead he would be dutiful and prudent.

For some six years after his retirement to Sumpu, Ieyasu's life proved to be a busy but peaceful one with a clear and purposeful rhythm. Every autumn after the farmers had cleared their fields, he left Sumpu on an extended hawking expedition. Such an expedition, typically involving his attendants, palanquin bearers, menial servants, commissary staff, and selected ladies-in-waiting, would head up the Tōkaidō, past Mt. Fuji, over the Hakone barrier, and down into the Kantō. For several days he would hawk here and there, staying in a local temple, a wealthy farmer's house, or a local castle. After gaining a feel for affairs in the countryside, he would arrive at Edo. There he would move into the western enceinte, a section of the castle containing a layout of rooms similar to those of Hidetada's huge residence in the main enceinte and similar to his own at Sumpu. He would spend a few days there, discussing affairs of state with Hidetada, greeting those daimyo who were in town, meeting with various and sundry other people, entertaining, and being entertained. Then he would leave again, hawking his way leisurely back to Sumpu, arriving there before year's end.

After his return he would attend to various affairs, and take a day or two off to hawk in the Sumpu vicinity. Then he would accept the flood of ceremonial greetings and visitors that came with the New Year. Shortly afterward, with his entertaining completed, he would set out on another hawking expedition. This would lead him west through Suruga into Tōtōmi and even as far as Mikawa. After exploring his old domain, he would return to Sumpu and devote himself to endless affairs of state: greeting daimyo, some of whom lived more or less permanently in Sumpu; maintaining his foreign correspondence; receiving visitors; settling disputes; arranging marriages and adoptions; and sending and receiving gifts. On successful hawking expeditions, he sometimes captured cranes and sent especially handsome specimens to the Court as gifts.

Thus it was that on this New Year's of 1611 Ieyasu was at Sumpu examining greeting cards, and not the heads of fallen enemies. On the seventh day of this New Year he set forth once more to hawk, heading west into Tōtōmi, accompanied by enough attendants, ladies, and others so that he could answer any belated greetings of the season and handle any government matters that might require attention while he was in the field. Several days later he returned to Sumpu with a catch of wild geese in hand. These he promptly sent to Kyoto as a New Year's Day offering to the Court. Another year of peace had begun smoothly.

100

CHAPTER XI:

Returns from New Connections

Ieyasu completed a piece of business while out hawking at the beginning of 1611. On January 11 he authorized a number of Japanese lords and merchants to mount commercial voyages to the Philippines, Siam, and the two states of Annam and Cochin (now Vietnam). He made these authorizations easily because by 1611 they had become almost as much of a routine as the receipt of New Year's greetings.

As soon as Ieyasu consolidated his position in the country after Sekigahara, he began soliciting foreign trade. During 1601 he corresponded with the ruler of Annam, reporting that affairs in Japan were stable again, that trading problems of the recent past should disappear, and that any Japanese traders who caused trouble should be punished according to the laws of the country involved. He also suggested regulations to apply to those merchants engaged in trade to that area. In subsequent years his trade correspondence grew to include the rulers of states in Vietnam (Tonkin, Annam, Champa, Cochin), Malaya (Patani and Dendang), and Siam. He eventually established official contact with a total of some twenty foreign cities and states, primarily in southeast Asia, but a few in Europe.

Ieyasu tried to expand commerce with China, seeking both government and private trade. We noted earlier his attempt to establish such trade through Okinawa. As another example, in 1610, he sent a message to Canton assuring Cantonese merchants that they were welcome to trade "in any province, any island, any inlet" in Japan and that if they were harassed by any Japanese while carrying on their trade, the troublemakers would be promptly punished. Some private Chinese trade was maintained, but no official exchange with the Ming state developed because it was under escalating assault from Manchu invaders who were pressing in from the north.

Ieyasu's trade dealt mainly with southeast Asia. Trade correspondence was usually carried by merchants, most commonly

East and Southeast Asia

TARTARY

KOREA

Edo

Nagasaki

CHINA

Okinawa

Macao •Canton

TONKIN

PHILIPPINE
Manila

SIAM

COCHIN

ISLANDS

CHAMPA

Patani

MALAYA

BORNEO

Chinese or Japanese. Some contacts were thwarted by shipwreck or other misfortune; some collapsed due to political disorder in southeast Asia. But enough commerce developed that Ieyasu pursued southeast Asian ties as frequently as opportunity permitted. A product he avidly sought, especially in his later years, was a type of aloe used in making incense. He repeatedly asked for the finest quality aloes, which were difficult to acquire because they had to be harvested and shipped promptly so that the aromatic nectar could be extracted before the tissue of the tree actually died.

A variety of people handled trade. Between 1601 and 1616 Ieyasu issued nearly 200 licenses enabling select persons to trade at ports in China and southeast Asia. He awarded them to several daimyo, to about sixty Japanese merchants and entrepreneurial samurai, and to about twenty foreigners who were in Japan for one reason or another.

So many people undertook trading ventures because they were immensely profitable—if one were lucky. Profit required luck because trade was risky and very expensive to initiate. The merchants who undertook it frequently pooled resources to obtain and outfit a ship and stock it with merchandise for a voyage. The cost of a venture, according to one study, could range from 100 *kanme* to 1600 *kanme*, averaging 500 *kanme* of silver in value, which (at one dollar per ounce or 0.00769 *kanme* of silver) would, for an arbitrary figure, have been worth about $65,000. Such investments were worthwhile because successful voyages returned profits ranging from 35% to 110%, averaging 50% of the investments on a six-month round-trip voyage.

Trade with southeast Asia, and from there, Europe, involved some exports. Items of Japanese origin included copper, iron, sulphur, wheat flour, lightweight garment material, padded silk garments, dyed goods, tea kettles, short swords, scissors, umbrellas, mirrors, folding screens, silver, lacquerware, and folding fans.

Desire for imports, however, lay at the heart of the trade. Ieyasu received an extraordinary variety of exotic goods: cinnamon, aloes, nutmeg, cloves, refined Borneo camphor, white sugar, brown sugar, honey, grape wine, woolen cloth, dark and white cotton cloth, calico, damask, satin, figured satin, velvet, carpets, pongee, figured gauze, yellow silk thread, deerskin, sharkskin, yak skin, ivory, rhinoceros horn, water buffalo horn, peacock feathers, gold, lead, copper, zinc, mercury, cinnabar, rice bowls, sandalwood, rosewood, betel nuts, chaulmoogra (seed oil used to treat leprosy), camphor, kapok.

Items also came from Europe. Some were brought directly by Europeans, and others came indirectly by way of Japanese traders and sailors in southeast Asia. Some of these imports amounted to very little. Timepieces did not find wide appeal for another three centuries, and lead pencils did not replace writing brushes. Telescopes, however, did acquire a certain value, enriching appreciably the lives of dedicated voyeurs. European clothing—raincoats, underwear, drawers, and buttons—did not find a wide market, but *pan* ("western bread"), a Castillian sponge cake *(kasutera)*, and some European pickles did attract considerable attention. Tobacco smoking caught on: the Japanese are still unable to shake the foul habit. From classical times Japanese have played a card game called *hana awase* (or *hanafuda*), and the Europeans introduced some of their own games, but to no great acceptance. Soap was introduced, and it may have alleviated women's washing burdens. Finally, sailors returning from southeast Asia brought home Irish potatoes, squash, and *tempura* (from the Porguguese *temporas*, "meatless Friday"), a dish the world now happily believes to be peculiarly Japanese.

One European who helped facilitate trade was Will Adams. He lived in Edo and was a shadowy figure whose path occasionally crossed Ieyasu's. After holding the crew of the *Liefde* in the Kanto for a few months, Ieyasu finally got around to releasing nearly all of them. Adams, captain Jacob Quaeckernaeck, and mate Jan Joosten were not allowed to leave, however. They, presumably, could be of use in one way or another. In 1605, hoping to contact the Dutch who had recently established themselves at Patani in Malaya, Ieyasu released Quaeckernaeck to carry a message to his countrymen, inviting them to trade with Japan.

Adams and Jan Joosten remained in Japan. Ieyasu furnished them with simple homes and modest stipends in Edo. It is commonly thought that Jan Joosten's residence was in the area now known as Yaesu, but once known as Yayosu, syllables derived from his name. A wharf area in Ieyasu's day, today Yaesu is a bustling commercial zone on the east side of the huge Tokyo Station and adjacent to the Ginza district. Adams' home supposedly was nearby but to the east along the former wharf area of Nihonbashi in a section that came to be known as Anjinchō or "Anjin's neighborhood." Adams came to be known in Edo as Miura Anjin. The name presumably referred to his role as pilot, or *an* "one who observes" *shin* "the compass needle." He was called Miura because his income derived from a piece of hilltop land that Ieyasu assigned him in the village of Hemi on Miura Peninsula south of Edo, in what is a section of the modern-day naval port town of Yokosuka.

Ieyasu found Adams helpful on occasion as an interpreter because he knew Portuguese and yet was no missionary. Indeed, he was able to provide Ieyasu with an alternative source of information and interpretation in his infrequent dealings with Europeans. As an expression of his appreciation for Adams' service, Ieyasu provided him not only with a house and income but also with a wife, the daughter of a pack-horse operator at a highway station. In the fullness of time she bore him a son Joseph and a daughter Suzanna. Adams' interpreting duties occasionally took him to Hirado, and he evidently left a son there as well. Ieyasu, of course, would have expected no less of him, but in any event, his contact with Adams was rare and inconsequential, except as it involved the advancement of foreign trade.

In 1609 the Quaeckernaeck message finally bore fruit, with Adams' help. That summer a Dutch trading vessel anchored at Hirado in Kyushu. One of the officers, Jacques Specx, soon made contact with Adams and Jan Joosten, who escorted him to meet Ieyasu at Sumpu. Adams served as interpreter. In July Ieyasu accepted a letter from the Dutch king and sent a reply agreeing to the request for trade and welcoming close relations between the two countries. He also authorized Specx to erect a trading station in Hirado and issued to another crewman, Jacques Groenewegen, a license authorizing Dutch ships to come and trade anywhere in Japan.

Imports were the core of this foreign trade, and Ieyasu was ready and able to pay cash for them. He could do so because he had an abundance to spend if he chose to spend it. He was mining precious metals in prodigious quantities and having the yield cast into coins for commercial use. A Spaniard living in Japan at the time reported that,

> There are many gold and silver mines in this realm, and at the present day only the king still works them. But there are mines everywhere and the metal is of high quality; the gold ore is so rich that they obtain ten taels (about fifteen ounces) of gold from every spadeful.

The "king", of course, was Ieyasu, and he worked the mines with vigor. Earlier, during his rise to power, he promoted mining in his own domain, just as had other lords in theirs. Hideyoshi had established some central control over much of the gold, silver, and copper mining in the land, and after Sekigahara, Ieyasu intensified that control. He imposed mining fees on those lords who continued to work mines on their own domains. Moreover, he obtained direct control of some major mining areas by confiscating them from daimyo who had chosen poorly in the weeks before Sekigahara. Most notably, the mines of Iwami province had belonged to Mōri Terumoto before the battle; and those of Sado Island, to Uesugi Kagekatsu. After Sekigahara they belonged to Ieyasu; everyone knew why.

Ieyasu dispatched an administrator named Ōkubo Nagayasu to

develop the largest mines. An interesting character, Nagayasu was originally the second son of a comic actor and had gained samurai status as a civil and financial administrator in the service of the Takeda of Kai. After their destruction in the 1580s, he joined Ieyasu, who found him an able manager. Ieyasu's close vassal Ōkubo Tadachika adopted him, hence his name. During the 1590s he rapidly assumed more responsible posts and by the early 1600s had become one of Ieyasu's most influential officials, to the irritation of hardened fighting men such as Honda Tadakatsu. Ieyasu chose to disregard the complaints of Tadakatsu and put Nagayasu in charge of such important tasks as developing the new bakufu's Edo city expansion program, its post-station system, land-tax policies, and bullion mines. In later years Nagayasu found the temptations too great. He surrounded himself with pleasures, including a bevy of twenty beautiful women and thirty entertainers. After his death in 1613 investigators uncovered a trail of peculation that ruined his reputation and the careers of his descendants.

Before his fall, however, Nagayasu was instrumental in making Ieyasu one of the world's richest men. When he took charge of the thirty-six mines on Sado, for example, they were producing very little. He opened major new veins, added manpower, tightened control of processing, and within two years had increased production so that in 1609 the island yielded some 10,000 *kanme* of silver bullion which at one dollar an ounce has a value of $1,395,200. In Iwami, production reached 4,000 *kanme* that year; other mines in Izu and elsewhere also produced substantial amounts of silver and gold. The mines on Sado reached peak production between 1618 and 1627. They yielded upwards of 100 tons of bullion annually for a few years, but some were later flooded out and others played out. They were of little value thereafter.

Mining was no picnic. In yielding up their treasure, the mountains exacted a heavy human toll. Most of the placers or surface deposits had long since been panned and sluiced; therefore Nagayasu's mines were underground, following seams of ore along convoluted courses to placers and veins hidden deep within. On Sado men dug the ore out of narrow tunnels and hauled it to human-powered inclined conveyors and hand-operated pulley hoists, raising the ore to levels where gravity could sluice it to the mine entrance as slurry. Hand-operated pumps prevented flooding of the mines and provided water for the sluice. At the mouth of the mine, workers processed the slurry and refined the ore, melting it and pouring it into molds to form bullion for shipment to Ieyasu's mints.

Mining accidents were common. Mines flooded and tunnels collapsed when earthquakes ruptured areas weakened by excavation, or when careless digging precipitated local cave-ins. The profits, however, were so great that besides the miners hired to work those mines directly controlled by Nagayasu's lieutenants, large numbers of independent men hired on to work their own areas, mostly placers, on a sharecropping basis. Miners cheated when they could, and supervisors punished them ruthlessly in vain attempts to stop it. Despite the risks, men stayed as long as the ore made it worthwhile. The operation was coordinated well enough to make Ieyasu a rich man, but poorly enough that much of the treasure flowed into the hands of miners, transporters, and the administrators themselves. That is one reason why Nagayasu came to such grief.

The lucrative mines were thus the creation of men who worked for Ieyasu; the same was true of the mints. In May of 1601, a month before his serious illness, Ieyasu instructed a merchant from the city of Sakai, near Osaka, to establish a silver mint or *ginza* in Fushimi to produce a standardized coinage for commercial use. Later the mint was moved to Kyoto. A second one opened in Sumpu and two others operated for a few years in Osaka and Nagasaki. Shortly after Ieyasu's death the Sumpu mint was moved to Edo, and eventually it was located just east of Chiyoda Castle in a section known even today as the Ginza, the heart of downtown commercial Tokyo.

During the preceding century coinage had proliferated. Many daimyo produced their own, and some 135 types of coins were in circulation. Nobunaga and Hideyoshi reduced that number substantially, but Ieyasu wanted to standardize the nation's currency in terms of regulated issues of gold, silver, and copper coins of designated relative values. The coins produced by his mints set standards of metallic purity, design, and usage against which later issues of coins were measured until the late nineteenth century. Even today, the gold Keichō *ōban* and *koban*, and the silver Keichō *chōgin*, are highly prized collector's items. Ieyasu's attempt to mint a standardized copper coin for daily use, the Keichō *tsūhō*, proved unsuccessful. Not until after 1636 was a new copper coin, the Kan'ei *tsūhō*, put into circulation, replacing a variety of older copper coins, and surviving today as a common collector's item.

Much as the comic actor Ōkubo Nagayasu had played a key role in developing Ieyasu's mines, merchants played a key role in minting. One such merchant was of a family named Gotō; another, a man known as Daikoku Jōze, "Daikoku the Assayer." Unlike Ōkubo, Gotō and Daikoku managed to keep clean reputations, and their descendants became major figures in bakufu minting operations for the rest of the Tokugawa period.

Their minting efforts were impressive. They produced so much more money than needed that Ieyasu cached vast quantities of coins new and old, copper, silver, and gold, in his treasure rooms in the donjon at Sumpu. On auditing his estate after his death, officials found vaults filled with 470 boxes of gold coins, 4,853 boxes of silver coins, and 55 large trunks of copper coins. He reportedly bequeathed to his successor, Hidetada, and his three young sons, Yoshinao, Yorifusa, and Yorinobu, coins and other treasure worth nearly 2,000,000 *ryō*, a sum equivalent to nearly twelve years worth of tax income from the entire Tokugawa domain. The hoard had a rice-purchasing power of nearly $300,000,000 in contemporary American money.

Even as his mines poured forth their wealth, Ieyasu did his best to avoid spending it. He relied heavily on daimyo in his massive construction projects. He pursued profitable foreign trade. When he gave gifts, they were usually simple items of symbolic value only, such as game taken in the hunt, fruit in season, or products of local fame. He repeatedly advised his vassals to live frugally and in his daily habits tried to serve as a model. When he went hawking, for example, he preferred simple baked lunches to elaborate banquets. Even at home he maintained a simple palate, to the occasional irritation of his household ladies, who yearned for finer things.

Popular wisdom credits Ieyasu's fondness for simple food with being the end of him. His final sickness commenced during a hawking expedition, and the customary story tells us that while he was hunting, his friend, the merchant Chaya Shirōjirō, visited to pay his respects. Talking idly, Chaya described a tasty dish then fashionable in Kyoto, the fish sea bream *(tai)* fried in sesame oil and garnished with shredded garlic. Ieyasu said it sounded delicious and promptly ordered two varieties of sea bream caught and prepared in the Kyoto manner. They were served, and he pronounced them excellent and ate his fill. Shortly afterward he became sick, presumably from spoiled fish, and never recovered. The story does not fit the details of his death, as we note later, but it does convey a sense of his frugal nature.

Despite the boxes of treasure he was accumulating, Ieyasu did not neglect the land tax. He took steps to prevent district administrators from levying excessive assessments on peasant producers. He was equally concerned that administrators collect fully--and forward to higher officials--the taxes that were properly due. After answering his New Year's correspondence in early 1611, going hawking, and licensing various men to trade in southeast Asia, he received and examined annual financial reports for the past year. Satisfied that all was in order, he sent his tax collectors audit vouchers certifying that payments had been received. Having done their share to maximize Ieyasu's annual returns, they had helped him start a good New Year.

CHAPTER XII:

The King-Maker at Work

Something was troubling Ieyasu at the beginning of 1611. His relationship with Emperor Goyōzei had gone sour, and late in 1610 he had reluctantly agreed to Goyōzei's retirement. The event was scheduled for the spring, and Ieyasu wished to assure that it was handled properly and that the new Emperor, young Go Mizunoō, took his position with an acceptable understanding of how his office related to that of the Tokugawa shogun.

Ieyasu's concern with the Imperial succession revealed his overall perception of the universe. In effect he viewed it as a gigantic watch, an organic whole consisting of many parts. When all the parts were fitted together correctly, the whole would function smoothly, which was characteristic of the Way as expounded by his Confucian mentors. However, if even a single piece were loose or out of place, the whole might malfunction. Because he was the master watchmaker, his task was to understand how all the pieces were to fit together, and to assure that they did so.

The problem of Goyōzei had taken shape during the previous year, and as much as Ieyasu wanted to, he could not dismiss it lightly. He had to pay attention, not only due to overarching Confucian considerations, but also because the Court was politically important despite its lack of military and economic power. Only the Emperor could appoint a shogun, as Goyōzei had appointed him shogun in 1603. Only an Emperor could transfer the title to one's son, as Goyōzei had transferred it to Hidetada in 1605--at Ieyasu's request of course. Nor could simply anyone be Emperor. Unless one were a son of an Emperor or had an appropriately close relationship so that one could be adopted as an Emperor's son, one could not become Emperor. At any given time, therefore, only a handful of people were potentially appointable as Emperor. To preserve peace, it was important to keep such people under control. Prudence dictated that one do this in such a way as to retain, as far as possible, the goodwill of those close to the Imperial title lest they start aiding and abetting malcontents.

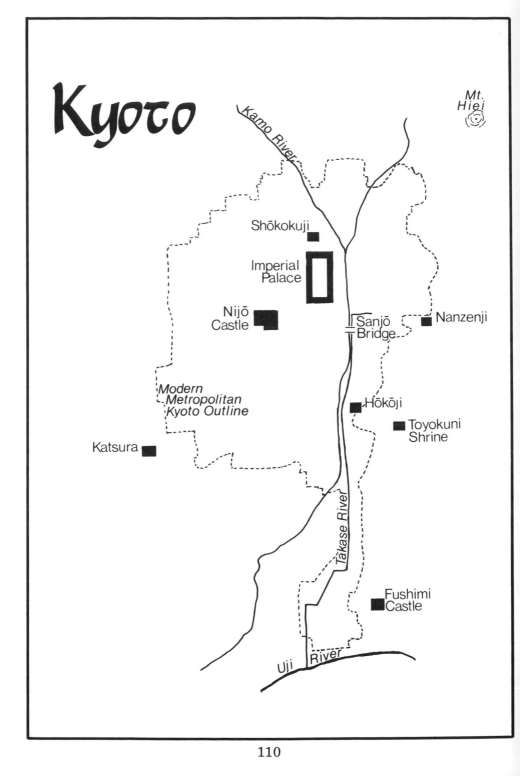

Kyoto

Mt. Hiei

Kamo River

Shōkokuji

Imperial Palace

Nijō Castle

Sanjō Bridge

Nanzenji

Modern Metropolitan Kyoto Outline

Hōkōji

Toyokuni Shrine

Katsura

Takase River

Fushimi Castle

Uji River

Ieyasu's appreciation of these realities led him to build Nijō Castle just a few blocks--a bit more than a cannon shot--from the Imperial Palace. He had the castle built in 1602-1603 as a simple but firm reminder to everyone that the new shogunate's presence was close, permanent, and generously paternal. The castle's moats, sculpted stone walls, parapets, gates, and towers were small by comparison with those of major castles, but by Kyoto standards they were massive. In later years much added work was done on Nijō, and the castle as it stands today is a work of art. The exteriors of its main buildings are decorated with gold leaf. The interiors are partitioned with great sliding doors covered with immense murals painted by leading artists of the seventeenth century.

Even in its simple original form, Nijō Castle stood as a message that none could miss. Moreover, Ieyasu permanently stationed garrison forces of swordsmen and pike-wielding patrolmen in the city. He installed city administrators assisted by investigators, accountants, and political facilitators, and stationed one of his best vassal commanders there permanently, to control all military forces in the vicinity, to supervise the Court, and to reinforce city administrators if necessary.

Along with Nijō and all its accoutrements, Ieyasu lavished both token and substantial gifts on the Court and aristocrats. He assigned lands to them to assure a regular source of income. Since he who gives can also take away, even his generosity had its coercive aspects.

Ieyasu's policy of velvet glove and mailed fist worked well for several years. He got on reasonably well with Goyōzei despite the Emperor's personal discontent with his preeminence. His generosity and strict attention to procedural correctness were appreciated by the titled aristocrats at Court, and in the early years after Sekigahara they were relatively cautious and presented him with few problems. He was even agreeable in 1603 when the Court issued self-governing regulations for the aristocrats.

By 1609, however, the comfort and security of the new order had eroded the caution of the Kyoto elite. Several members of the Court were found guilty of sexual indiscretions with one of the Emperor's favorite ladies. Goyōzei was furious; the affair was quite unacceptable to the Court's leaders. They asked the shogunate to advise them on the matter but were told to handle it themselves. They recommended the death penalty. Ieyasu felt the penalty to be a bit extreme, so he intervened, reducing the punishment to exile for five and pardons for two of the nobles.

Goyōzei was severely embarrassed by the outcome and angered by this reversal of shogunal policy. Perhaps this eruption of political tension exceeded his strength because he was reported to be seriously ill with a nervous affliction. His eyes troubled him, his chest throbbed, he vomited when trying to eat, his stomach ached,

111

he suffered from diarrhea, and when left alone in a room, he grew hysterical. Just before year's end he indicated his wish to retire and in early 1610 dispatched officials to Sumpu to arrange with Ieyasu for abdication and for the coronation of a new Emperor. At that time the sudden death of his youngest child, Ichihime, was distressing Ieyasu and he made no reply. A month later, however, he informed Goyōzei that for reasons of procedural correctness he could not agree to abdication at that time.

During the autumn Ieyasu addressed the matter again. He indicated that the succession would be executed in the following spring and sent advice to Kyoto concerning the training of Goyōzei's successor. He also decided to visit Kyoto to oversee the event. He departed Sumpu on March 6, 1611, making his first trip to the Kyoto area since the autumn of 1606. Not being a shogun, he did not take an army of 100,000, as Hidetada had done in 1605, but assembled 50,000 and a covey of accompanying daimyo. Neither the Court nor anyone enroute could mistake the message: an Imperial succession occurs only with Tokugawa approval.

He travelled for eleven days and on the sixteenth of the month entered Nijō. Ten days later Goyōzei formally retired and Go Mizunoō succeeded to office. The former was forty years old; the latter, fifteen.

Ritual visits filled Ieyasu's days at Kyoto. Several of his sons came to Court and received new titles and promotions. Toyotomi Hideyori and Hideyoshi's widow, Kōdaiin, called on him, and he sent sons to Osaka to pay a return visit. Ieyasu presented a number of generous gifts to the Court, and during March he ordered daimyo to commence a major program of construction to expand and improve the buildings and grounds of the Imperial Court. The most famous product of that project was Katsura Detached Palace, one of Japan's greatest architectural masterpieces.

Ieyasu intended this construction project to restore some of the Court's former grandeur. The Kyoto Imperial palace grounds of today are in basic outline the product of that effort, except that the area once covered by residences of the aristocrats is now open park surrounding the palace proper.

Ieyasu's construction project was so extensive as to require the bringing of vast quantities of lumber into Kyoto. Not to do things by half measures, Ieyasu decided to expedite the transport. He ordered that a new river be dug, running directly south from between Sanjō Bridge and the Imperial Palace through Fushimi to the Uji River. Suminokura Ryōi was put in charge and construction was undertaken. The twelve-kilometer canal was dug and water from the Kamo River diverted into it. The new river then filled with barges hauling logs into the city for construction of the Hōkōji and the Imperial Palace. From the type of vessels that plied it, the river came to be known as the Takasegawa (Takase River), and food, firewood, lumber, and other commodities were hauled up to Kyoto on it until well into the twentieth century.

The king-maker who could amass an army of 50,000, install an Emperor, build a palace, and create a river also had the political strength essential for the completion of other enterprises. Indeed, on the very day Ieyasu left Sumpu for Kyoto, Hidetada in Edo issued orders to the daimyo to launch a major new phase of construction on Chiyoda Castle.

During 1592-1593 Ieyasu had converted his rickety little castle into a modest yet solid defensive bastion, but only after Sekigahara did the town of Edo and its castle really begin to grow. This growth was propelled by Ieyasu's decision to locate his bakufu there and his determination to transform his castle from a rustic hovel into a bastion worthy of a shogun.

Near the end of 1601 a fire erupted in Edo. Driven by the gusty dry winds of winter, it roared through the town and reduced most of it to ashes, undoing several years of urban development. Some reconstruction occurred during 1602, but the town hardly looked fit to house a bakufu. Therefore in March 1603, shortly after being named shogun, Ieyasu ordered the daimyo to provide laborers and materials for urban reconstruction and improvement. Honda Tadakatsu and others were put in charge, and work orders issued. The high ground in the modern Surugadai district was leveled, transported to the coastal area, and dumped, to form the Nihonbashi-Ginza area. Canals were dug, streets laid out, and buildings erected.

By the end of 1604 the basic geographical preparation was complete and new shogunal orders instructed the daimyo to enlarge Chiyoda Castle. The lords had to contribute labor crews according to fixed scales of obligation, sending them to specified places to dig, hew, and haul. Flotillas totalling some 3000 ships were built, taken to Izu Peninsula, loaded with great stone blocks cut out of a mountain there, and towed up to Edo. Each ship could carry two such blocks per trip and could make two trips per month. In Edo the vessels were pulled through the canals to the work site, where the stones were levered into position on the massive walls that were taking shape. Other lords had the task of skidding and rafting huge logs out of forests in Shinano, Ise, Izu, and other provinces, and transporting them to Edo for use in the construction.

Through 1605 and 1606 the immense project continued. When Ieyasu returned from his last regular visit to Kyoto in the fall of 1606, the *honmaru*, "central keep," with its sprawling shogunal residence *(ōoku)* and the outer ramparts and moats *(gaikaku)* were complete. In later years, as in 1611, further construction projects added more walls, moats, enceintes, gates, barbicans, and a tower-

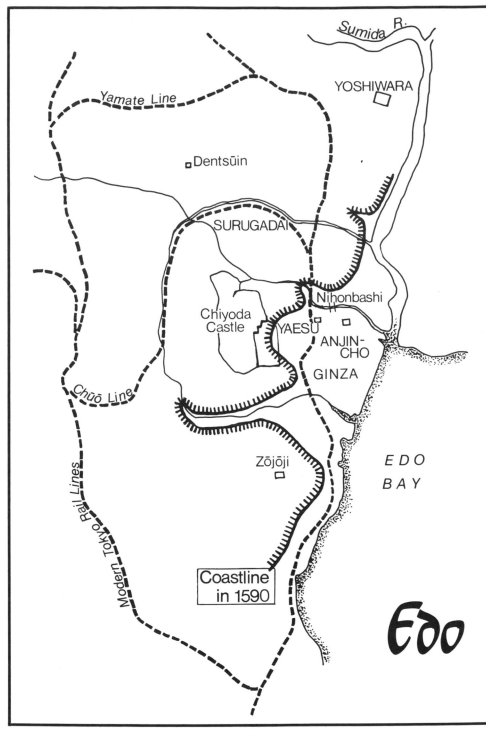

ing donjon *(tenshukaku)*. And around the castle an endless process of construction continued, adding streets, houses, inns, warehouses, canals, wharfs, and store fronts. By 1700 the work had transformed the rather small castle town of Edo into a great city; by 1800 it was the largest city in the world, a metropolis of over 1,000,000 residents, the heart of what has become modern Tokyo.

As of 1611 that gargantuan outcome lay far in the future, but Chiyoda Castle was already a bastion worthy of a shogun. No daimyo would think lightly about attacking it. Nevertheless Ieyasu wanted military might to function as his regime's last line of defense, not its first. The first line of defense was to be habit and conviction, habitual adherence to peaceful behavior based on the conviction that such behavior is right as well as prudent. And there were other lines of defense.

One was bedroom politics. By 1611 Ieyasu had arranged so many marriages and adoptions that he was related to almost every major daimyo in the country. He was always ready to do more. Thus, while in Kyoto that year, he adopted a daughter of Ikeda Terumasa, whose wife was his own daughter Tokuhime, and gave the girl as wife to the adopted son of Date Masamune of Sendai. Ikeda, incidentally, had been rewarded for his loyal service in 1600 by a transfer to Himeji, west of Kyoto. Himeji Castle stands today as the most well known and the finest example of an original Tokugawa era castle. The castle commonly appears on "wish-you-were-here" picture-postcards.

Another line of defense was rules and regulations. In 1611 Ieyasu seized the occasion of Go Mizunoō's enthronement to require assembled daimyo from central and western Japan to promise compliance with a simple three-clause set of regulations that were announced at Nijō in April. First, he suggested that it would be prudent for them to observe carefully all instructions coming from Edo. They were issued, he said, in the tradition of regulations that had appeared periodically since the days of Minamoto Yoritomo. He warned that those who broke the law or disobeyed their superiors must be prevented from travelling about. Finally, he ordered that no one should employ a person known to have engaged in sedition or murder. He warned that disobedience would be investigated and punished severely. The following year Hidetada had lords from the Kantō and northeast Japan swear to comply with these same regulations.

In his manner of informing the assembled daimyo about these regulations Ieyasu tried to kill two birds with one stone. He wished to deter the daimyo from unseemly political activity, obviously; but he was also giving the new Emperor a lesson. He could have informed the daimyo by courier or in audience at Edo or Fushimi. Instead, he announced the regulations to assembled lords in Kyoto on the very day he made a ceremonial visit to the new Emperor. Doubtless he wished to impress upon Go Mizunoō's young mind the authority of the bakufu, lest, in an excess of adolescent energy, he confuse the nature of his relationship with this short, pudgy old man.

In the course of the enthronement ceremonies Ieyasu encountered more petty quarreling among the Court nobles, but he decided to disregard it, hoping perhaps that once the succession was settled, things would quiet down. Two days after visiting Go Mizunoō, he invited the nobles to the performance of a Nō drama at Nijō.

He still retained his taste for Nō acquired during the 1590's. With its origins in the medieval period and its close associations with the Ashikaga shogunate and the Buddhist tradition, he found Nō thoroughly admirable. He appreciated its stately grace, subtle power, and demanding technique. Its sedate, strictly controlled manner and its themes of vigor and virtue were entirely appropriate to the orderly and righteous realm Ieyasu sought to leave his descendants.

The same could not be said for certain flourishing forms of popular entertainment. He and Hideyoshi were to blame for this problem, because their success in pacifying the realm allowed it to rise. Peace proved a blessing for the general populace. No longer were the able-bodied subject to conscription for war as foot soldiers and menial laborers. Looting by armies had ended. Instead, construction boomed as cities grew and castles expanded. More dependable jobs became available as lords fostered production. Villagers were left to run their own affairs--within limits. It is true that tax collectors had more time to conduct closer land surveys and that local administrators were better placed to regulate with more precision. But spared the harsh requirements of war, the demands of the rulers were less onerous and arbitrary than during the preceding years of war. Performing corvee work on the highways and in peacetime construction was not a radical improvement over corvee service with an army in the field, but the pay was more regular, the work schedules more orderly, and the risks fewer.

The tenor of public affairs was evident in the proliferation of leisure activities. Folk dancing gained great popularity, festivals abounded, and in province after province local dance traditions established themselves. In the cities, popular entertainment flourished, as migrants introduced dances from several provinces. A shrine maiden named Okuni introduced a corrupted version of a shrine dance from Izumo Shrine to Kyoto in 1603. The dance became known as *Okuni kabuki.* Bold and lascivious in both its story line and the dress and movement of the female dancers, it quickly attracted large crowds. In a yet more corrupted form it soon appeared at Sumpu and other castle towns all across the country as *onna kabuki,* "women's *kabuki."*

A cleaned-up version evolved into legitimate *kabuki,* but during Ieyasu's lifetime *kabuki* meant *onna kabuki,* and in Sumpu, specifically, it bothered him. Shortly after he retired there in 1607, an *onna kabuki* troupe moved into town and began giving performances near the castle. What attracted the women's *kabuki* to Sumpu was the swelling populace of young, able-bodied, unattached, and under-employed samurai and servants who moved into town with the daimyo and officials who came to call on or work with Ieyasu. And what the women offered was not so much the action on stage as action offstage. This was the problem. By the middle of 1608 Ieyasu had enough. If Sumpu were to serve as a model for the new order he was coaxing into being, something would have to be done. He expelled all the *kabuki* women as well as other less artistic harlots from town.

In later years the prohibition was modified and such women were permitted to live and practice their profession in a designated neighborhood. Similar licensed quarters were gradually established in most of the major cities of Japan, one of them the Yoshiwara district in Edo. There, geisha of many sorts entertained guests of equal diversity in all kinds of activities, clever and not so clever. New genres of art and literature sprang up around this *ukiyo* "floating world" of meretricious fun and games.

Women were eventually excluded from participation in the *kabuki,* and it evolved into a highly sophisticated, legitimate all-male stage entertainment. As colorful and noisy as Nō was solemn and sedate, it enjoyed immense popularity among commoners and samurai alike.

For Ieyasu, however, Nō, not *kabuki,* remained real theatre. On April 14, 1611, he invited Imperial princes, aristocratic prelates, and other nobles to see a Nō drama in Nijō Castle. Just as he had used the occasion of his visit to Go Mizunoō to lay down the law to assembled daimyo, he seized this occasion, when the nobles were all before him, to deliver a lecture on the importance of propriety in all matters relating to rank and status within the aristocracy.

With that task completed, his mission to Kyoto was finished. Four days later he headed back toward Sumpu. He planned to go home, rest, and see how things were progressing. Perhaps in Keichō 16, with a new Emperor, a new palace, new rules for the daimyo, and new advice to the nobles, the realm would finally conform to the Way.

CHAPTER XIII:

Establishing the Way--Utilitarian and Universal

Ieyasu's army of 50,000 headed home from Kyoto by way of the Tōkaidō. Ieyasu himself, however, chose an unusual route home. He made a scenic and sentimental journey, conscious perhaps of the real possibility that it might be his last trip that way. He had reason to suspect as much: so many of his old comrades in arms were already dead that he must have felt himself to be living on borrowed time. Torii Mototada had died eleven years earlier. Ii Naomasa was gone nine; Sakakibara Yasumasa, five; and ornery old Honda Tadakatsu, a year. He had travelled too many hard roads and cracked too many hard nuts with them. He missed them. He recollected old days and old adventures with nostalgia.

From Kyoto the old man went up the Nakasendō by way of Sekigahara to Gifu, then cut south to Atsuta near Nagoya. This was the route he took at the time of Sekigahara, when he ran it in the opposite direction. But at Atsuta, instead of heading east on the Tōkaidō, he boarded ship and sailed down Ise Bay, as he did earlier in 1600 after fleeing Natsuka Masaie. He disembarked near the lower end of Chita Peninsula, visited a temple there, sailed again to the very tip of the peninsula, which thrusts eastward toward Atsumi Bay, and disembarked again. He then returned to the highway, made a leisurely trip through his old home territory of Mikawa, rejoined the Tōkaidō, passed through Tōtōmi and Suruga, and reached Sumpu on April 28.

The trip took only ten days. Its speed and comfort testified to one more aspect of his labors of the past decade: his fashioning of an improved highway system.

While consolidating his hold on the country in 1601, Ieyasu had ordered Ōkubo Nagayasu to begin establishing a regular packhorse system of designated way stations and licensed stable operators along the highways between Edo and Osaka. The main roads were widened to about nine meters and smoothed and covered with a gravel surface. In 1604 the bakufu ordered the highways measured and markers placed at 1 *ri* (4 kilometer) intervals, starting at Nihonbashi ("the Bridge of Japan") in Edo. Along the high roads rest-stops were erected at the 1 ri markers, and plantings of pine and nettle trees were made on both sides to protect highway and traveller alike from wind and rain. In later years cryptomeria and other trees were planted and maintained; some still stand today, giants towering over the wayfarer below. Nowadays most highways bypass those avenues of giants (which saves the trees from auto emissions), but for over two centuries they offered shade to all sorts of governmental, commercial, and private travellers.

As the years passed, daimyo bound to and from Edo on alternate attendance and merchants travelling on business used the highways more and more. The 26 post stations linking Edo and Osaka in 1601 grew to 75 in 1616 and over 100 later on. To accommodate the increasing traffic, Ōkubo and others extended the highway system until it linked all parts of the Tokugawa realm. The post horse operators offered their services in accordance with regulations that specified how many horses to maintain, the size of stables, and the sections of highway on which they could operate. Hiring arrangements were also specified. For example, daimyo were authorized to rent post horses at set fees, with the weight limit per horse set at 280 pounds maximum. Merchants could rent pack horses at negotiated, usually higher rates with a load limit of 350 pounds. Porters were available for hire at half the cost of a horse.

Those highway stations flourished, as Oliver Statler tells us in his charming book, *Japanese Inn.* An elaborate system of inns developed to feed, wash, and shelter the myriad travellers, from the shogun himself and the most elegant daimyo, down to the most obscure couriers and artisans. Most of the travellers were men, and their wishes were accommodated by a large population of cooks, manservants, cleaning women, entertainers, bath attendants, and assorted ladies of the *onna kabuki* variety.

Travel took place on routes other than highways, moreover, as Ieyasu's trips on Ise Bay demonstrated. In 1603 he licensed a regular shipping service on the Yodo River between Kyoto and Osaka, which was the first link in what Suminokura Ryōi and other merchants would develop into an elaborate river and coastal shipping system.

Ieyasu did not build bridges very often. A sense of military preparedness dominated his thinking: he wanted no enemy to have easy access to his domain. Instead, he established systems of ferry boats and porters at fords along the high roads. Travellers hired boats and porters for set fees--or waded across themselves if the water or their purses were low and their spirits high.

The Japanese word for road is *michi.* Its ideograph or character is 道 . In Chinese the character is pronounced *dao* and means "the way," not only in the tangible sense of a road, but also in the philosophical sense of a moral order or universal mode of conduct (as in Taoism). In Japanese the word *michi* has a comparably broad usage. When used with other characters to form complex words, it also has the pronunciation, *dō*, derived from the Chinese *dao*. Thus the Tōkaidō is the highway of the Tōkai or "eastern sea" district, and the Nakasendō is the highway of the Nakasen or "mountains of the interior" district. The same *dō* shows up in *Butsudō*, the "way" of Buddhism, and in *bushidō*, the "way of the warrior" (which, incidentally, was not formulated until several decades after Ieyasu's death). The word *dō* appears, bent slightly into *tō* in *Shintō*, the "way of the gods."

Ieyasu's interest in the "way" extended well beyond the road system and into the realm of political thought. It was the "way" of Confucian thought that most attracted him. He began serious examination of Confucianism during the 1590s, and in the years after Sekigahara he occasionally listened to lectures by the Zen monk and Confucian scholar, Fujiwara Seika. It was Seika who lectured to him on the art of government in 1593 when he was in western Japan during Hideyoshi's first invasion of Korea. Seika was a widely-read scholar, versed in various Chinese doctrines as well as Japanese poetry and literature.

Seika found particular merit in the teachings of the Sung Confucianist Chu Hsi (1130-1200). In Chu Hsi's view the universe, "heaven above and earth below," was a harmonious whole when it functioned properly. Its myriad parts fit together in mutually beneficial ways. The ruler's task, he held, was to understand how the pieces of the universe, especially the human pieces, ought to fit together and, through the exercise of benevolent and dedicated rule, to keep them prosperous, peaceful, and in their proper places.

To Ieyasu, Chu Hsi's ideas seemed wonderfully sensible. He wished Seika to serve him as a regular advisor, but when he invited the scholar to move to Edo for that purpose, Seika declined, preferring to stay with his students in Kyoto. In 1603, Ieyasu heard of an even brighter and younger scholar. His name was Hayashi Razan, and he was twenty that year. Like Seika, Hayashi had studied Zen and then turned to Confucian studies, which he found much more satisfying.

Ieyasu met Razan not at that time but two years later, in July of 1605, when visiting Nijō Castle in conjunction with Hidetada's succession. Old Ieyasu summoned young Razan, together with a critic of the scholar, and Ieyasu's two learned advisors, Saishō Shōda, abbot of the Shōkokuji, and Kanshitsu Genkitsu, master of the Enkōji. Ieyasu assembled the group in order to test young Razan's knowledge of Chinese history. He was probably looking for an advisor who could be of future service to the newly-minted shogun. To his great satisfaction, Razan proved more versed in the details of Chinese history than the three senior scholars sitting with him, and Ieyasu decided to employ him.

In the following months he summoned Razan for occasional discussions, and a year later the young scholar assisted in negotiating the resumption of Korean-Japanese relations. In the spring of 1607 Razan went east and at the age of twenty-four began to lecture to Ieyasu and Hidetada from a number of Confucian texts on government. He served actively as advisor, travelled about on assignments, lectured, handled negotiations, drafted documents, and gave advice on numerous matters.

Even more than Seika, Razan saw the correctly ordered universe as a seamless whole in which all parts have their proper places:

> *Heaven is above and earth is below. This is the order of heaven and earth. If we can understand the meaning of the order existing between heaven and earth, we can also perceive that in everything there is an order separating those who are above and those who are below. When we extend this understanding between heaven and earth, we cannot allow disorder in the relations between the ruler and the subject, and between those who are above and those who are below. The separation into four classes of samurai, farmers, artisans and merchants, like the five relationships [of ruler and subject, father and son, husband and wife, older and younger brother, and friend and friend], is part of the principles of heaven and is the Way which was taught by the Sage (Confucius).*

"Those above and those below" all had their proper places, as did other parts of the universe, including all forms of learning. The art of the good ruler was to fit the pieces together, reconcile differences, and end discord. To reconcile discordant views successfully, however, one had to understand them, and such understanding depended, in turn, on having access to sufficient information. Information came in written records, and these were scarce. One of the tasks of the good ruler, therefore, was to promote the reproduction of those historical records and learned works that would contribute to understanding the universe and its proper governance.

The idea was not original. The vision of total harmony in the world of ideas and human affairs was pervasive in medieval Japan, probably in great part because reality was so different and cried out so painfully for some way of bringing order and peace to the disordered realm. A number of scholarly endeavors had flowed

121

from this vision and the corresponding quest for a harmonious order. During the 1590s, for example, Hideyoshi encouraged scholarship by erecting temples and enriching archives, most notably his own. Emperor Goyōzei promoted the publishing of precious works, his effort facilitated by a novel device that had recently come to his attention: the moveable-type printing press.

The press that Goyōzei was familiar with used wooden type and was a Korean invention. Hideyoshi's army brought a model back to Japan, and when Goyōzei learned of it, he set people to work with it, making copies of a number of volumes, both Chinese and Japanese, scholarly and literary, including the *Tale of Genji*.

In 1599 and 1600 Ieyasu first became involved in book-printing when he had Genkitsu reproduce some Chinese works on good government. While in Fushimi in 1605 he had Shōda and Genkitsu produce two more works, using a Korean-style press at the Enkōji. One of these was a Confucian work which, in the view of Shōda, demonstrated the harmony of Buddhism and Confucianism. As Shōda wrote in his preface: had Gautama the Buddha been born in China and taught there, he would have been like Confucius; and if Confucius had been born and taught where Gautama lived, he would have been like him. Buddhism and Confucianism are like the two wings of a bird or the two wheels of a cart. Like Razan's understanding of the proper relationship of those above and those below, Shōda's understanding of the relationship of Buddhism to Confucianism was ideally suited to Ieyasu's needs. It made room for both schools of thought and provided an intellectual basis for overriding the dogmatic arguments of disputatious monks, priests, and scholars.

The two scholars reproduced something even more satisfying to Ieyasu that same year: his favorite historical work, the *Azuma kagami* or *Mirror of the East*, the history of the founding of the Kamakura shogunate. In the preface Shōda wrote that the work recorded both the good and bad deeds of great men, and so left a record for posterity. As all good Confucianists know, histories should provide a set of guidelines in the form of examples that people of a later age may emulate. The lessons of the *Azuma kagami* were clear; a shogun ruled. He ruled from the east. He ruled through his vassal bands. He ruled justly, punishing insurgents and rewarding loyal followers. He kept the peace. And through the action of a grateful and cooperative Court he received--and at the proper time passed on to his heir and descendants--the title of shogun.

This printing work was politically useful, needless to say. It was also culturally important, helping to preserve works that otherwise might be lost to humanity. For example, the copy of *Azuma kagami* that Ieyasu instructed Shōda to reproduce came into his hands only a year earlier. It was a rare and precious treasure that had been in the possession of a daimyo named Kuroda. In 1590 Kuroda helped negotiate the surrender of Odawara Castle, and as an expression of gratitude for his part in the settlement, the Hōjō, who had owned the *Azuma kagami* as a family treasure, gave it to him. They were able to do so, of course, because the castle had not been stormed and burned, and the book had not been destroyed. Many other equally precious records were lost in the savage wars that had rippled incessantly across Japan during the sixteenth century.

Even the copy that came into Ieyasu's hands was incomplete. In the summer of 1604 Saishō Shōda asked to borrow the forty-fifth fascicle. Ieyasu replied, "I do not have fascicles 38, 41, and 45 here. I do have the others, and if you have use for them, I shall loan them to you." Doubtless that situation encouraged the men to produce new copies, presumably locating copies of the missing fascicles to make a complete edition.

The printing efforts of Goyōzei, Ieyasu, and others thus replenished a stock of historical records that had diminished in the decades of war. They also helped preserve parts of the Chinese intellectual heritage that otherwise might have been lost. In 1616 Ieyasu had a valuable fifty-volume compendium of Chinese writings reproduced, a work that had long since disappeared from China. Only one copy survived in an archive called the Kanazawa Bunko, located on the coast of the Sea of Japan in the castle town of Ieyasu's great ally, Maeda. By reproducing it, Ieyasu assured posterity access to a major work of Chinese scholarship.

Ieyasu was probably aware of the cultural significance of his publishing activity, but clearly its political value was uppermost in his mind. The *Azuma kagami*, republished in 1605, provided historical justification for his regime. In 1606 he had Genkitsu publish, on his press at the Enkōji, a set of seven Chinese works on military matters. In the preface Genkitsu declared these works to be the most useful of many on military affairs because they showed how military and civil affairs meshed to sustain a tranquil realm and a contented populace.

Fitting things together to make a peaceful realm was what Ieyasu saw himself doing, and the reproduction of works illustrating the "way" of the good ruler was part of the task. He also believed that once he had the pieces properly in place, the task of his successors would be to keep them in harmonious balance.

Ieyasu went to Kyoto early in 1611 to improve the fit of some pieces that were still out of line. After his return to Sumpu in April he continued to work toward a permanently ordered realm. He knew how valuable the *Azuma kagami* had been for himself, and he believed that his descendants, in turn, would have the best chance of maintaining stability if they realized what he had done and why. They would need a full historical record to use as precedent in distinguishing right from wrong and good governance from bad. On August 1, the twenty-first anniversary of his move to the Kantō, he ordered archivists in Sumpu to begin a daily record of his own actions, decisions, and orders.

Besides establishing an authoritative record of his own times, Ieyasu wished to have for use as extensive a record of the past as possible. It was the Kamakura shogunate, and not its successor, the Ashikaga, that he admired; but he was ready to learn from all sources, so in September he had Hayashi Razan read to him from the *Kenmu shikimoku* "Code of the Kenmu Year-Period." This was the basic code of laws compiled by the first Ashikaga shogun, and Ieyasu and Razan considered its merits and weaknesses.

The precedents embodied in the genealogies of families were just as important as lessons derived from past codes. They established what lineages had legitimate claim to what titles and perquisites. Earlier Ieyasu had shown interest in obtaining proper information on genealogies, and on October 1 three scholars arrived at Sumpu from Kyoto, delivering a folding screen that diagramed genealogies of the major aristocratic families, to help clarify their relationships.

Shortly after receiving this screen of noble genealogies, Ieyasu addressed two matters of his own lineage. It evidently occurred to him that his claim to Minamoto ancestry could stand some consolidation. On November 9, while at Edo on a hawking trip, he dispatched the abbot of the Zōjōji together with two key Tokugawa vassals to the site in Kōzuke province (at Tokugawa village near Ojima town on the Tone River in modern-day Gunma Prefecture, to be precise) where his distant Tokugawa ancestor reputedly lived before moving to Mikawa and being adopted by the Matsudaira family. This Tokugawa ancestor supposedly descended from the Minamoto by way of the Nitta family, which lived nearby. To Ieyasu's delight, the abbot reported the discovery of evidence presumably demonstrating the existence of that Tokugawa family and its ties to the Nitta. How much of the report was a happy invention of the moment is unclear, but Ieyasu ordered a family temple erected on the site as permanent testimony to the Minamoto ancestry of the Tokugawa rulers.

A problem regarding the future of his lineage also arose. Hidetada's wife, Tatsuko, was the sister of Hideyoshi's concubine, Yodo. Like Yodo, she was a strong-willed woman and exercised considerable influence on her husband. Due to her influence, it is said, Hidetada was partial to his clever and endearing third son, Tadanaga, born in 1606, rather than to his second and eldest surviving boy, Iemitsu, born in 1604. Mindful of the Toyotomi experience, Ieyasu wished the more mature son to succeed. It is said that Iemitsu's wet nurse, a woman named Kasuga no Tsubone, was upset that the boy she was raising might be passed over. She arranged to make a pilgrimage to the Ise Shrine and on her return stopped at Sumpu and complained to Ieyasu. He was concerned, and while in Edo that fall dealt with the matter. On October 24 and (as the incident has been described) while Hidetada was hosting a banquet for him, Ieyasu took the seven-year-old Iemitsu by the hand, placed him on a higher dais, then placed his little brother Tadanaga before him on a lower dais, and explained to the children that Iemitsu was to be lord and Tadanaga his vassal. After that display Hidetada understood that Iemitsu would succeed. And Tatsuko, who was the mother of both boys but had not reared the elder, ceased her agitation.

By the end of 1611 Ieyasu had reason to hope that the universe was sufficiently in order. He was not leaving the future to chance. He had done his best to assure that foreign trading relations would flourish, that domestic producers and tax-collectors would tend to their proper duties, that the Court and nobility would hold to their proper roles, that the daimyo would abide by the regulations he had given them, and that his descendants would make sound use of the legacy he was recording for posterity. Through his efforts the "way" was being made known, and thereby secure. Those who would travel between the rows of trees on his highways would be able to comprehend and abide by the larger "way" that gave them reason for being.

PART III

THE NINETEENTH YEAR OF KEICHŌ (1614)

CHAPTER XIV:

The Stench of Sedition

Ieyasu put on the best face possible for the situation. He was spending New Year's in the western enceinte of Chiyoda Castle at Edo, and he hadn't planned it that way. The situation was patently outrageous, and his spirits were not particularly improved by the customary exchanges of greetings with Hidetada or Hideyori; or the other daimyo, nobles and prelates; or even by the Nō drama Hidetada provided for his entertainment in the main enceinte on the fifth of the month.

Nevertheless he tried to feign ease and contentment. He went out hawking one day, licensed a series of trading expeditions to southeast Asia another day, and handled a few ceremonial affairs. He did his best to give his life the appearance of calm routine because he wished, through his example of adherence to routine despite disruptions, to serve as a model for others, an exemplar of the "way."

As he looked at the world on New Year's of 1614, it seemed substantially less promising than it had three years earlier. Even then there were some worries--whose life is free of them?--but the numbers and forms of worry had proliferated.

From about 1610 various developments began to oppress him. From all sides troubles seemed to intrude themselves. People seemed more irascible, less ready to compromise. In Kyoto, in the daimyo domains, and everywhere one might turn, there seemed to be increased restlessness, more discontent, and in response, more attempts by rulers to suppress disorder and retain control. In Edo gangs of toughs marauded, caroused about, and collided with police units. Only harsh punishments brought them under control. The veterans who knew the agonies of war were dying off, while the stories of their heroism lived on. Young men had no prospects for similar glory. Peace was safe, but it was dull, so people quarreled, schemed, shoved, strutted, and got into trouble. The realm seemed to be disintegrating.

Ieyasu grew even more worried as he counted the years of his life and saw the remaining time dwindle. Would he lose, just as

Hideyoshi had lost, the struggle to forge a permanently ordered world? Would Hidetada or his successor finally be reduced, as Hideyori had, to the tedium of doing as directed? Or worse yet, would failure lead, as it had for the Toyotomi, to renewed warfare, or even to chronic disorder? What would future chroniclers then say of Ieyasu and of the Tokugawa? What would such failure mean in terms of Ieyasu's immortality? Would such an outcome preclude the chance of his experiencing the saving grace of Buddha? Would it be proof that he had failed to master the Way?

The shadows that spread across Ieyasu's life encroached from many directions and seemed to threaten him in many ways:

(1) *His most trusted vassals quarreled and seemed bent on dragging him into their disputes. In the process they sabotaged the quality of his political judgement.*

(2) *The Iberian missionary presence, which he had tolerated for years as one price of foreign trade, became deeply entangled in his thinking about the proper order of the universe, his worries about his family and its future, and his concern with Court and daimyo behavior.*

(3) *His family situation, which had seemed so secure in 1606 - 1607 (when he made plans for his life as ōgosho or "retired shogun" in Sumpu), had worsened, much to his distress.*

(4) *The Court, which he had tried to set straight in 1611, had continued to bother him periodically.*

(5) *Religious questions, which had never before been of any special interest to him, mushroomed into soul-consuming problems that tormented him both as a mortal man and as the aspiring maker of an orderly world.*

(6) *And finally, the Toyotomi-Tokugawa relationship, which he had been trying to make habitual since Hideyoshi's death, suddenly disintegrated during 1614.*

All of these problems manifested themselves in one way or another during the years after about 1610, and what kept Ieyasu at Edo on New Year's of 1614 was an incident that seemed a culmination of malign trends.

During the autumn of 1613 Ieyasu left Sumpu for his customary leisurely hawking trip of two or three months around the Kantō. This had gone smoothly, and on December 3 he left Edo for an equally leisurely trip back to Sumpu, planning to arrive sometime before the end of the month. As he headed southwest toward Odawara, he received word that Ōkubo Tadachika, the lord there, was angry with him and was perhaps engaged in sedition. It seemed possible that Tadachika would attack his nearly-unarmed party as he passed the castle, so Ieyasu abruptly halted his westward progress and returned circuitously to the safety of Chiyoda Castle.

Sixty-one-year-old Tadachika had long been one of Ieyasu's finest vassals and staunchest supporters. The anger that supposedly was turning this man into a dangerous enemy related in part to the growing rifts among the advisors of Ieyasu and Hidetada. As the old veterans died off, new men took their places, and these included a father and son, Honda Masanobu and Masazumi. Neither Honda has enjoyed a good reputation among historians in recent years. Masanobu has been likened to Ishida Mitsunari as an upstart who lacked military prowess and rose to power through political maneuver and intrigue. He was given to fanaticism and was notorious for conniving. As a young man he embraced Ikkō doctrine and fought against Ieyasu in Mikawa in 1563. When defeated, he chose to flee rather than yield, and only later did he again become a vassal of Ieyasu. Eventually he became a political confidante, a rival of several of Ieyasu's senior advisors, and finally, it is said, a dogmatic advocate of Confucianism, as sure of its univeral truth as any Christian missionary was sure of the universal truth of his own creed. Masanobu's son, who also became a political advisor to Ieyasu, inherited his father's enemies and possibly his persuasions. His entanglement in internal political feuding proved to be as intense as that of Masanobu.

The Hondas came into particularly sharp collision with Ōkubo Tadachika and his protege, Nagayasu. Tadachika had a nasty dispute with Masanobu earlier in his career, when Masanobu's criticism of his battlefield tactics led to the disgrace of Tadachika's son and the suicide of one of his advisors.

In 1612 Ōkubo Nagayasu and Honda Masazumi, who already disliked one another, became entangled in an ugly scandal at Sumpu, and each tried to protect himself by maligning the other. Before year's end Nagayasu fell ill, and on April 25, 1613, he died. With his death Ieyasu learned that the man had engaged extensively in peculation and abuse of authority. Ieyasu ordered his fortune confiscated and instructed his heir to disembowel himself. A large number of other people associated with Nagayasu were punished harshly, and one suspects that the Hondas had a hand in the purge.

With good reason Tadachika saw this attack on Nagayasu's family and associates as an intolerable assault on his own dignity. It also was a threat to his wellbeing and that of his family because, as Nagayasu's sponsor, he could be held responsible for his conduct. The Hondas, in turn, had some reason to fear Tadachika since he was one of the most renowned of the surviving colleagues of Ieyasu. He was famous for his generous kindness to visitors, a

131

generosity that may have been supported by Nagayasu's peculation. Perhaps as a result of that generosity, he enjoyed great popularity among Tokugawa retainers. To make an enemy of Tadachika was to make an enemy of many swift-sworded men. In any event, the Honda appear to have maligned Tadachika. Indeed, a questionable record dating from nearly a century later asserts that Masanobu purposely and ruthlessly set Ieyasu and Hidetada against Tadachika through a campaign of slanderous innuendo. Even if the Honda-Ōkubo relationship was not that deadly, it was still one that made it very difficult for old Ieyasu to get a clear picture of the real situation.

Another element in the Honda-Ōkubo dispute soon expressed itself: Ieyasu's fear of the Iberian missionary presence. One of the charges leveled against Tadachika was that he was sympathetic to Christian activities. If indeed he had become cool toward Ieyasu and Hidetada as charged, and if he were sympathetic with Christians, then in view of his popularity, his military prowess, and the size of his castle and vassal force, he was a dangerous man indeed.

Accordingly Ieyasu treated the warning about Tadachika seriously, returned to Chiyoda Castle, and took a number of preventive measures. On December 14, the day he reentered the castle, he rushed a trusted vassal to Sumpu to protect his children, Yoshinao and Yorinobu. He also ordered reinforcements from Sumpu to come and escort him home. On the same day he ordered daimyo in Ise and Mikawa Provinces to stay home and not plan trips to Edo that year.

Five days later he sent instructions to Tadachika, informing him that he was to proceed to Kyoto shortly to supervise the expulsion of all missionaries. At Sekigahara, Ieyasu gave Kobayakawa and other turncoats an opportunity to prove their devotion by leading the assault on Ishida Mitsunari's castle at Sawayama, and subsequently he honored Mōri Terumoto by permitting him to lead the expedition to suppress the Shimazu. Now he would see if this man, suspected of complicity with Christianity, would accept the duty of expelling its teachers.

Ieyasu designated Tadachika sōbugyō, "Magistrate-General", in charge of deportation with instructions to leave for Kyoto on January 3. Tadachika did in fact leave nearly on schedule, heading west from Odawara on the fifth. Almost as soon as he reached Kyoto, the bakufu deprived him of his fief at Odawara and put him under house arrest in a secluded place. Ieyasu justified the action on the ground that Tadachika had arranged a marriage with another lord's family without proper shogunal authorization. With that matter settled, Ieyasu at last set out for Sumpu, surrounded by a substantial escort force. He moved as rapidly as possible, passed Odawara in a state of high alert, and crossed the

Hakone barrier without delay, reaching Sumpu on January 29. Three days later he ordered the castle at Numazu, between Sumpu and Odawara, torn down. If one of his most able, most powerful, and most trusted vassals were about to turn against him, he did not want that man--or anyone else for that matter--to be able to establish a forward position close to Sumpu.

Ieyasu selected the issue of Christianity to force Tadachika out of town because he had reached the limits of his patience with the alien creed. As it seemed to him by the end of 1613, the missionary activity had become an intolerably subversive force that was sabotaging his efforts to establish a stable order. The hand of the missionaries seemed to show up everywhere: in some of his troubles with daimyo, in his problems with the Court, and even among members of his own household at Sumpu. Rumors linked them to trouble in the domain of his son, Tadateru, and to the troubles with Ōkubo, one of his most trusted vassals. If there were a key to his troubles, one single item to be isolated and expunged as a step toward easing a whole range of vexing problems, it seemed to be the expulsion of the missionaries and the containment of their ideology.

Ieyasu had never welcomed the Iberian missionaries. Too often they had managed to present themselves as quarrelsome, intolerant fanatics from abroad who sowed dissension among people of all races and callings in Japan. He had put up with them only because that seemed necessary in order to retain his foreign trading connections. By the end of 1613 enough avenues of trade had developed that there no longer seemed need for tolerance. He decided to get rid of them.

Foreign missionary activity had generated resentment and distrust in Japan as early as the 1580s when Hideyoshi half-heartedly ordered the Jesuits to leave the country. More trouble occurred from the 1590s on as other Iberian missionaries, initially Spanish Franciscans and, after 1602, Dominicans and Augustinians, challenged the Jesuits. Nevertheless, during the first years after Sekigahara, Ieyasu tolerated the missionaries because he wanted to continue trade with both Portugal and Spain and believed he could not have the one without the other.

Ieyasu preferred to have trade without dogma because, even at its best, foreign trade was a rough business. Japanese mariners who sailed with unemployed samurai and other tough characters handled much of that trade. Some trade was carried by Chinese ships, some by Korean, some by Ryukyuan and some by European. It was in all cases a dangerous business, and the men who went to sea were a hardy, brawling lot, not averse to piracy and violent encounters all along the coasts of east and southeast Asia. Ample grounds existed for trouble: cultural differences, language barriers, rivalry for women, too much liquor, and conflicting economic interests. Adding religious bigotry to the mixture could only exacerbate an already explosive situation. Having the religious element closely linked to political power multiplied the risks.

Ieyasu did his best to keep religious matters out of his relations with foreign lands. During 1605, shortly after rumors of daimyo-missionary scheming came to his ear, he wrote the Spanish governor of the Philippines, Don Pedro de Acuña that he would approve trade with the Spaniards but that missionary activity was forbidden. This prohibition had no effect, however, and for the next four years he allowed the Iberian missionaries to continue their activity. In 1606, for example, while in Kyoto, he received in audience the Jesuit Bishop of Japan, Luis de Cerqueira. In Sumpu in the spring of 1607, he received the Jesuit Vice-Provincial Francisco Pasio. Two years later, in September 1609, the retiring governor general of the Philippines, Don Rodrigo de Vivero, visited him en route back to Spain via Mexico. Wishing to promote trade with Spain, Ieyasu disregarded Vivero's haughty conduct and gratuitous denunciation of the Dutch and assured him that he would not persecute missionaries and would welcome Spanish trading vessels warmly.

Nevertheless Ieyasu kept trying to develop avenues of trade that avoided religious complications. The Japanese and other Asian trading ventures that he continued to encourage were his most important avenues. But he sought more. In 1605 he sent Jacob Quaeckernaeck, captain of the *Liefde*, to Patani in Malaya to develop a Dutch trading connection. This attempt finally bore fruit in 1609 when an official mission from the Netherlands arrived at Hirado and formal Japanese-Dutch trading arrangements were established.

Even as this new trading avenue was being developed, Ieyasu found his patience with the Iberians strained further. At his behest a Kyushu daimyo named Arima dispatched a ship to Malaya in 1609 to purchase aloes for use in making incense. On the return trip the ship docked at Macao, where the grew got into a major brawl with local Portuguese gendarmes. The first reports reaching Ieyasu described the Japanese seamen as the trouble-makers, and on July 25 he sent a notice to Macao stating that Japanese ships would be prohibited from stopping there. Later, however, Arima and others presented versions more critical of the Portuguese, and Ieyasu, having just acquired new hope for trade with the Dutch, gave Arima permission to obtain redress from the next Portuguese vessel to reach Nagasaki.

In December a ship arrived, but when Arima's men moved to impound it and interrogate the ship's captain, the latter understandably attempted to sail out of the harbor. After three nights of indecisive battle, the ship was surrounded. In renewed fighting a fire started aboard ship. Recognizing that his ship would soon be overrun, the captain ignited its powder magazine and blew it to pieces. Ieyasu rewarded Arima for his efforts, but not nearly as richly as Arima wished.

Despite this altercation, which shogunal officials in Nagasaki reported in grim detail, Ieyasu still wanted Iberian trade to continue and even urged the Spanish to conduct it in the Kantō rather than in western Japan. The Dutch were unable to keep their promise of the year before to start trade in 1610, so in 1611 Ieyasu negotiated a set of trade arrangements with the Spanish as well as the Dutch and also with traders from China and other Asian countries. Trade with Portugal halted temporarily following the Arima affair, but it was of sufficient value to both Ieyasu and the Portuguese that in July of 1611 a reconciliation was negotiated, and that trade, too, resumed.

Still, the Iberians were becoming increasingly unwelcome. In 1611, shortly after Ieyasu's reconciliation with the Portuguese, the Spanish navigator Sebastian Viscaino reached Japan from Manila. In accordance with authorizations given by Ieyasu in 1609 and 1610, he anchored at Uraga, not far from Edo, and visited Ieyasu at Sumpu in September. He requested permission to chart the coastline of Japan. Ieyasu agreed to the request, although he was angered by Viscaino's arrogant behavior and refusal to abide by local custom. Moreover Viscaino--whose real intention was to find the fabled gold and silver mines of Japan--indicated that he had no serious interest in trade and wished solely to promote the Christianization of Japan. That explanation may have been an intentional smoke screen, but it was poorly designed to win Ieyasu's approbation.

The missionary enterprise was thus compromised by its association with problems of both trade and aggressive Iberian state power. When those factors became involved in domestic Japanese politics, they became intolerable. Probably Ieyasu's doctrinal advisors, with their vision of a harmoniously integrated universe, took exception to both the philosophical intolerance in missionary doctrine and the related missionary denunciation of differing doctrine. For Ieyasu, doctrinal issues mattered because of their political implications.

There was, for example, the worrisome propensity of some daimyo, primarily in Kyushu, and especially among those who had not been his allies at Sekigahara, to embrace Christianity. Although some of those lords may simply have been using the missionary contact to promote their own trading interests, the fact remained that they seemed to be forging political links which might one day be dangerous. As early as 1604 reports circulated of an attempt to organize a strong Christian political force in Kyushu, and while nothing came of it, such a development seemed at all times plausible and possible. That year, therefore, when a bakufu official in Nagasaki worked with local daimyo to erect a Buddhist temple as a religious counterweight to the local Christian churches, Ieyasu approved.

Beyond the problem of Christian daimyo was the broader question of popular faith. Ieyasu had experienced enough trouble with religious communities in quelling Ikkō resistance earlier in his life. Now, as his days grew few, he hardly needed such trouble again. And yet with each passing year there were more and more converts to Christianity. The number of resident missionaries did not change noticeably (129 in 1603, 124 in 1606, and 117 in 1611) but the numbers of baptized Japanese kept growing: 793 baptisms in 1605 according to one source, some 8,000 in 1606, dropping to 4350 in 1613 after proselytizing was forbidden, according to another source. Other sources speak, very imprecisely, of 300,000 Christians in 1600 and 700,000 in 1610.

In 1612 the missionary problem finally seemed to materialize in domestic politics. Ieyasu learned that Arima, the Christian daimyo in Kyushu who recently held the shoot-out with the Portuguese, was dissatisfied with the subsequent expression of Tokugawa gratitude. In pursuit of a larger domain, Arima bribed and connived with some officials and members of Ieyasu's household, even implicating his favorite consort, Lady Ōta. The scheme, which included talk of murdering Ieyasu's senior official in Nagasaki, entangled Ōkubo Nagayasu and a man by the name of Okamoto who was in the pay of Honda Masazumi. Ieyasu was enraged by the talk of murdering one of his officials. And he was distressed to learn that Okamoto was a key broker in the whole corrupt business because Okamoto's father had been the man whom Ieyasu sent to execute his first wife, Tsukiyama, in 1579. By subtle connection this sordid affair with Arima thus revived painful memories that Ieyasu only wished to leave at rest. And Okamoto, it turned out, was a Christian, like Arima.

Honda knew Ieyasu distrusted Christians, and perhaps to save his own skin, he seems to have promoted the view that the Ōkubos (rather than Okamoto) were the Christian sympathizers creating the trouble. And rumor also spoke of Lady Ōta and others in Ieyasu's household as harboring Christian sympathies. For Ieyasu it mattered little who in particular was associating with the alien creed; what troubled him was the evidence that the insidious doctrine seemed to be penetrating his closest circles. He resolved to eradicate it. He did so by prohibiting missionary activities and proscribing practice in places of political importance, namely Edo, Sumpu, and Kyoto, and in the area of greatest missionary success,

Nagasaki and its environs. In March 1612 his spokesman in Kyoto ordered all Christian proselytizing halted and all churches in and near the city closed. A month later the shogunate ordered that fourteen Tokugawa vassals living at Sumpu, who had been convicted of being Christian, be stripped of their rank and stipends and denied permission to live and work anywhere in the country. In Edo, meanwhile, a new system of neighborhood governance was initiated to expose secret religious practices.

This first attempt by Ieyasu to proscribe the religion was neither complete nor altogether successful. In Kyoto the Jesuits managed to obtain exemptions, so that only Spanish missionaries had their churches closed. In Nagasaki the effort bogged down in uncertainty and confusion. Arima, whose fief was near, was stripped of his domain in March and ordered to commit suicide in May. Shogunal officials at Nagasaki put pressure on his son and successor to eliminate Christian activity in his domain. The whole matter was messy, riddled with rumors, charges, and counter-charges, and little was accomplished. The more Ieyasu heard, the more concerned he became about the apparent links between foreign governments, foreign priests, and uncontrollable domestic forces that even reached into the Court and his own household.

Some of Ieyasu's growing concern may have been a reflection of changes in his advisory group. Saishō Shōda had died at the end of 1607 at age fifty-nine; and Kanshitsu Genkitsu, the summer of 1612 at age sixty-four. Ishin Sūden (who was forty-three in 1612) and Hayashi Razan (who was twenty-nine that year) survived as chief advisors on matters of philosophy, and they may have insisted on the dangers of the alien creed. Among Ieyasu's lay advisors, most of the trusted old veterans were gone and the Hondas had acquired great influence. With Masanobu's strident Confucianism and Masazumi's conflicts with Ōkubo, they were ill equipped to guide Ieyasu through complex and ambiguous issues.

Ieyasu's hardened attitude toward missionary activity was reflected in a communication to Spanish authorities in Manila in September 1612. In a letter that Sūden wrote, Ieyasu confirmed his agreement of the previous year with Viscaino: that he might survey the coast; that shipwrecked personnel would be aided; and that ships might take refuge wherever necessary along the coast. Ieyasu took the occasion to have Sūden lecture the Spaniards. He informed them that Japan is a land of Buddhism and Shintō, between which two are no disagreements. Both uphold the principle of loyalty between lord and vassal, as do all righteous people. The meritorious are rewarded, the erring are punished. Confucian virtues are upheld. He then continued:

The doctrine followed in your country differs entirely

*from ours. Therefore, I am persuaded that it would not
suit us. In the Buddhist sutras it is said that it is difficult to
convert those who are not disposed toward being converted. It is best, therefore, to put an end to the preaching of
your doctrine on our soil. On the other hand, you can
multiply the voyages of merchant ships, and thus promote
mutual interests and relations. Your ships can enter Japanese ports without exception. I have given strict orders to
this effect.*

Clearly Ieyasu hoped he need not write off trade with Spain, but
equally clearly he was no longer willing, as he had been in 1609, to
accept missionaries as the price for that trade.

He also hoped to preserve commercial ties with Portugal. Letters
that he and Honda sent to the Portuguese in Macao in the autumn
of 1612 expressed satisfaction with the most recent trading vessel
and urged ships to continue coming in future.

During 1613 Ieyasu established a foreign trading connection that
seemed completely free of the religious complications inherent in
trade with Iberians. In the summer of that year an English ship of
the East India Company, commanded by John Saris, sailed into
Hirado Harbor. During August Saris travelled overland to Sumpu
with Will Adams, whom Ieyasu had sent west to fetch him. Saris
presented Ieyasu a letter from King James I.

James' letter began, "James, by the Grace of Almightie God,
Kinge of Great Brittaine, France, and Ireland, Defender of the
Christian Faithe etc., to the Highe and Mightie Prince the Emperour of Japan etc., Greeting." After commending "emperour" Ieyasu for "the reputacon and Greatnes of yor Power and Dominion" and "your Princelie Magnanimitie and Disposition" and
"yor accustomed Benignitie and Favor," he asked that Ieyasu allow British merchants to establish trading facilities in Japan and
assured him that Japanese merchants would be welcome in "or
kingdomes and Countres."

Despite its prolix style and imaginative spelling, James' letter
seemed to be just what Ieyasu was looking for. After gleaning
such information as he could from Adams and discussing the matter with his advisors, Ieyasu drafted a friendly letter in response to
James and issued Saris a patent of authority to trade. In the patent
Ieyasu specified that,

*(1) Englishmen are authorized to carry on trade in Japan.
(2) Ship's cargo should be itemized by contents.
(3) English may choose ports of trade. Ships in trouble
may freely anchor in any inlet.
(4) Merchant residences and warehouses may be estab-*

138

lished in Edo. Return to England will be unrestricted.
Residences may be owned outright.
(5) The possessions of any Englishmen who die of illness
will be returned intact.
(6) Compulsory purchase of goods will be forbidden.
(7) Law-breaking Englishmen are to be punished in accord-
ance with the decision of their English commander.

In such clauses one can see both Ieyasu's wishes and his concern to allay English suspicions. He wanted trade to center on Edo. Lest the experience of Adams and his colleagues frighten them off, he assured the Englishmen free passage (at the same time allowing Adams to return to England if he wished; he didn't). He also assured them possession of their facilities and security in their goods. He protected them against coerced trade and promised them exemption from the rigors of Japanese law. In effect, he was offering to build into his relations with the English those privileges of extraterritorality that later became hallmarks of European imperialism.

In any event, Adams and Saris returned to Hirado. By that time the two disliked each other intensely. Saris apparently resented Adams' deracinated behavior as a "naturalized Japanner" who not only consorted with Japanese and his Dutch rivals but even with the Portuguese and Spanish, for whom Adams worked as an interpreter and marketing agent. Moreover, Adams wished the English trading station to be located in the Kantō near his home. Saris wanted it at Hirado, and it was Saris, not Adams, who had the power to decide. Saris named a merchant, Richard Cocks, to head the trading post, and after some hard bargaining Adams agreed to serve as an assistant to Cocks.

By the end of 1613, then, Ieyasu had in the Dutch and the English two promising new avenues to European trade, and both obviated the necessity of continuing to tolerate the troublesome Iberians. At that juncture the Ōkubo Tadachika matter blew up, and Ieyasu resolved to turn it to advantage as a way of ridding himself of the missionary problem.

Having decided to test Ōkubo, and in the process to resolve the series of problems that seemed linked with Christianity, Ieyasu needed a document to explain his action. On December 21, seven days after Ieyasu's return to Chiyoda Castle, Sūden reached Edo from Kyoto. He met Ieyasu, they discussed the situation, and the next night Sūden prepared a statement for Hidetada, who in turn issued it on the twenty-third.

In this hurried, late-night document, Sūden expanded on the main thesis contained in his letter of 1612 to Manila. Starting with the hoary proposition that "Heaven is father; earth is mother;

humans live between the two," he then introduced Shintō and Buddhist propositions leading to the argument that in Japan there was no discord between the two doctrines. He went on, however, that Christian sectarians came to Japan, not simply to trade, "but also hoping to spread their evil doctrine without permission, to confound true religion, change the political order of the realm, and make it their own." Just as the virtuous are fully rewarded, Sūden continued, those who create trouble should be severely punished. The perpetuation of an orderly and virtuous society is difficult under even the best circumstances. Because the missionary bands are lawless and engage in injurious and unethical activities, if they are not proscribed promptly, they will certainly be a source of future grief for the realm. Hence they must be expelled, and any who fail to enforce this edict must be punished. Thus will the country prosper and the people be at ease now and in future.

Clearly, times had changed. In 1609 Ieyasu had been ready to tolerate Iberian missionaries as the price of trade. By 1612 he was ready to say that trade must flourish without religion. By the end of 1613, he wanted to be completely rid of the missionaries and did not even bother to encourage the Iberians to continue trading.

During 1614 he pressed his attack on the missionaries. After ousting Tadachika from Odawara, he put others in charge of the missionary round-up. Officials were encouraged to uproot Christianity from the Nagasaki area and in the domain of Arima. Ieyasu instructed Kyushu daimyo to deploy all the forces necessary to achieve that objective. During the summer about a hundred members of the mission establishment were rounded up, put aboard ship, and deported to the Philippines. Many others went into hiding, some taking shelter with Toyotomi Hideyori in Osaka Castle, and the proselytizing continued. Then the whole deportation project went into abeyance, overshadowed by another matter.

CHAPTER XV:

Of Children and Courtiers

It was no accident that one of Ieyasu's first acts, after hearing of Ōkubo Tadachika's anger, was to take special precautions for the safety of his sons, Yoshinao and Yorinobu. The vitality and well-being of his progeny had been an enduring concern throughout his life. In that regard he was simply a man of his age. But after 1607 he became more anxious about his offspring than he had previously been.

Few things could dismay him as much as the thought that his children were in danger or the news that they were in trouble. Certainly he had not forgotten that terrible day in 1579 when he ordered his eldest son, Nobuyasu, to rip his belly open. Hideyoshi's brutal destruction in 1596 of his nephew and heir, Hidetsugu, and his family, also seems to have made a lasting impression on the Tokugawa chief.

His first major loss after Nobuyasu was his fifth son Nobuyoshi, who died in 1603 at the age of 20. Nobuyoshi had been given to the Takeda family years before, thus leaving the Tokugawa family anyway, and Ieyasu still had other sons who could preserve his lineage. They were Hideyasu, born in 1574; Hidetada, in 1579; Tadayoshi, the following year; Tadateru, in 1592; and the three infants: Yoshinao, born in 1600; Yorinobu, in 1602; and Yorifusa, in 1603.

Nobuyoshi's death did not seem to threaten his family's prospects, but certain deaths in 1607 did. Within two months of one another, two of his adult sons suddenly died. In March, a few days after Ieyasu moved down to Sumpu, Tadayoshi, who as daimyo of Kiyosu anchored his domain at the midpoint between Sumpu and Fushimi, died unexpectedly. Two months later death claimed the brave but callous and frustrated 33-year-old Hideyasu, who governed a vast domain on the Sea of Japan and who was also serving as castellan at Fushimi.

A few months later death stalked Ieyasu into his very bedchamber. Construction of his handsome new residence at Sumpu was completed by summer, and he moved in on July 3. Five months later, just a few nights after he returned from a hawking expedition in the Kantō, and while he was sick in bed, a fire broke out near his quarters. Close attendants hustled him to safety, and his son Yorifusa was saved from the flames, but several waiting ladies died in the blaze and his new home was utterly destroyed. The fire evidently started from a candle that ignited a wall, and while it seems to have been accidental, it was no less dangerous or costly. And it might not have been accidental. The burning of an enemy castle was a customary tactic, and saboteurs were part of every able lord's arsenal of weapons.

What was happening? Were there saboteurs in his midst? His sons Hideyasu and Tadayoshi, two key figures in his defense line from Edo to Fushimi, were dead. Yorifusa and Ieyasu himself were nearly burned to death. Fushimi, Kiyosu, Sumpu: Were Chiyoda Castle and the shogun the next targets? Or was it a devious plot at all? Was it just bad luck and bad health? If the problem at Kiyosu was the location of the castle, he would build a new one there, so that Tadayoshi's successor, young Yoshinao, would be safer.

At Sumpu, as well, he responded by putting men to work at once on a new residence. During 1608 he ordered a massive construction effort to make the castle more secure. The suspicion of sabotage seemed borne out by later reports, and in June of 1609 charges of arson in the castle were brought against two serving girls in his household. As a lesson before the world, he had them burned at the stake, and two senior women attendants who were responsible for the hapless girls were banished.

The deaths of Hideyasu and Tadayoshi left Ieyasu with dependable Hidetada at Edo and Tadateru at Matsushiro in Shinano, plus the three little boys. Then in 1609, even as he dealt ruthlessly with the arson case in his own castle, Tadateru's political worth came into question. Tadateru was born with a birth defect on his face, a deep slash running back from one eye and badly discolored flesh. Ieyasu had a vassal rear the child, and Tadateru was later adopted by one of Ieyasu's Matsudaira kinsmen. Early on he showed emotional problems and was a violent and domineering young daimyo at Matsushiro. When he was seventeen, he developed an intense affection for a Nō actor, and soon the actor and Tadateru's senior advisors were bitterly at odds. The issue was brought to Ieyasu's attention, and at the end of October 1609 he stripped two of Tadateru's principal advisors, whom he had appointed himself, of all their lands and ordered a third to commit suicide. A few months later, hoping to start the young man anew under better circumstances, he transferred him to a larger but more isolated domain at Takada in Echigo on the Sea of Japan.

There were other family worries. Nine days after he transferred

Tadateru, Ieyasu's equanimity was shattered by the death of his last child, the three-year-old girl, Ichihime, born of his beloved consort, Lady Ōta, who was also raising his six-year-old son Yorifusa at Sumpu. One by one his children seemed to be dying before his eyes. His response to this newest blow was to show even greater concern for his other youngsters. He ordered Hidetada to take direct personal responsibility for the wellbeing of Yoshinao and Yorinobu, aged nine and seven respectively. Meanwhile Ieyasu and Lady Ōta would continue to look after Yorifusa.

A year later the old man again showed his keen sensitivity for the health of his children. In the autumn of 1611, a few days after making it clear to Hidetada that the third shogun was to be Iemitsu and not Tadanaga, Ieyasu was happily hawking in the northern Kantō. Reports reached him that his son Yoshinao, who was visiting Sumpu, was ill with smallpox. He cut his trip short and rushed homeward. His palanquin bearers and retinue headed south to Kawagoe where Hidetada met them for a briefing. The shogun then returned to Edo and Ieyasu headed directly home, going cross-country to Fuchū, where a messenger from Sumpu caught up with him. The messenger reported that the illness was mild and not a cause for alarm. Much relieved, Ieyasu halted his headlong dash, and instead sent a letter off to Yoshinao's mother, Okame (Lady Shimizu) and his other favorite consort Achaya (Lady Kawamura), both at Sumpu. He wrote, in his own cursive script:

> *Yes indeed, what fortunate news! I hear that Yoshinao is much improved. Good news! I am delighted. You can imagine my joy. He had a very mild case and now is well, so my mind is at ease. Such good news! I am so relieved, as you surely realize.*
> *Glad tidings. And best wishes.*
> *To: Okame; Achaya*   *From: Ie*

After dispatching this message of unsuppressed relief, Ieyasu returned to hawking and did not get back to Sumpu for another ten days.

This intense concern for his children was a reflection, no doubt, of Ieyasu's advancing years. When younger, he could have responded to the problems of endangered progeny by siring more. Those days were gone. He must now carefully nurture those who remained, and do what he could in the time still left him to see that the realm would be safe for them.

In early 1614, after looking to the wellbeing of his children, disposing of Ōkubo Tadachika, and confronting the missionary problem, Ieyasu turned to another matter of periodic concern: the Imperial Court.

He had tried to settle affairs there in 1611 when he made his grand trek to oversee the enthronement of Go Mizunoō and to admonish the courtiers about their behavior. The aristocrats evidently continued to be a nuisance, because in June of 1612 Ieyasu sent a message to Kyoto, advising them to study diligently their family's traditonal learning, to be discreet in their conduct, and to stop hawking, which was a samurai sport and unseemly for Imperial aristocrats. Still, petty quarrels continued. For example, Ieyasu had to have his delegate in Kyoto persuade Goyōzei to return to the Court certain treasured articles that he had removed from the Palace when he abdicated.

Ieyasu's impatience with the nobility grew, and in June of 1613 he issued a five-clause code of conduct for the Court. Modeled in part on the Court's own code of 1603, it admonished the nobles to study assiduously, perform their duties, avoid crowds, troublemakers, gambling halls, and other improper places, and abide by appropriate regulations--or be banished. Banishment, of course, was the new twist. With it he served notice that he would no longer permit the Court to police itself. The bakufu would do that henceforth, and it would no longer tolerate misconduct.

Even then, Ieyasu's efforts proved insufficient to stop back-biting and scheming at Kyoto, so in 1614, after returning to Sumpu, he again tried to manage the Court. He pursued two separate avenues of manipulation. One involved bedroom politics; the other, bureaucratic management.

Late in 1612 someone had proposed, with Ieyasu's approval no doubt, that a daughter of Hidetada could be strategically placed in the Court as wife of the young Emperor. In March 1614, when an Imperial delegation delivered to Sumpu a notice of a promotion for Hidetada, Ieyasu was also told that the Court intended to arrange just such a marriage. Ieyasu was fittingly delighted. Should such an arrangement come to pass, his granddaughter Kazuko, who was born in 1607, might well deliver a boy who might then become Emperor. That would be one way to assure a Tokugawa role in the Imperial Court. Ieyasu saw himself as a samurai, a *bushi*, certainly, but in this instance he was using a political stratagem primarily associated with that greatest of *kuge* families, the Fujiwara. As matters worked out, a series of incidents delayed the marriage, but finally, despite much resistance in Kyoto, Kazuko entered the Court in 1620. Three years later, at the age of sixteen, she gave birth to a boy who succeeded to the throne in 1629 as Emperor Meishō.

Long before this venture in bedroom politics bore fruit, Ieyasu intensified his efforts at bureaucratic management. Early in 1614 he instructed Ishin Sūden and other monks to study Court affairs more deeply in order to draw up a thorough and more solidly grounded set of regulations for *kuge* and priestly behavior. At Sumpu he already had genealogical information on the major noble families, but he wanted complete data. During March he assigned monks the task of assembling those data. During April he instructed Sūden, Honda Masazumi, and others to gather all existing records in all the archives and storehouses of the Court and aristocratic families so that they might be used by the scholars who were preparing a new code for the *kuge*. He ordered scholar-monks from the great Zen temples of Kyoto to prepare new regulations to guide both *kuge* and *buke*. He specified that they should draft the codes on the basis of precedents in the *Gunsho chiyō, Jōgan seiyō, Shoku Nihongi*, and *Engi Shiki*. The first two were Chinese works, the latter two were works of the classical period in Japan.

The scholars did their job, and while the family records were being assembled, they exchanged and discussed a series of drafts. During May tentative plans were made for Ieyasu to go to Kyoto in about three months to express appreciation for the Court's responsiveness in the marriage matter and to promulgate permanent codes for the guidance of members of the Court and for temples and shrines.

Ieyasu did not devote such attention to the Court because he believed maneuvering by a handful of powerless aristocrats constituted a direct threat to his regime. It did not. The Emperor, after all, had no more divisions than the Pope. But the intrigues did suggest that Tokugawa control of the Court was not sufficiently complete and that there might be room for rivals to maneuver and subtly erode the regime's base of legitimacy in the Imperial appointment of successive Tokugawa shogun. In the long run it was important that the relationship of the Court and Ieyasu's successors be so regularized that no rival could exploit courtly dissatisfaction to challenge Tokugawa rule.

CHAPTER XVI:

The Quest for Eternal Order

During his unplanned sojourn at Edo during January, Ieyasu took care of the necessary New Year's ceremonies. After his return to Sumpu at month's end, he attempted to reestablish his routines there. He went hawking around Sumpu, but not very far away. He did some entertaining in the castle, but not much. He met a few daimyo and other visitors, and started people working on regulations for the Court. But what really consumed his time was a seemingly endless series of discussions with prelates of the major Buddhist sects. This series was without precedent in his life.

Ieyasu's interest in religion did not simply burst forth in 1614. It began to appear in 1611, grew steadily during the next two years, and by 1614 seemed almost morbid. He listened to three lectures on religion in 1612; six in 1613; and twenty-eight during the first nine months of 1614.

Surely part of his interest in theological matters sprang, as did his heightened concern for his progeny, from an old man's growing consciousness of his own mortality. For years he had enjoyed philosophical discussions, but Confucian commentaries interested him most. The issues of enlightenment and salvation that are central to Buddhist discourse had not elicited his attention. From about 1611, however, perhaps in reaction to the troubles that seemed to be pressing in on him--the general discontent, the trade and missionary problems, the family worries, the Court complications--religious issues began to gain new significance. Unquestionably, the deaths of so many old comrades and friends also took their toll on his spirit. At the end of 1612, after all, he had turned seventy (seventy-two by his own calculations), and he may have had a growing fear that his life's efforts were coming undone and that he had too little time left to do all that was needed, unless he could get a little help from elsewhere.

Ieyasu's family had long been associated with temples of the Jōdo sect. The Daijūji at Okazaki had been the Matsudaira family temple since the fifteenth century, and it had not been neglected.

Ieyasu's grandfather Kiyoyasu expanded its holdings during his lifetime, and in 1602 Ieyasu endowed it suitably with additional land. It was a Jōdo temple, and burial tablets of the family's deceased were maintained in its graveyard. In Edo, Ieyasu established and fostered the growth of another Jōdo temple, the Zōjōji, as the family's main temple. One of the earliest expressions of his growing interest in theology dates from 1608 when he instructed the Zōjōji abbot and a large group of acolytes to travel down to Sumpu to discuss Jōdo doctrine. Evidently satisfied with what he heard, he continued to promote the temple's interests, assigning it lands, honors, and scholars. In 1611, when he ordered a family temple erected to that hoary Tokugawa ancestor of his in the northwest Kantō, it was supposed to be designated a Jōdo temple.

In its popular formulation, Jōdo Buddhism involved a simple doctrine. The faithful were encouraged to celebrate the saving grace of the Buddha Amida by uttering the invocatory expression "Namu Amida Butsu" in a mood of utter and trusting faith. By doing so with complete sincerity one could assure one's salvation and contribute to the salvation of all others. Ieyasu adhered to the practice of Jōdo, and in his final years seems to have identified himself with Amida, at least to some extent. Perhaps he saw his own role in bringing peace to the realm as a manifestation of Amida's benevolent grace.

Surely this was a gratifying thought, but it was only one of the many riches of Buddhist theology. Beginning early in 1611, Ieyasu's religious interest began to deepen and broaden, and as he investigated other Buddhist teachings, he found even greater religious challenges and rewards awaiting him. In April 1611, while in Kyoto for the enthronement of Go Mizunoō, he had Shingon priests from Mt. Kōya lecture on their doctrines. That autumn he received a set of Tendai doctrinal writings.

Perhaps these first contacts with Shingon and Tendai doctrine piqued his curiosity, for during 1612 his interest in Buddhist theology commenced to grow. From about the middle of the year he began summoning monks of the Shingon sect to lecture on their teachings. Through the next year and into early 1614 the message of Shingon monks dominated his religious interest.

Shingon embraced a demanding, nearly inaccessible mode of religious action. Its doctrine held that one could not know the nature of Buddhahood by study and discussion. It was not accessible to the rational mind. Rather, it could be grasped only by richly cultivated sensibilities. One must be initiated into the secret rituals of Shingon, be taught the religious meaning of the mandala (or religious diagrams), and appreciate the significance of all the gestures, invocations, gongs, and implements that helped one perceive the Buddha nature. Such esoteric stuff must have seemed excessive

147

to the earthy Ieyasu. Shingon, however, also provided rules and regulations and an elaborately detailed cosmology, and those qualities probably appealed to his desire for an orderly universe.

During 1613 Ieyasu also began to listen to lectures on Tendai, and by the middle of the following year Tendai seemed to displace Shingon as the focus of his religious attention--perhaps because it offered rules and regulations, just as Shingon did, but with a much less intimidating doctrine. Prodded, perhaps, by Sūden, a Zen monk, and by others among his close advisors, he also heard lectures by proponents of the Sōtō sect of Zen, the Jōdo sect, and the Hossō and Kegon sects. Tendai, however, seems to have proved most satisfying.

Tendai's apparent triumph was ironic. Monks of the Tendai persuasion, after all, had been slaughtered by Ieyasu's mentor, Oda Nobunaga, on Mt. Hiei in 1571. Oda was able to destroy the organization of Mt. Hiei, its people, its treasures, and its great library, but he was unable to kill the iridescent message of the Lotus Sutra, the basic text of Tendai, with its bold assertion that the Buddha nature is found in all sentient beings and that all may in the end attain the state of enlightenment and thereby transcend the impermanence of this life.

In Tendai doctrine the means to enlightenment were not tightly regulated. In place of the closely guarded rituals of Shingon, Tendai held that all three classic forms of sacred action--faith, doctrinal study, and good works--had religious merit. Even if he had no sure faith, certainly Ieyasu qualified on the other two counts. He was making diligent inquiry into the nature of Buddhahood, which surely satisfied the requirement for doctrinal study. And his whole life--if peace should endure--could be seen as a good work. Had he not ended murder and rapine? Had he not brought tranquility to the land? Had he not benefited the myriad sentient beings? And more directly, had he not granted land and benefit to innumerable temples and shrines? Had he not rewarded monks for their service and encouraged study and learning? It was a record of considerable merit. In terms of Tendai doctrine, it all made good sense. If only he could keep the peace.

In his religious quest the old man surely had one eye cocked to his own prospects. But Ieyasu, the crafty old politician, had another eye that was clearly focused on another of his problems: that of disputes involving temples and monks. Oda had ravaged Mt. Hiei, and Hideyoshi, Ieyasu, and others had bent considerable energy to the crushing of other politicized temples and sectarian groups. At the same time, however, Ieyasu had taken care to guarantee those lands of temples and shrines that accepted his leadership. With clear evidence that cooperation paid off, monks bowed to these realities during the 1590s and the first decade after Sekigahara.

To sustain this cooperative attitude among men of the cloth, Ieyasu issued sets of regulations to guide abbots in administering major temples. In 1601, for example, he issued such a set to the powerful Shingon temple on Mt. Kōya, and in August of 1608 he issued a set to the reviving Tendai temple organization on Mt. Hiei. In the latter set he ordered the following rules adhered to faithfully:

(1) Those who do not study the doctrine may not reside on Hiei, except for those returning to the mountain and engaged in building themselves shelter.

(2) Those who, despite their study, do not abide by the spirit of the teachings must leave the mountain promptly.

(3) Those with distinguished special training should be nurtured.

(4) No one is to belong to more than one monastic residence, and vacant residences are to be closed.

(5) Except for the chief priest, no one may try to auction off monastic residences and lands.

(6) Deeds and titles of sale on monastic dwellings and lands will have no legal worth.

(7) Any monks who lawlessly plot to assemble and do wrong are to be expelled.

In these regulations one can see Ieyasu's lasting concern lest the temples again become hostile and powerful political forces. To some extent, this concern reflected the disorder of Ieyasu's early years in Mikawa, but the rules also revealed his growing concern for the future. With peace and the passage of time, monks, like the aristocrats of Kyoto, the young toughs of Edo, and others as well, seemed to become more restless. Not only Buddhists, but other men of religion such as priests of Shintō and Shugendō (mountain ascetics) gave him headaches.

From about 1610 on, Ieyasu found himself drawn into more and more religious quarrels and called on to resolve them. When disputes pertained to practical matters, such as land and income, he could act. The particular characteristics of various sects and of specific temples, however, compelled him to issue regulations that seemed to differ endlessly even when concerned with minor details. When issues involved questions of doctrine, precedent, and ritual practice--and much of the disputation and consequent adjudication did--Ieyasu was ill-equipped to settle them. His knowledge of theology was inadequate. His solution to the dilemma was to study doctrine, hear arguments, and then issue such sets of regulations as would bring more order and consistency into the chaotic world of clerical administration. He began doing so about the middle of 1612, issuing regulations to selected temples or to doctrinal groups such as Tendai, "old-school" Shingon, and "new-school" Shingon.

After his return to Sumpu in early 1614, he began to summon groups of monks to discuss theology and temple practices. Men from Kōya came to Sumpu to explain Shingon in a series of seminars. A number of monks from other temples discussed Sōtō Zen doctrine. During the following months Ieyasu heard more lectures and discussions on Shingon texts, on Hossō doctrine, on Tendai, and on Kegon. By late May he had sufficient grasp of the various doctrines to begin planning a general theological conclave. He hoped, it appears, to hammer out a theological position or set of relationships that would be generally acceptable and could help give doctrinal and administrative order to the intricate world of Japanese Buddhism. Ieyasu might not gain Buddhahood directly, but if he left his descendants an ordered world, it would be quite an achievement; enough, perhaps, to have the corollary effect of gaining him access to the state of enlightenment.

CHAPTER XVII:

Crisis in the Established Order

While Ieyasu pursued religious discussions and supervised the preparation of codes of conduct, his officials in Kyoto and Nagasaki, as well as daimyo elsewhere in Kyushu, were tearing down churches and rounding up missionaries (missing many who changed to lay attire and pretended to be traders).

This was the most dramatic aspect of the Ōkubo affair. Another side of the affair existed, however, that may have contributed to certain events in 1614. A report suggested that Tadachika was conniving with Toyotomi Hideyori at Osaka. Years before, Ishikawa Kazumasa had defected to Hideyoshi. Was Ōkubo now planning to defect to his son? Those who had not been with Ieyasu at Sekigahara might understandably feel ties to the Toyotomi, but if Tokugawa vassals also were beginning to drift away, there was cause for alarm.

Most probably with this report in mind, Ieyasu ordered lords in Ise and Mikawa Provinces (between Hideyori and Tadachika) to stay there rather than visit Edo in 1614. He then sent Tadachika west with a handful of men to Kyoto and on into political oblivion. That settled the immediate problem, but during the summer the broader Hideyori question rapidly came to the fore and dominated Ieyasu's attention until finally resolved in blood and violence.

The fundamental issue was the unsettled problem of the Tokugawa-Toyotomi relationship. It had existed since Hideyoshi's death and was inherent in the history of the two families. Ieyasu had been Hideyoshi's subordinate and in 1598 swore to serve faithfully the Taikō's successor, Hideyori. But events of 1599 and 1600 so altered Ieyasu's position that his subordination to little Hideyori became patently empty. When he took the title of shogun, he abandoned all pretense of subordination, and with the transfer of the title to Hidetada in 1605, it was obvious that the Tokugawa would never willingly accept any Toyotomi claim to supremacy.

During the first decade after Sekigahara the issue was quiescent. Young Hideyori lived quietly in his immense bastion at Osaka, sustained by his large domain of some 650,000 *koku*. Ieyasu, meanwhile, was getting along famously with the Court. Foreign relations were conducted almost without incident. The priests and administrators of temples and shrines seemed content with the arrangements the new regime afforded them. Those daimyo who had chosen the winning side at Sekigahara were rewarded. The losers paid their penalty; or they did their best to avoid trouble and salvage what they could from an awkward situation. Subordinates seemed well enough off, or sufficiently well controlled by their lords, to present few problems.

Given the pervasive acquiescence in the new peace, anyone who might have sought a Toyotomi revival, whether out of dedication or a desire for self-advancement, would have been hard pressed to develop a following. Hideyori had done nothing to encourage anti-Tokugawa activity. Born in Osaka on August 3, 1593, of Hideyoshi's beloved consort, Lady Yodo, for several years after Sekigahara he was too young to be politically active. Under the guidance of cautious advisors, he closely observed protocol in his dealings with Ieyasu, the Court, and other figures of consequence.

The same cannot be said of his mother. Lady Yodo seemed unable to reconcile herself to Tokugawa supremacy, and seems to have bent her efforts toward preparing Hideyori for the day when he could assume his rightful position.

Ieyasu had tried to preclude such ambitions. In 1598 he promised the dying Hideyoshi that he would marry his granddaughter to Hideyori. True to his word, In July 1603, a few months after being named shogun, he sent six-year-old Senhime, Hidetada's eldest daughter, to Osaka as Hideyori's bride. However, because of the changed circumstances of the two families, the marriage bore political implications very unlike Hideyoshi's intentions. Instead of a ruling Toyotomi family sustaining ties with its powerful vassal, there was a ruling Tokugawa shogun magnanimously giving a granddaughter to a boy, in memory of former ties with his deceased father. Hideyori's supporters at Osaka were not pleased by this arrangement. Although aware that those around the boy were unhappy with the trend of events, Ieyasu allowed the boy to live quietly at Osaka, simply advising daimyo to discontinue paying courtesy calls on Hideyori when travelling to and from Edo.

Yodo remained adamant. Ieyasu encouraged her to build temples, but her energies were not sufficiently absorbed; her ambitions were not quieted. In 1605, at the time Hidetada was named shogun, daimyo sent ritual greetings and congratulations, but none came from Hideyori. Therefore Ieyasu urged him, by way of Hideyoshi's gracious widow, Kōdaiin, to come up from Osaka to Kyoto

152

for a visit. Yodo, who probably resented Kōdaiin's favored position, refused to permit it, recognizing that such a trip would constitute a gesture of consent to the new order. Indeed, she was said to be ready to kill herself and to have her son disembowel himself to avoid capitulation. The rebuff fueled more rumors and worry, so as a conciliatory gesture Ieyasu sent his son, Tadateru, who was Hideyori's age, to Osaka to extend greetings to him. The strain was eased momentarily.

Later, Ieyasu ordered Hideyori, as he did other daimyo, to participate in construction of Sumpu Castle. Yodo and some of Hideyori's supporters were outraged at such degrading and burdensome treatment. In 1610 Hideyori and Yodo wrote Maeda Toshinaga, whose father had ably served Hideyoshi, asking his assistance in the name of the dead Taikō. Toshinaga knew who ruled and was scarcely in a position to behave like a vassal of the Toyotomi. He responded by letter, acknowledging that his dead father was indeed grateful for Hideyoshi's benevolence and observing that he himself, out of respect for the Taikō, had done no ill to Hideyori at the time of Sekigahara. But having been named lord of three provinces by the lords at Edo and Sumpu, he could not contemplate serving anyone else. Hence, it would be impossible to aid the Toyotomi. But, he added, if they were truly impoverished, he would give them some gold and silver. This certainly was not the answer Lady Yodo wanted.

In 1611, when Ieyasu was in Kyoto supervising Go Mizunoō's succession, he again invited Hideyori to visit. Lady Yodo objected, arguing that her son's life would be in danger if he left the castle. Ieyasu responded by sending his young sons Yoshinao and Yorinobu to Osaka in a compensatory gesture. The exchange constituted a sort of hostage arrangement that Yodo found acceptable, and the visit was carried out. Lest his visit be misconstrued as capitulation, however, Hideyori also took the occasion to visit the Toyokuni Shrine and Hōkōji. The former was the Shintō shrine of the Toyotomi family; the latter, the Buddhist temple dedicated to Hideyoshi's memory.

It was not Hideyori's life that was being risked by visits of this sort, but Lady Yodo's dreams for his future. Even so, when Hideyori returned safely to Osaka, there was a popular sense of relief, which suggests the extent to which people saw an irreconcilable clash developing because of Tokugawa determination to prevail and Toyotomi determination never to give up Hideyoshi's legacy. Even major political figures were fearful. The daimyo Katō Kiyomasa, who had loyally served Hideyoshi and later Ieyasu, played a central role in the meeting. He escorted Hideyori to Kyoto, was present during his two-hour exchange of pleasantries and refreshments with Ieyasu, and escorted Hideyori to Fushimi, where he saw him safely off to Osaka by boat. Throughout the meeting in Kyoto, Kiyomasa had kept a dagger hidden in his shirt with the intention of dispatching Ieyasu if by any chance anything untoward befell Hideyori. Kiyomasa knew full well the enormity of the risk he was running, and when at last Hideyori was safely off, he took out the dagger amidst a torrent of tears of relief, saying, "Ahhh, at last I have fulfilled the obligation I owed Hideyoshi."

During the next three years the Toyotomi-Tokugawa matter rested quietly. Hideyori continued to work at temple construction, and Ieyasu regularly approved his activities. Through the spring of 1614 the temple work seemed to present no problems, but soon thereafter things started to change.

Ieyasu was at Sumpu in April, listening to monks explain religion, seeing two Nō presentations, instructing scholars to prepare codes for nobles, prelates, and daimyo, and hearing of the plan for Hidetada's daughter to marry the Emperor. At Kyoto, meanwhile, Hideyori's most cherished temple project was nearing completion. Final steps were being taken for the casting of a great, deep-toned, sonorous bell to be installed in the nearly rebuilt Hōkōji.

The Hōkōji was not a venerable fane like those on Mt. Kōya and Mt. Hiei. It held no particular cultural importance, only political significance. In 1587 Hideyoshi had subdued the independent daimyo of western Japan, and the following year most of the eastern lords had also submitted. To celebrate, and perpetuate his pacification of the country, Hideyoshi ordered the erection of a giant Buddha image. It was to be held together with bolts cast from the weapons of war confiscated by daimyo from peasants and townsmen in their domains.

Hideyoshi explained that in erecting the temple he wished to assure the wellbeing of the people. He wrote,

> *In other lands, such as China, the ruler Yao converted swords and sharp weapons into agricultural implements after he had established peace. In our country such an experiment has never been made. Thus, all the people should abide by and understand the aims of this act and give their undivided attention to agriculture and sericulture.*

Hideyoshi's version of "swords into plowshares" would not only give Japan an enduring monument to peace and Toyotomi glory but would also deprive the general populace of the power to rebel. Clearly Hideyoshi had not forgotten the politically troublesome Ikkō militants and ambitious local samurai.

The temple was erected and the image formed, but Hideyoshi's project was ruined by the great Fushimi earthquake of 1596. In 1602 Hideyori, encouraged by his mother, undertook the rebuilding of the Hōkōji. Ieyasu made a gesture of encouragement, ordering woodsmen to select a proper tree from near Mt. Fuji and fell it to obtain a ridgepole. The tree was felled; getting the giant piece of timber safely out of the forest and by sea to Osaka required three months of painstaking labor. Despite such exertions, before the temple was completed, it was destroyed by another fire.

Hideyori was unwilling to give up and placed his trusted vassal Katagiri Katsumoto in charge of a renewed effort. In 1608 the preparatory work of assembling money and materials commenced. This time Ieyasu did not provide the ridgepole and Hideyori had to buy it. The one he found had originated in a forest in Kyushu. It measured 26 meters in length and required a month to travel by sea from Kyushu to Osaka. At the Osaka timber market the piece cost Hideyori 90 *kan* of silver, or about $12,000 (at one dollar per ounce of silver).

Despite the difficulties and costs entailed, Hideyori pressed on with his project. By 1612 the new Buddha, a huge bronze image, was completed. It was immense. The eyes were some seven feet across. The ears, with their long lobes of Buddhist wisdom, were some fifteen feet in length. The thumb was too large to be encircled by a person's outstretched arms. A huge temple was erected around the image, its roof towering more than 45 meters in the air. A bell tower and gates were added, and by 1614 the construction was finished. It cost 824,585 *ryō* in gold, or $6,625,000 (at one dollar per ounce of silver and 16 gold *ryō* per *kan* of silver).

By May the bell was cast and Hideyori began planning a dedication service for the temple, to be held in August. He sent messengers to Sumpu to obtain Ieyasu's approval of the proposed procedures. Some initial questions were raised, minor changes were made, and until July all seemed well.

July, however, was unsettling. For months Ieyasu had heard lectures on Shingon, Tendai, and other sectarian Buddhist teachings, and he was engaged in drawing up codes of conduct to regulate temple life, hoping thereby to resolve quarrels among stubborn monks. He found that project thorny enough, but it was only an addition to the list of troubles making him uncommonly suspicious in the summer of 1614: he had recently confronted the Ōkubo issue, with its freight of factionalism and alleged betrayal. He fretted about his children and their future. He was thinking about his own worth and dealing with an insidious foreign ideology.

Into this sea of troubles sailed Hideyori's delegates in July. They proposed that Tendai monks be given charge of the Hōkōji dedication ceremonies. Disagreements promptly erupted. Ieyasu's advisors, Ishin Sūden and Honda Masazumi in particular, argued that both Tendai and Shingon monks should be involved. Hideyori suggested that both could be there but that only Tendai monks should officiate. Ieyasu replied that precedent clearly called for two ceremonies, a dedication of the temple building and a dedication of the Buddha image. One ought to be held according to Tendai precepts; the other, by Shingon. Moreover, they should be held fifteen days apart. In reply Hideyori proposed to hold the ceremonies on the same day, to avoid a schedule conflict with memorial services for his deceased father. Ieyasu could hardly fault that reasoning, but he did note that the date Hideyori had suggested was by tradition an unlucky day for dedicating buildings, and in any case the inscription to go on the $12,000 ridgepole was wrong because it omitted the name of the master carpenter.

Not only were the dedication ceremonies planned improperly; there were problems with the inscription on the great deepthroated bell that Hideyori had cast for the temple a few months before. It had been prepared by a monk who was not of the proper rank or a member of the proper temple, so that the procedure followed in preparing the inscription did not conform to the 800-year-old precedents set in the erection and dedication of the great Buddha image at Nara.

By themselves these issues were trivial and scarcely worth arguing over. But shortly before, Ieyasu had learned about the bell inscription itself, probably from Sūden. The syntax of the inscription permitted differing interpretations when read as Chinese or Japanese. Moreover, the ideographs chosen for the inscription included those for Ieyasu's given name, part of Hideyori's family name, and others that could be read as referring to lord and vassal, and the Toyotomi in the west and Tokugawa in the east. Depending on one's handling of the syntax, a suspicious mind could find in the phrasing evidence of a scheme to claim a Toyotomi superiority over the Tokugawa.

Developments of the past half-year had made Ieyasu very suspicious. He was ready to put the worst reading on the evidence, and as he and Hideyori argued over the trivial procedural problems, he seemed to have become more and more convinced that the worst interpretation was the correct one. At the very least Hideyori was willfully confounding his attempts to routinize temple affairs; at worst he was seditious. And the young man's stubbornness in the face of explicit instructions from Sumpu was clearly intolerable. On July 26 Ieyasu angrily denounced Hideyori's proposal, that of holding the ceremonies on the same day, as contrary to established practice and disruptive of his attempts to standardize temple procedures. He ordered the entire dedication postponed.

The old man was thoroughly upset, his general mood reflected in comments he made in August to some Iberians protesting his earlier expulsion order: "If Christianity spreads, the people of the realm become rebellious. Therefore, to stamp out the evil at its source, not a single Portuguese will be permitted to remain in the country." Ieyasu's evidence for this proposition, like that for his assessment of Hideyori's intention, was cumulative and of uncertain validity, but in the summer of 1614 he was ready to believe the worst of missionaries, just as he was of Hideyori.

Ieyasu's advisors may have tried to direct his anger toward the missionaries as a means of deflecting it from Hideyori. During August some of them, as well as vassals of Hideyori and various monks, tried to calm the old man, persuade him that Hideyori meant no harm, and induce him to let the Hōkōji dedication proceed. But on August 18 Ieyasu received evaluations of the inscription from scholars at the major Zen temples of Kyoto. They found more that was improper. And Hayashi Razan read it as positively disrespectful and seditious. His own deepest suspicions reinforced, Ieyasu refused to meet Hideyori's advisor, Katagiri Katsumoto, who reached Sumpu seeking a compromise the next day. Instead he had Sūden and Masazumi inform Katagiri that the inscription was unacceptable and must be erased. Then he had them add a new and devastating item to his litany of complaints. Why, he demanded to know, was Hideyori summoning *rōnin*, unemployed fighting men, to Osaka? What was he up to?

With that query it became crystal-clear. Ieyasu suspected that Hideyori was preparing an insurrection. Several days later he abruptly ordered a halt to the major construction work then under way at Edo castle and shortly thereafter sent a notice to all daimyo, ordering them to give oaths of allegiance to himself and to Hidetada. While these steps were being taken, Katagiri returned to Osaka with his understanding of Ieyasu's requirements for a pacific settlement. The inscription was to be eliminated; an appropriate apology was to be rendered; Hideyori and his mother were to leave their bastion in Osaka and go to Edo or settle out in one of the provinces.

Had Hideyori been his own master, he might have counted noses and concluded that a quiet home in the country was exactly what he wanted. He was not his own master, however. His vassals were badly divided, but none found Katagiri's message acceptable. Some urged that Ieyasu be conciliated just a bit longer, because he would die soon and Hidetada would be an easier figure to challenge. Others called for resolute defiance, and they found their champion in Lady Yodo.

In the autumn of 1614, as the Hōkōji dispute deepened, Lady Yodo grew agitated. When she learned of Ieyasu's demand that she and Hideyori leave Osaka, she refused. It was clear to Hideyori's advisors that Ieyasu believed the Osaka situation could no longer be left unchanged, and tensions in Osaka Castle grew intolerable. During September, Katagiri and other proponents of conciliation fled the fortress, leaving the hard-liners in control of Hideyori and the destinies of the Toyotomi house. On October 1, Ieyasu received a report of the situation in Osaka from his representative in Kyoto, and he concluded that with hard-liners in control, an acceptable peaceful resolution of the dispute would not be forthcoming.

The tragedy taking shape at Osaka did not come as a surprise to everyone. As long ago as 1601 Date Masamune, daimyo of Sendai, had predicted it, and over the years others had anticipated it. In April of 1601 Date had written a letter to a man in Kyoto, hoping the man would relay it to Ieyasu and thus forestall trouble. In the letter Masamune warned:

> *While Hideyori is young, he should stay at Edo or Fushimi, or somewhere near Ieyasu. Although he is Hideyoshi's heir, Ieyasu will never let him rule Japan, but he will grant him two or three provinces in perpetuity. If, however, Hideyori remains at Osaka, sooner or later some ambitious character will foment rebellion in his name. And even if Hideyori knows nothing about it, he will be blamed and forced to commit suicide, to the grief of Hideyoshi's ghost.*

A period of worsening affairs and political decay that had begun in about 1610 culminated in the autumn of 1614 when an angry, worried Ieyasu became convinced that he could preserve peace and perpetuate his family's supremacy only by trimming Hideyori's military capacity to acceptable dimensions. Within the course of three months trivial matters of ritual had laid bare the elemental conflict still pitting Tokugawa against Toyotomi. Ieyasu became convinced that sixteen years of management had failed to persuade the Toyotomi that their best choice was to enjoy great daimyo status under Tokugawa rule. He was finally resorting to war, an instrument he had not used for nearly fifteen years. Things were not working out as he wished.

PART IV

THE FIRST YEAR OF GEN'NA (1615)

CHAPTER XVIII:

Rituals and Reckonings of the New Year

Ieyasu was tired of the place. He did not really wish to spend the first days of another New Year in Kyoto. He had been in and around the city since October 23, and now, two months later, he wanted to leave. He wanted to go home to Sumpu, to be done with the current nastiness and pick up again the comfortable routines of the recent past.

Kyoto simply could not compare with Sumpu. The city was cold and damp in winter, whereas Sumpu was warmed by the sea and sheltered by hills west and north. Kyoto sprawled out, and getting to the hills was a tiresome ride. Moreover, Nijō Castle, where he was staying, was situated within the city and despite the castle's elegance, the view had little to recommend it. Sumpu, by contrast, was a small town. Open countryside for hawking was near at hand, and the majestic beauty of sea and mountain was ever visible. Besides, Kyoto reeked of pretense and pomposity. People made too much of even simple entertainments such as Nō or the tea ceremony. At Sumpu a man could enjoy them. And there he could eat simple foods with gusto, wear comfortable clothes, and chat amiably with old friends, free of the more onerous requirements of propriety.

As the last month of 1614 drew to a close, however, he realized he must stay in Kyoto until the New Year's greetings had been exchanged. Given the political importance of the Imperial Court, and given the tumultuous events that had just transpired, it behooved him to stay in town a while yet to pay his respects to Go Mizunoō and everyone else, and in the process to keep a close eye on them.

Accordingly, he stayed in the damp, cold city. On New Year's, the first day of the first month of the twentieth year of Keichō, he presented appropriate gifts to the Emperor. During the day he also received at Nijō a messenger who conveyed season's greetings and proper regards from Toyotomi Hideyori, who still lived in his great family castle at Osaka. Then came a stream of messengers conveying greetings from countless lords, prelates, and vassals. On the second day Imperial emissaries arrived, conveying the Emperor's greetings, and then representatives brought appropriate messages from the families of courtiers. Finally with these rituals finished, Ieyasu clambered into his palanquin and left the city for home. At the age of seventy-two (seventy-four by his reckoning) he had started another new year properly, and he was going home to enjoy it.

As far as nomenclature was concerned, it was just another year, Keichō twenty. But in time that would change, and it would come to be known as the first year of Gen'na. The change in name was no more fortuitous than the changes that Matsudaira Takechiyo's name underwent on the way to becoming Tokugawa Ieyasu. The change mattered because the calendar was not regarded as an inert recorder of time. True, it did record time, but it was not uninvolved in the times. It was part of the wholeness of being. It had to be kept in harmony with that wholeness, and it was the duty of a virtuous ruler to keep it harmonized. Therefore, occasionally it had to be changed.

Fifteen hundred ninety-six, for example, had begun innocuously enough as the fifth year of Bunroku. Bunroku, like most calendrical labels for year-periods in east Asia, consisted of two ideographs. In the case of Bunroku they meant something like "culture and beneficence." This name was chosen late in 1592, when Hideyoshi's invasion of Korea was in full flower and an era of unparalleled glory abroad and flourishing peace at home seemed to be opening.

Things did not work out well for Hideyoshi, however, and by 1596 they had gone completely sour: the great Fushimi earthquake, the trouble with the Spanish Franciscans, the worries about little Hideyori, and then the "insolent" Chinese embassy's refusal to submit. Hideyoshi took steps to slash through this forest of troubles by crucifying the Franciscans and renewing his war on China. A few weeks after reviving the war, he had the official astrologers at Court change the year-period name. The soft-sounding era of Bunroku was replaced by the more vigorously assertive Keichō, "rejoicing eternal", in which the ideograph for *chō* also had overtones of leadership or command. As Hideyoshi set out again to put the world in order, he did so in the auspicious era of "rejoicing eternal."

When Ieyasu emerged supreme in 1600, he had no doubt that the period-name was in tune with the times, and it remained more or less in tune for the next fourteen years. One has to say "more or less" because life was no more tidy in Ieyasu's day than in ours. Problems are inherent in the process of getting through a day. But from about 1610 on, matters began to worsen, until 1614, when Ieyasu finally sailed head-on into a sea of problems, trying to over-

162

whelm them much as Hideyoshi had done in 1596. By the summer of 1615 they seemed to be under control, and it was then that Ieyasu decided to bring the calendar back into harmony with the rest of the universe.

Accordingly, astrologers examined their charts and reported that the proper name for the times was Gen'na, which means "elemental peace" or "basic reconciliation." Clearly it was appropriate and auspicious. There was a ring of firmness about it, but firmness to a compassionate purpose. Less effeminate than Bunroku, less pretentiously assertive than Keichō, Gen'na seemed to bespeak an orderly world. So the sun that set on the twelfth day of the seventh month of the twentieth year of Keichō rose a few hours later to begin the thirteenth day of the seventh month of the first year of Gen'na. Without a moment's interruption the times had begun anew.

Just to keep matters straight, writers in a later day would backdate the first year of Gen'na to New Year's. But as Ieyasu's retinue wended its way through the streets of Kyoto heading back to Sumpu on January 3, he could not anticipate all that would occur in the next few months before Keichō would give way to Gen'na.

CHAPTER XIX:

Hideyori Confronted

From Kyoto, Ieyasu began a leisurely trek east, enjoying scenery he had not seen for nearly four years. He stayed overnight on the shore of Lake Biwa, took a boat across the southern tip of the lake, and then on the fourth, rode to Minakuchi near the eastern edge of Ōmi province.

He spent the night there, enjoying the sleep. After seventy-two years his old bones were no longer up to the joggling of the palanquin. It had been years since he had done much long-distance touring, and it was not particularly pleasant. From Minakuchi he proceeded slowly, reaching Nagoya on the seventh. He spent two days there.

Nagoya made an excellent rest-stop. It boasted a very new castle, one of the largest, most formidable, and most elegant in Japan. Ieyasu had decided to erect it in 1609 to replace the smaller fortress at nearby Kiyosu. That fortress had been the original headquarters of his early mentor, Oda Nobunaga, and most recently it had been the castle of his son Tadayoshi, who had died suddenly of illness in 1607. The Kiyosu fortress had military disadvantages because its location made it subject to flooding, and it was uncomfortable and perhaps unhealthy. Ieyasu decided to build a great new castle, which he would assign to Yoshinao, his third-from-youngest son. It would serve as the western anchor of the domain he oversaw in his hawking expeditions. It would give him a powerful barrier fortress facing the Toyotomi domain to the west, and it would link his bastions at Fushimi and Nijō with those at Sumpu and Edo. With it he would have an unbreakable chain of strong points stretching from the Kantō to the Kinai, dominating the entire expanse of fertile plain that constituted the central breadbasket of Japan.

Construction of a monstrous castle would also enable him to employ the daimyo. Reports reaching him during the year indicated that some of the western daimyo were expanding their castles. In irritation he asked, "Are they expecting disorder to erupt before long?" He issued no formal ban on such castle work, but word of his disapproval spread and the work stopped, one lord even tearing down some partially-completed fortifications. Wryly concluding, perhaps, that if the daimyo wished to build so badly, he would let them, during 1609 and 1610 he ordered large numbers of them, including Maeda, Mōri, Katō, and Ikeda, to deploy forces, funds, and material resources for the construction. He assigned experts to supervise the work and visited the project himself during the winters of 1611 and 1612. As the work progressed, he sent occasional token gifts to the participating daimyo, and in 1614 the massive enterprise was finally completed. The castle then became the citadel of Yoshinao, supervised by selected vassals who were close to the old man himself.

The fortress at Nagoya was nearly two kilometers in circumference. Broad, water-filled moats surrounded two sides, a deep, unfilled moat, a third. Within the moats were immense walls made of boulders, and these surrounded open lists bordering interior moats and walls. At the center was a towering main donjon and a smaller secondary donjon. Built on the open areas of the enceintes were rambling residential buildings that housed the lord, his household, his stable of waiting-persons, his advisory officials, and numbers of samurai at their guardposts and workplaces. Running along the great stone ramparts were roofed parapets regularly pierced with apertures from which shot and arrows could be poured out upon attackers. At strategic points on the ramparts there arose towers that could house large numbers of samurai and military stores. These towers were equipped with slits that permitted a raking fire on any who might seek to cross the moats or penetrate outer barbicans and cross the lists to assault inner defenses. At the entries were great gates constructed of massive posts and planks faced with thick iron plates held on by heavy rivets. The gigantic gates were set into massive gate-houses lined with firing slits and large enough to hold both munitions and their users.

As Ieyasu rested in his massive and elegant new castle, he had every reason to congratulate himself on his timing. No sooner had it been made ready than he had use for it. But the very existence of the castle, the mere fact that Ieyasu had decided to build it at all, betrayed the darker side of his life, the worries that stalked him as he grew older. Those worries culminated in the Hōkōji imbroglio, which precipitated his resort to armed force. The resort to arms disrupted his routine and led him west just at the time of year when, had matters gone more smoothly, he would have set out eastward into the Kantō for a few leisurely weeks of hawking and visiting at Edo.

On October 1, 1614, Ieyasu learned that those controlling Osaka Castle would not compromise. With that news, he made up his mind to go to war. He notified Hidetada at Edo that he had decided to use force against Hideyori and had instructed daimyo in central Japan to dispatch troops toward Osaka. Having made his decision, he felt again the warrior's exhilaration that he had known in past years when he had resolved to cease the maneuvering and slash through the Gordian knot. As Honda Masasumi described him in a letter of that day:

Ieyasu has learned that he must settle affairs by war, and he is feeling very spirited about it. Orders are being dispatched promptly here and there. He enjoys this process, and since it is his specialty, all is well. Moreover, just yesterday Hidetada was feeling a bit ill, but hearing of the decision for war, he has recovered completely.

One suspects that Masazumi painted the rosiest picture he could (he had no way of knowing so soon how Hidetada at Edo felt about it, for example); within a few weeks Ieyasu would feel considerably less pleased with affairs. But for the moment at least he could revel again in the exhilaration of a resolute decision. During the next few days orders were sent out, forces mobilized, chains of command set up, and shipping rounded up for a sea blockade and logistical support. Contradictory orders from Edo and Sumpu were sorted out and duty assignments specified. Gradually, the somnolent giant of a bakufu army began to materialize from the groups of semi-deactivated samurai scattered about the country at Edo, Sumpu, Kyoto, Fushimi, daimyo castle towns, local administrative centers out in the countryside, and in dwelling places on the little fiefs of minor vassals.

After eleven days of preparation, Ieyasu headed west with a token force of about 400 men. He sent his second-from-youngest, twelve-year-old Yorinobu, on ahead, evidently figuring that if there were to be a battle or a castle investment, it was well that the lad be there to learn a bit about how to conduct one. He left his smallest boy, Yorifusa, aged eleven, in nominal charge at Sumpu.

Ieyasu did not follow up his prompt departure from Sumpu on October 11 with a rapid move westward. The daimyo were still unorganized, and as in 1600, he did not wish to venture too far until he knew where they stood. Moreover, he still hoped that a show of strength would obviate the need for an actual assault on the mighty Toyotomi bastion. He moved slowly, taking time to hawk as he advanced, and receiving more reports on the turmoil within Hideyori's ranks.

By the time he reached Hamamatsu three days later, reports indicated that Hideyori was calling on major daimyo to come to his aid but that the lords were declining to do so. On the seventeenth he reached the great new castle at Nagoya, shortly after Yoshinao departed for Osaka with an army of his own.

Two days later Ieyasu reached Gifu, and there he received the first hint that Hideyori might be looking for a pacific settlement. A nearby daimyo showed him a letter from Hideyori in which the young Toyotomi lord asserted that he had no evil designs against Ieyasu or Hidetada and requested the lord to mediate on his behalf. It was a hint, but nothing more. There was no indication that Hideyori would accept the conditions Ieyasu had stipulated, and Ieyasu ignored the letter. Three days later he heard of an Osaka plot to burn Nijō Castle and have snipers gun him down. The would-be arsonist was caught, and Ieyasu kept advancing, reaching Sawayama, formerly the castle of Ishida Mitsunari, on the twenty-first. Two days later he entered Nijō Castle with Yorinobu. There he held a council of war with assembled commanders. They decided to deploy an enveloping force around Osaka Castle and then await the arrival of Hidetada, who was leaving Edo at the head of the main shogunal army. The delay would also give daimyo forces from the west time to get into position.

Ieyasu was not pleased with his situation. He would have preferred a peaceful settlement. Had Hideyori gone quietly, the problem would have been solved with no complications. But now he had more troubles than ever. Punishing Hideyori created enemies at Court, where he wished to leave only a legacy of goodwill for Hidetada. Moreover, he had to dun many people for money for the campaign. City merchants, local administrators, daimyo, temples, and shrines were all called on to help cover the costs of fielding an army that eventually numbered nearly 100,000 men. Not all the daimyo were eager to participate, and some were procrastinating in an unseemly manner. Also, the army was out of condition. While the forces already assembled in the Kyoto-Fushimi district waited for others to come, they tended to be rowdy. Worse yet, Hidetada was delayed because so many of his men fell sick during the forced march that he had to halt while the illness ran its course.

Hidetada was nervous, too. Evidently he remembered the nearly-fatal outcome of his tardiness in 1600, because as soon as he realized he was being slowed again, he sent a letter to Ieyasu urging him to hold off an attack until the main army arrived. The next day, more worried than ever, he sent another letter saying he would proceed ahead with an advance guard. Hidetada's fears were groundless because Ieyasu was in no hurry to tackle Osaka Castle, which was even larger than the one at Nagoya. He wanted Hidetada's forces there merely to intimidate.

What he really wanted was to wrap the whole messy business up

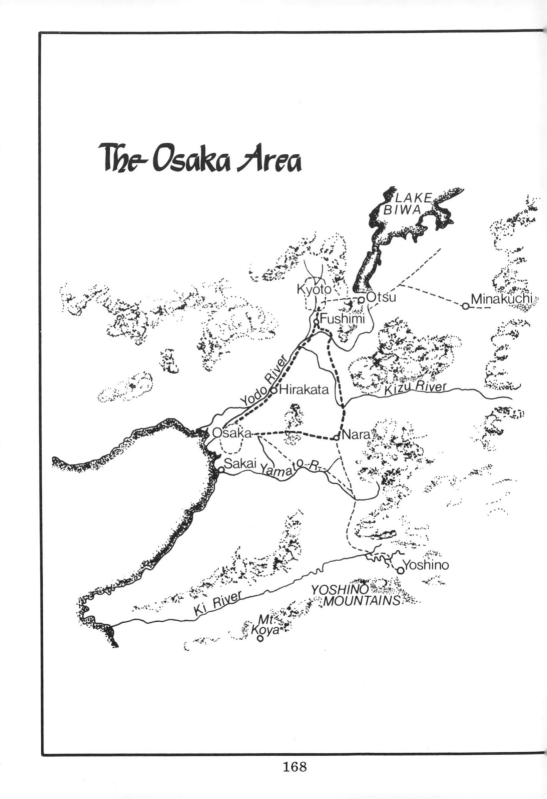

The Osaka Area

LAKE
BIWA

Kyoto ○ Otsu

Fushimi

○ Minakuchi

Yodo River

Hirakata

Kizu River

Osaka

Nara

Sakai Yamato R.

Yoshino

YOSHINO
MOUNTAINS

Ki River

Mt.
Koya

quickly with a minimum of fighting so he could get his army back to its home bases. By November 5 he had obtained detailed information on the defensive arrangements within the castle, so he gave his advance forces their tactical deployment orders. Five days later Hidetada and his army reached Fushimi, and in consultation, father and son fixed November 13 as the day for deployment. Daimyo forces continued to arrive, however, and the deployment was postponed until the fifteenth. On that day Hidetada led his army southwestward from Fushimi, down the Yodo River, through Hirakata, to the outskirts of Osaka, while Ieyasu took his force south to Nara and then west toward the city.

As the two armies approached the city, they wheeled around to the southeast of the castle, thereby cutting off retreat to the Yoshino Mountains. As Ieyasu knew very well, anti-Ashikaga forces had held out in those mountains for half a century before 1393, propping up an Imperial line that challenged the Imperial regime that was sustained by the Ashikaga shogunate in Kyoto. He wanted no such problem to develop again. Blocked to the north and west by the Yodo River and the sea, the Osaka forces were trapped. Like Uesugi Kagekatsu in 1600, they could choose to sally forth, fight, and fail in blood and fury; or they could seal up their huge fortress and fail in hunger and desperation. This time there was no second front to divert Ieyasu from the investment.

On November 18 attack forces took up forward positions. On the nineteenth the first assault was made, and a fortified area near the castle was overrun. The Osaka leaders still showed no signs of yielding. Their numbers had risen to some 90,000, including many *rōnin*, men who had lost their positions after Sekigahara and the subsequent punishment of daimyo. The great size of that force, together with the belief that many daimyo wished to defect, gave the Toyotomi leaders hope for the future.

Such considerations gave Ieyasu pause. He knew the immense casualties his forces would incur if they attempted to storm the gigantic castle, so he looked for other means of breaking the defenders' will. Two days later he found a small opportunity. Some of his men captured a saboteur sent from Osaka with forged documents designed to foment a quarrel between Ieyasu and the commander of his advance force. At Ieyasu's order the hapless messenger had his fingers chopped off, was branded on the forehead, and sent back to the castle for the edification of its inhabitants.

Meanwhile Ieyasu devised other ways to weaken the castle's defense. On the twenty-third he ordered the Mōri, who were on his side this time, to construct pontoon bridges where the castle defenders could see them and to commence damming up the Yodo River to divert it from the moats around the castle. He intended to lower the water level in the outer moats enough to move his own

169

forces across them on the bridges. Or so, at least, he hoped the enemy would believe, because in fact he was not at all sure how to crack the formidable egg that lay before him.

He consulted his commanders, discussed strategies with noted military theoreticians of the day, and debated his general situation with Ishin Sūden and other scholars whom he summoned to his encampment. Reports of continuing disorderly conduct among the troops sustained his wish to conclude the venture quickly. On the twenty-sixth a second sharp battle erupted, but again no real gains were made.

Earlier, Ieyasu had inquired if the foreigners at Nagasaki might have any useful equipment, and on the twenty-seventh he was told that the Dutch would shortly be arriving with some heavy cannon. At that time he was deporting Iberian missionaries and he would have no traffic with people of their ilk, but the Dutch suppliers would be welcome.

Two days later his forces mounted a new assault and succeeded in forcing the defenders back. His scheme of diverting the Yodo still wasn't working, and he ordered his advance forces to commence bombarding the southwest tower and ramparts, which he regarded as the most vulnerable point of approach.

This bombardment, like the Yodo damming, pontoon bridge construction, and branding of the message carrier, was more an act of psychological warfare than part of a real military assault. Even before ordering it, Ieyasu had dispatched a messenger to seek a settlement, and by December 3 the messenger learned that Hideyori was ready to compromise. While those negotiations were in progress, he continued to deploy inspectors among the assembled armies to insure that they would hold to their posts, present a fearsome aspect to the castle, and keep out of trouble. The next day, both Hidetada and Ieyasu moved their headquarters closer to the castle.

Whatever propaganda value those moves may have had was dissipated the same morning. Elements of the attacking army, impatient that Ieyasu had not ordered a full-scale attack, mounted an open assault on a portion of the castle walls only to be repulsed amidst heavy casualties. This setback only intensified dissatisfaction, and on the next day Hidetada objected to Ieyasu's diplomatic maneuvers and tried to persuade him to mount a general assault and overrun the castle. Ieyasu refused and ordered his disgruntled son to make sure that henceforth attacks be mounted only with his authorization.

One suspects that the old man wished to avoid bloody carnage not only because it was distasteful to him, but also because it would entail massive obligations. Many men would claim rewards, and unlike Sekigahara, even victory would provide him with very modest lands to distribute. So he racked his brain for less costly means of achieving his ends. The castle defenders had lands here and there, and he began confiscating them. They had wives and children, some of whom had been at Osaka and had fled to Nara to hide. He ordered his administrators in Nara to hunt them down and confine them. This would give husbands and fathers in the castle something to think about and likely add to the dissension in their ranks. While chopping away at enemy morale, Ieyasu tried to maintain that of his own forces. After the setback of the fifth he tried to minimize future losses in assaulting the castle walls by ordering commanders at the front to construct earthern breast-works and tough bamboo shelters. These constructions would stop incoming musket shot while permitting sappers, scalers, and assault forces to deploy and pursue their tasks in reasonable safety.

Negotiations proceeded slowly. An exchange of letters occurred on the eighth, but Ieyasu wanted to speed things up. With every passing day he had to call for more money from the townsmen of Osaka, Fushimi, Kyoto, and elsewhere. No resolution could come too quickly, so on the ninth he began organizing a general assault. By way of worrying the castle's inhabitants, he planned to have his armies launch a coordinated assault every night. It would consist of a castle-girdling set of war whoops and cries and a concerted bombardment by cannon and musket. The racket would unnerve the inhabitants of the castle and disturb their sleep. The shower of gunshot would hit some of the crowded people in the castle and start a few fires. And the attackers would not be endangered. Then he had messages on arrows fired into the castle, inviting all and sundry to surrender, assuring them that they would be permitted to do so in safety.

In the event these moves did not suffice, on the eleventh he ordered work battalions to begin tunnelling into the castle, using techniques employed in his mining operations. By then the Yodo diversion was working and the outer moats were emptying. On the thirteenth he ordered engineer battalions to commence building ladders for distribution to the assembled forces, and he ordered daimyo to start filling in some of the outer moats that had drained and been overrun.

Negotiations for a compromise continued, but the gulf separating the two sides was still immense. The castle leaders replied on the fifteenth to Ieyasu's proposal that Lady Yodo move to Edo. They suggested that in exchange for her going to Edo, it would be proper for Ieyasu to increase Hideyori's domain to support the *rōnin* who had joined him. Ieyasu replied, in irritation no doubt, "On the basis of what loyal service to me should I reward *rōnin*?" While it was an absurd proposal from Ieyasu's perspective, it did reveal that the private interests of *rōnin* had replaced Toyotomi ambitions as the principal concern of the castle defenders.

Ieyasu had postponed the implementation of his assault plans for several days, but that night, after receiving the proposal on *rōnin* support, he ordered the first general bombardment of the castle. The bombardment alarmed Hideyori and Lady Yodo, and they expressed much more readiness to compromise. The hard-liners refused, however, and mounted an unsuccessful assault on the daimyo forces that had started filling in the outer moat.

By then the Imperial Court was growing tired of the whole inde-cisive struggle and saw in the apparent stalemate an opportunity to enter the political fray. On the seventeenth, Imperial delegates in-vited Ieyasu to come up to Kyoto to negotiate a compromise. It was a most unwelcome suggestion. Ambitious nobles had been of concern to Ieyasu before the Hōkōji imbroglio developed. For years he had tried to regularize affairs in such a way as to insulate the Court from all politics, and thus from all rivals to Tokugawa rule. To have the Court attempt to interpose itself in a struggle between himself and the Toyotomi, the one foe who constituted a serious threat to the basic legitimacy of the Tokugawa regime, was outrageous. Nobles were nobles, however, and adherence to deco-rum was a cornerstone principle of Ieyasu's notion of good gover-nance. Instead of branding and mutilating these meddlesome mes-sengers as he may well have wished to do, he courteously thanked them for their solicitude, and regretfully declined on the ground that it would be disrespectful of the Court if he approached it before a settlement was assured.

On the day after this reply, the nineteenth, Ieyasu opened a new line of communication with Lady Yodo through one of his con-sorts. Sobered by the nightly bombardments, the Lady and her son were ready to offer new terms, and these proved acceptable to Ieyasu. As agreed on the twenty-second, Hideyori would not have to leave Osaka Castle. He would retain the main enceinte, but the outer moats would be filled. His main advisors would send hos-tages to Ieyasu. Ieyasu would guarantee his rank and would par-don all supporters, both old and new, who had come to the aid of the Toyotomi. Finally, Hideyori would swear that he would here-after harbor no malice toward the Tokugawa.

The agreement was ratified the next day and the hostages were provided. Ieyasu ordered the bombardment terminated and noti-fied local townsmen and villagers that it would be safe for them to return to their homes in the battle zone. He ordered advance forces to pull back to their base camps, appointed officials to oversee the castle demolition, and designated occupying forces to hold the outer castle areas pending their destruction. He began distributing rewards, excused the daimyo from all service levies for three years, and instructed a number of major lords to start home-

172

ward. He gave aid to local people disrupted by the siege and granted lands to temples and shrines that had made contributions to his war chest.

Even as these steps were being taken, Ieyasu turned his attention directly to the issue of unruly courtiers. During the next several days he discussed codes of conduct and questions of rank and propriety for Court officials and Kyoto aristocrats in general. In those matters he used advice from both Hayashi Razan and Sūden, whose knowledge of classical precedent and Confucian principles was deep and profound.

Ieyasu then put Hidetada in charge of the castle dismantling at Osaka and prepared to turn homeward. On the twenty-fifth he went up to Kyoto. Three days later he reported formally to the Court on the settlement at Osaka and presented appropriate gifts to members of the aristocracy. Again he discussed rules and regulations for the aristocrats and had the Court's officers of ceremony draw up for his examination and approval a 7-clause code that was in conformity with classical precedents and that would guide aristocrats in the future. Then he went to Nijō Castle to rest for a few days.

Thus it came to pass on New Year's day of 1615 that Ieyasu was at Kyoto, having just settled his quarrel with Hideyori and having made progress in disciplining the Court. There were the usual exchanges of greetings, and on the third day of the new year, Ieyasu left Nijō Castle, heading for his beloved Sumpu.

He crossed the end of Lake Biwa by boat, rode to Minakuchi, and then proceeded onward via the Tōkaidō to Nagoya, where he rested for two days before moving further.

CHAPTER XX:

Hideyori Confounded

While at Nagoya during the early days of the first year of Gen'na, Ieyasu received messengers sent from Osaka by Hidetada. They brought reports on the progress being made by the lords who were filling in the moats of Hideyori's castle. The reports indicated that matters were proceeding according to agreement.

Hearing that, Ieyasu continued his journey, riding east to his original home castle of Okazaki in Mikawa, arriving there on the ninth. For ten days he rested, receiving more reports on the moat-filling at Osaka. From Okazaki he proceeded slowly, ever watchful of the Osaka activity, reaching Hamamatsu on the twenty-ninth. He spent ten days in that vicinity too, receiving more messages from Osaka, and on February 8 talked secretly with Hidetada, who had left Osaka some days earlier to return to Edo. Ieyasu finally reached Sumpu on the fourteenth, the same day Hidetada reached Edo, having spent over a month on a strip of road he could have covered easily in ten days.

One probable reason for lingering was that his old bones protested any attempts to hurry his palanquin on its way, but that was not the main cause of his snail-like progress. What primarily caused his cautious movement was the question of the moat-filling. The December agreement stipulated that moats would be filled in, but it did not specify precisely which ones. From a contemporary letter written by Ishin Sūden, it appears that the Tokugawa side understood the agreement to mean that the moats of the second and third enceintes would be filled in. At least Hidetada's men filled in the moats of both enceintes and leveled their defenses, and as Ieyasu learned of Hidetada's actions, he approved them.

The Toyotomi leaders protested the leveling of the second enceinte and the filling in of its moats, calling those actions a violation of the agreement. In view of Ieyasu's calculating ways, it is entirely possible that he chose knowingly to exploit to the hilt the vagueness of the agreement and to fill in as much as he could to see whether Osaka would acquiesce in a *fait accompli*. In any

174

event, he left Hidetada in charge of the filling, instructed him to finish the job as rapidly as possible, and kept a close watch on developments as he moved eastward slowly and in stages. By January 19 Hidetada had completed the task, and the Osaka leaders only fumed bitterly, and belatedly sent an angry delegation east to protest directly and ineffectually to Ieyasu. In the short run Ieyasu's gamble had paid off: Osaka Castle no longer was an impregnable fortress. Whether in the long run his cavalier use of guile would help him win the peace remained to be seen.

On the day Ieyasu reached Sumpu, rumors began to sweep the Kinai region that he and Hidetada would shortly be visiting Kyoto again. Despite such rumors, the month passed uneventfully. But on March 2 a messenger from Hidetada at Edo brought secret news to Ieyasu at Sumpu, and on the fifteenth, representatives of Hideyori and Lady Yodo reached Sumpu. Other messengers arrived from Kyoto shortly thereafter, and on the eighteenth Ieyasu again consulted secretly with Hidetada's messenger.

Behind these rumors and secret consultations was a growing set of accusations and denunciations. The principal grievance of the Osaka side pertained to the moat-filling, which had effectively destroyed the defensive capacity of their castle. The Tokugawa on their side charged that the Osaka people were producing gunpowder and amassing provisions in the castle. Moreover, they accused Osaka not only of refusing to dismiss the assembled *rōnin*, but of actually recruiting more.

The charges and counter-charges were well founded, but the explanations of behavior may not have been as simple as the protagonists supposed. To examine his behavior first, Ieyasu was just exploiting vagueness in the agreement, employing again that guile for which he had long been known. He was not deliberately violating the agreement to provoke further fighting. Indeed, he had powerful reasons to seek a peaceful resolution: it would cost less; create fewer strains between himself and the daimyo; and leave far fewer wounds to heal. Moreover, it would reinforce his claim that the Tokugawa ruled benevolently and righteously; and closer to home, avoid painful heart-wrenching among people dear to him. Hidetada and his wife Tatsuko were getting on well and raising a good family. But Tatsuko was the younger sister of Lady Yodo and the aunt of Hideyori. Her daughter Senhime had been married to Hideyori for over ten years, which entangled the two families even further. If Ieyasu were to destroy Hideyori and Yodo, what would happen to Senhime? If she were to die, what would be the effect on her parents, or, for that matter, her brothers, Iemitsu and Tadanaga, who were still children?

Certainly Ieyasu had no intention of permitting a Toyotomi challenge to persist. And clearly he was willing to risk antagonizing

Toyotomi supporters as the price of crippling their fortress. But the terms of the December agreement and his subsequent behavior suggest that he still hoped to win by habituating Hideyori to the status of a daimyo in a peaceable Tokugawa order. Thus, after learning of the Osaka military preparations from his representatives in Kyoto, he met a delegate of the Toyotomi leaders. He told the man,

> *If Toyotomi family members really bear no ill will toward the Tokugawa, they can prove it by leaving Osaka Castle and moving to Yamato or Ise, or else by dismissing all the* rōnin, *retaining only their original vassals. Take your choice.*

Superficially, Ieyasu's alternatives were entirely reasonable. But in fact they did not constitute a workable solution because Hideyori and his principal advisors were not the main proponents of revitalized resistance and were not free to choose. Rather, it was the assembled *rōnin* who advocated a renewed effort. They, after all, had the most to lose. If dismissed by Hideyori, they would again become unemployed and would have to fend for themselves in a workaday world for which they were poorly equipped at best, and dangerously vulnerable as the survivors of a failed rebellion. Even if Hideyori had wished to dismiss them, he lacked the vassal forces necessary to oust them from his castle. He probably could not even leave the castle himself if he chose. He had become the pawn of his supporters.

The December settlement decayed, and rumors and suspicions proliferated. Reports about activity at Osaka continued to reach Ieyasu, and by March 28 rumors indicated that he and Hidetada would soon lead an army west. Shortly thereafter rumor gave way to action.

By April Ieyasu felt he had to move, but he still hoped to avoid an actual military clash and initiated a calculated policy of escalating pressure. On April 4, while still awaiting the Osaka response to his instructions to dismiss the *rōnin* or move out of Osaka Castle, he left Sumpu for the west. He did not say he was going to confront Hideyori, however. Rather, he travelled to Nagoya for Yoshinao's wedding. Yorinobu accompanied him, and he again left Yorifusa in nominal charge at Sumpu. The day before he left Sumpu, he instructed a delegation of Hideyori's, which was then in town, to proceed to Nagoya and await him there. They, presumably, would send news of Ieyasu's movements to Osaka, which might help give the Toyotomi leaders pause.

The day after he left Sumpu, however, a messenger from Osaka informed him that Hideyori had refused to leave his castle. There was no evidence that *rōnin* were being dismissed, so Ieyasu ordered daimyo in central and western Japan to prepare again for war. At Edo, Hidetada shortly led his army westward. On the tenth, Ieyasu reached Nagoya, where he talked with the Osaka representatives who had preceded him from Sumpu. He told them he had learned Hideyori would neither move nor dismiss the *rōnin* and that he and his mother obviously still regarded the Tokugawa as their enemy. He then instructed some of the representatives to report his understanding of affairs to Osaka while others were to proceed to Kyoto to await his arrival.

While those added pieces of psychological warfare were having their effect on the Osaka group, he participated in Yoshinao's wedding ceremony. After a five-day stay in Nagoya he continued on his way. As he advanced, he received more reports of war preparation and the hiring of *rōnin* at Osaka, and in response he issued more orders to daimyo. Three days later he entered Kyoto, where on April 24 he met Hideyori's representative and gave him another statement to deliver to Osaka, reiterating the existing choices.

The following day Hidetada's main force arrived, and in consultations he and Ieyasu set the twenty-eighth for an advance on Osaka. Within hours they learned of plans by the Osaka defenders to burn Kyoto; city patrols rounded up scores of people implicated in the plot. That venture was thwarted, but elsewhere in the Kinai region fires broke out as *rōnin* guerrilla forces attempted to provoke a general uprising. The effort failed, but it delayed Ieyasu's advance on Osaka. Reports that people in Tanba Province northwest of Kyoto were ready to join the insurrection led Ieyasu to order more stringent surveillance there--and later to order a daimyo to commit suicide for alleged complicity in the situation. Finally, on May 5, after reassuring himself that a general insurrection was not about to erupt, Ieyasu led his armies toward Osaka.

One force of Osaka *rōnin* that had been out marauding had by then encountered a daimyo army and been badly mauled. As Ieyasu's main armies approached Osaka, they encountered other such forces and smashed them in two days of bloody open-field battle. On the seventh a fire of incendiary origin destroyed the heart of Osaka Castle, and by nightfall, despite extraordinary effort and bravery, the Toyotomi *rōnin* had been crushed. After this there was no effective resistance in the ruined fortress. On the morning of May 8 Osaka Castle fell. Ieyasu's granddaughter Senhime was returned safely to her father. Yodo and her son committed suicide. She was about forty-eight; he was twenty-two.

It was a pathetic, unnecessary end for the Toyotomi family. Ieyasu had no stomach for this last tawdry drama, and within four hours of the castle's surrender he had left the battlefield, returning to Nijō Castle in Kyoto by midnight of the same day. Then, by way of minimizing the significance of the whole sad affair, he promptly turned his attention to other matters.

CHAPTER XXI

Ordering the Realm

As soon as the challenge from Osaka was dealt with, Ieyasu directed his attention again to issues that had consumed his interest in the two previous years. Most notably, he focused on matters of religion, reviving the intense study of doctrine that had been interrupted in the autumn of 1614. He also gave attention to arranging Court procedure and continuing the elaborate pattern of audiences, gift exchanges, and rewards and punishments that was the heart of his relations with the Court nobility and daimyo.

He found time to reward those who had served him well at Osaka and to issue a few harsh words designed to prevent a recurrence of the Toyotomi tragedy. Hideyori had a son, Kunimatsu, and a daughter, Chiyohime, by a consort. Both children survived the fall of Osaka Castle and fled with a wet nurse to Fushimi. There they were captured, and at Ieyasu's order the boy was slain, along with his attendants, and the little girl placed in a nunnery in Kamakura. Ieyasu was determined that no one could ever claim to be a legitimate successor to the great Hideyoshi. In the same ruthless spirit, surviving *rōnin* were rounded up, executed, and their heads posted along the Fushimi highway. Presumably their fate would serve as a warning to other men that in a world at peace they should no longer aspire to careers as samurai. Two months after the castle fell, he erased one of the principal memorials to Hideyoshi by abolishing the Toyokuni Shrine, moving its main sanctuary to the Hōkōji, and putting it in the charge of a reliable abbot.

Three days later, on July 13, lest the meaning of the struggle and its outcome be misunderstood, he had the name of the year-period changed. Keichō, "rejoicing eternal" obviously had not been the appropriate label for the unhappy year just past; Gen'na or "basic reconciliation" or "elemental peace" might now be right on the mark and hence conducive to happier prospects. A month later, in the spirit of the new era, he ordered pardons for all the long-established vassals of the Toyotomi family who had been at Osaka and instructed daimyo to release them from detention.

There were other, much more significant expressions of the new era. "Elemental peace" would not be left to chance. Before leaving Kyoto, Ieyasu resolved to issue new, and presumably final, codes to regulate the daimyo, Court, aristocrats, temples and shrines.

For two years before the Hideyori imbroglio, he had worked on codifying rules for the guidance of these groups. He studied questions of Court ceremony, of shogunal tradition, and of religious principles and practices at great length. He issued some sets of regulations and had scholars working on still others. The work, particularly that relating to daimyo, was nearly complete when interrupted in mid-1614. During the interregnum between the winter and summer battles at Osaka, he renewed discussion of the codification of Court behavior in conversations with Hayashi Razan, Ishin Sūden, and delegates from the Court.

Six days after Hideyori's suicide, and his own return to Kyoto, Ieyasu revived his intensive study of religious doctrine and practice. For nearly three months he received presentations from spokesmen for major temples and discussed Tendai, Shingon, and Jōdo teachings with them. Beyond the teachings of those sects, he even probed the principles of *inmyō* or Hindu logic, the bedrock of all Buddhist teachings.

During the same months he summoned nobles to discuss Court practices. At last he was satisfied that he knew how to proceed with both Court and temple regulations, and he ordered Sūden and other scholars to prepare the necessary codes of conduct.

While those codes were being hammered into final form, Ieyasu dealt with the daimyo. On July 2, Sūden showed him a draft of a code for daimyo which he accepted. Five days later Hidetada assembled the daimyo in Fushimi Castle for a Nō performance, and while they were gathered, he had Sūden inform them of the new thirteen-clause *buke shohatto* or "Laws for the Military Houses." The code drew on precedents and phrasing that dated to the dawn of Japanese civilization and Prince Shōtoku's seventeen-article "constitution" of 604 AD, and some aspects derived directly from China. It instructed lords to pursue "the civil and military arts," to behave themselves, to adhere to rituals proper to their station in life, to employ no suspicious characters--Toyotomi *rōnin* being a case in point, no doubt--and to inform on seditious neighbors. The daimyo were forbidden to make unauthorized marriage arrangements or to engage in castle construction without permission, and they were held accountable for the conduct of their vassals and the tranquility of their fiefs.

On July 17, ten days after informing the daimyo how things were to be thereafter, Hidetada journeyed from Fushimi up to

Nijō Castle. There, he and a senior Court official jointly delivered to assembled courtiers the *Kinchū narabi ni kuge shohatto* or "Laws for the Court and Nobility." The "Laws" were in seventeen clauses, in keeping with the ancient work of Prince Shōtoku. They spelled out clearly the status relationships of Court officials and other nobles, defined patterns of succession and inheritance, specified criteria for punishing offenders against established Court procedures, gave the bakufu *de facto* control of Court affairs, and effectively excluded the *kuge* from any political role.

Seven days later Ieyasu settled the third major set of regulations, the laws for temples and shrines. While one set of laws could be applied to all daimyo and one to all aristocrats, diversity of religious practices led to the issuance of a great number of specific sets of regulations with idiosyncratic stipulations accommodating the traditions of particular temples and sects, including Shingon, Tendai, Jōdo, Sōtō, and Rinzai. Nine codes were issued that day, bearing titles such as *Kōyasan shūto hatto* "Laws of Members of the Mt. Kōya Monastery," *Gozan jūsetsu hatto* "Laws for the Five Monasteries and Ten Temples of Zen," *Daitokuji hatto* "Laws for the Daitokuji," and *Jōdoshū seizanto hatto* "Laws for the Western Sect of Jōdo."

During the same month Ieyasu issued a series of regulations for Shintō shrines. He had not shown much interest in Shintō before, but he had some reason to mend fences. For years one of the most influential Shintō priestly families, the Yoshida Shintō line, had been associated with Hideyoshi and Hideyori, and they had headed the Toyokuni Shrine. When Ieyasu's relations with Hideyori disintegrated and war erupted in 1614, Yoshida Shintō priests tried to salvage their position by cultivating Ieyasu's friendship. He welcomed their efforts and made arrangements for the family to flourish in other shrines. By the end of July 1615, he had succeeded in separating the Toyotomi family legacy from Shintō and had established a regularized system for governing the shrines without losing the goodwill of the important Yoshida Shintō line. A year later, Shintō sensibilities were taken fully into account with the establishment of the Tokugawa Mausoleum at Nikkō.

By August 1--the twenty-fifth anniversary of Ieyasu's triumphal entry into Edo in 1590--his work at Kyoto was done. Only time would tell, of course, whether this newest attempt to give permanent form to the realm would prove to be a correct, and therefore a durable, ordering of the "way." But at least he had done his best. He had been utterly exhaustive in his pursuit of information, and he had used the best minds he could find to work out the codes. Now he could only wait, watch, and hope for the best.

Ready to go home, after the usual ceremonies of departure were executed, on August 4 he headed east. He was seventy-two. He would never see Kyoto again.

CHAPTER XXII:

Last Flight of the Falcon

Ieyasu had reason to feel some satisfaction as he left Kyoto in August of 1615. He had resolved the Toyotomi problem with fewer complications than he had feared. The affair had given him a good opportunity to issue a new and more substantial body of regulations for Court, daimyo, and religious groups. The problem of Christianity seemed on the way to solution, and he had not had to give up foreign trade to accomplish it.

His family situation was vexing. His intemperate sixth son, Tadateru, was in trouble again. He had gotten into difficulty in 1609, when he was seventeen, but Ieyasu had been able to blame his advisors, and had transferred him to a new domain. Tadateru was twenty-three now, and he was charged with murder. Worse yet, the murdered man was one of Hidetada's vassals. As Tadateru and his men had been heading for Osaka and the final battle with Hideyori, a group of three of Hidetada's vassals cut in front of the retinue. One of Tadateru's men challenged them on the ground that they had been disrespectful toward the shogun's brother. They pointed out that they were the shogun's direct vassals. Words soon gave way to swords and one of the shogun's vassals was slain.

Ieyasu heard of the incident when he was at Minakuchi. He decided that the case involved a daimyo's man murdering a shogun's vassal, and that was unacceptable. He could not bring himself to order his son to commit suicide--once in a lifetime is enough for that sort of task. But he could not pardon him either, so he ordered him to surrender his large domain at Takada on the Sea of Japan and go into strict confinement at a small castle not far from Edo. When Ieyasu rendered that judgement, he said, "Even when I, his father, am living, he is disposed to assault the shogunal dignity. After I die, such disdain for the government will be even more intolerable." The comment reveals both Ieyasu's public concern that attitudes subversive of the regime be discouraged and his private concern lest Tadateru get into similar trouble after his own

182

death and be punished severely for it. His judgement therefore removed Tadateru from a politically vulnerable position but spared his life. Tadateru knew well enough not to refuse that order. Later he was officially censured for the incident, took the tonsure, and became a monk. He spent the rest of his life at temples in the custody of others. He lived a reasonably peaceful existence and died quietly at the age of ninety-one in 1683, during the reign of his grand-nephew, Tsunayoshi, the fifth Tokugawa shogun.

For all practical purposes Ieyasu had lost another son. However, his three youngest were thriving, and Hidetada's several surviving children were also doing well. It was understood by all that his child Iemitsu would succeed. Having done about all that was humanly possible to assure his family's continued vitality, Ieyasu was able to absorb the disappointment of Tadateru's misbehavior. On the whole, his family was healthy and strong.

Ieyasu reached Minakuchi on August 5, only to be detained there by three days of downpour. He didn't particularly mind. It was not the Minakuchi of fifteen years earlier, when he had headed east to chastise Uesugi Kagekatsu. Then the castle was held by Natsuka Masaie, who had tried to sell him two hundred guns. But that had proven to be the least of Natsuka's mistakes, and by year's end his head was propped on a post in Kyoto. His castle and domain had then been given to one of Ieyasu's supporters. So during those rainy days in the summer of 1615 Ieyasu slept soundly, untroubled by the sort of plot that had prompted him to fly by that same castle in the dead of night fifteen years before.

Not even the Tadateru matter could ruin this interlude. After discussing the issue thoroughly and making his decision, he had time for philosophical discourse. He was accompanied by Hayashi Razan, who was now thirty-two years old, and the two men engaged in sustained discussion of that classic work, *The Analects of Confucius* (*Rongo* in Japanese).

After the rain ceased, he moved on, stopping at Nagoya for a two-day visit with Yoshinao, who was nearly fifteen. He then poked along the Tōkaidō, reaching Sumpu on the twenty-third, after nineteen days on the road. There he picked up the happy routine that had been abruptly interrupted a year earlier by the Toyotomi crisis. In the following weeks he pursued the usual affairs, such as granting several licenses to trade in southeast Asia, hearing lectures on Sōtō Zen Buddhism, hawking now and again, and even meeting Will Adams and a visiting English ship's captain.

In September, on schedule, he left for his hawking tour of the Kantō and stayed a while at Edo Castle with Hidetada. He met various people, heard a lecture on Jōdo teachings, hawked across the Kantō, heard a lecture on Tendai during a visit to Kawagoe

Castle, visited sites in the eastern part of the Kantō, and at the end of November returned again to Edo. For a seventy-two-year-old man he was certainly flourishing.

Ieyasu then headed back toward Sumpu, hunting on the way. Smoothly his palanquin bearers carried him by Odawara Castle and up the tortuous trail over the Hakone mountains. From there he could see Mt. Fuji soaring skyward, its cone covered with the snow of another winter. The mountain was harder to see than it had been a few years before, however, because the rows of trees that he had planted along the highway were beginning to shut out the vistas.

Descending the western slope, he stopped at Mishima on December 4, near hot springs at the foot of the Hakone pass. He remembered his first visit to Mishima. It had been in the spring of 1586 when he rode there to join the Hōjō of Odawara in a lavish banquet signifying the establishment of friendship and alliance. In following years he passed through the town countless times, but this time he stopped. He was looking for a quiet and pleasant place in which to erect a retirement hermitage in the coming spring. There he would take the tonsure and genuinely retire to pursue in earnest his quest for true enlightenment.

Ieyasu spent the night at a nearby temple. Then, satisfied with the plans he had made, he headed toward Sumpu. He was met by his son Yorinobu at Shimizu, and happily he went the last ten kilometers of the way together with him.

On his return to Sumpu he heard that a delegation from the Imperial Court was preparing to come east to pay a formal visit to Hidetada and him. He promptly sent a notice advising them to cancel the trip; he had better plans. He intended to take his grandson Iemitsu, who would be twelve in the summer of 1616, to Kyoto to introduce him to the Emperor. The old man was already planning for the day when Hidetada must pass the reins of government on to his successor, and he wished that successor to be well-versed in affairs of state and well recognized as the rightful third Tokugawa shogun.

Meanwhile he had heard that his eighteen-year-old granddaughter, Senhime, was ill at Edo. She had reason to feel out of sorts. She had been Hideyori's wife and had watched with horror as her husband and grandfather drifted into irreconcilable conflict. She had been at Osaka Castle during the summer siege, failed to mediate a settlement, and was there during the castle's final burning and capitulation. Her husband and mother-in-law had committed suicide, but she had been rescued and returned to Edo to recover from the tragedy. All of this had occurred just six months previously. Ieyasu showed the same concern for her that he had shown for his own children. In one letter he wrote at year's end to her seventeen-year-old waiting lady, Chobo, he said:

> *I have been really worrying about Senhime and wish to be reassured about her condition. I am so thoroughly worried that I am sending Tōkurō to gather full details about anything you can tell him. Please inform him fully about Senhime's condition.*

In January 1616 he sent a longer letter full of reiterated endearments and expressions of relief that she was feeling better. Through Chobo he assured Senhime that he would pray for her good health and would visit her in Edo in the coming autumn when he made his next trip into the Kantō. And shortly after that, he sent yet another letter to Chobo:

> *Truly, your frequent letters please me greatly. This spring I am happy that Senhime is so well. It is wonderful to hear of her full recovery; I am delighted. Here we are all fine, so I wish you to feel at ease about us. Congratulations and many thanks.*

Retirement to Mishima; a trip to Kyoto with Iemitsu; a trip to Edo to visit Senhime; grandfather was planning a busy second year of Gen'na. If his energy held out, there were the younger grandchildren, Tadanaga and Kazuko, to think about also. Gen'na was a good name for the era. Of that there could be no doubt.

The first year of Gen'na ended. The usual greetings of the New Year were exchanged, and Ieyasu busied himself planning for his retirement home. On the ninth day of the new year he sent a vassal to Edo to inform Hidetada that he was thinking of visiting to observe the ceremony for initiating Iemitsu into manhood: the hair cut to samurai style, the outfitting in proper Court garb, and the granting of an adult name to the boy who was still known, as his grandfather had been before him, as Takechiyo.

Two days later he granted some Chinese merchants licenses to conduct trade. The following day he suddenly changed his mind about retiring near Mishima and cancelled his order for construction of a hermitage there. With grandchildren to think about, why take the tonsure?

Seven days later, on January 19, he ordered Razan and Sūden to publish the great Chinese compilation *Gunsho chiyō (Collected Works on Government)*. A fifty-volume work on government dating from the seventh century, it had long been lost in China, and only one copy survived, that at the Kanazawa Bunko or Library in Japan. The work had originally been compiled at the behest of T'ai Tsung, the illustrious second emperor of the T'ang dynasty.

Its purpose was to demonstrate the principles of good government; in particular, the virtue of firm lord-vassal relationships. Clearly, its intent fit Ieyasu's desires perfectly, and he ordered Razan and Sūden to reproduce it for the edification of future generations.

They were able to do so, using a printing press then at Sumpu. It was different from the press Genkitsu had used at Fushimi a few years earlier. His was of Korean origin and used wooden type. This one was of European design, which the Jesuits first brought to Nagasaki in 1590. Later they operated two such presses, one in Kyushu and one in Kyoto, turning out religious propaganda in both European and Japanese script. When the missionary activity was proscribed in Kyoto in 1614, it appears the press was confiscated and brought to Sumpu with some 80,000 Japanese characters *(kanji* and *kana)* in metal type.

At that time Ieyasu was deeply engaged in his Buddhist studies, and in August of 1614, just as the Hōkōji affair was approaching a climax, Sūden presented him with a rare work, a major compilation of Buddhist doctrine called the *Daizō ichiranshū (Digest of the Tripitaka)*, a collection of Buddhist writings selected from the Tripitaka by Ming scholars because of their particular usefulness in teaching Buddhist doctrine. Ieyasu saw in this work the key to eliminating monkish sectarianism. If he made it available to temples throughout the country, he reasoned, all monks could study it, and on the basis of a shared source of religious instruction, all would reach, presumably, a shared understanding of religious truth. The Osaka crisis had diverted his attention, but, in March, 1615, when he was back in Sumpu briefly following the winter siege, he ordered Razan to produce some 100-200 copies of the work on the metal press for distribution to temples throughout the land. He must have derived some satisfaction, too, from the thought that the machine that had for years produced works on Christian doctrine would be used to issue a definitive text on Buddhist teachings.

Razan had set to work on the printing, assembling some eighteen artisans to do the typemaking, typesetting, aligning, proofreading, printing, and binding. The typemakers produced another 10,368 characters and set them up for use. By the time Osaka Castle had fallen and Ieyasu was in Kyoto preparing regulations for Court, daimyo, and temples in the summer of 1615, Razan was able to show him a sample of the work. Ieyasu was pleased with its quality, and the printers ran off 125 copies of the six-volume edition of *Daizō ichiranshū*, distributing them to temples throughout the country.

In January 1616, when Ieyasu instructed Sūden and Razan to print the *Gunsho chiyō*, the experience with *Daizō ichiranshū* gave him reason to except a prompt and high-quality product. The two men set out at once to provide him with just that. They installed the press in the third enceinte of Sumpu Castle, adjacent to the Nō stage where Ieyasu entertained visitors. They assembled the necessary copper to make more type, the ink pans, paper-drying racks, boxes and storage chests for the type, chisels, hammers, and other paraphernalia. By February 23 they had assembled about twenty technicians and were ready to begin the work.

In the meantime Ieyasu fell ill, so they proceeded rapidly and quietly, trying to have the new edition ready as soon as possible without disturbing him. To keep their employees under control, Razan and Sūden issued a set of five work rules:

(1) Work hours are sunup to sundown.
(2) Loud debate and argument are forbidden.
(3) All must be diligent. Don't neglect this rule!
(4) Work is not to be done on any of the tatami-*floored rooms, on the No stage, or in the dressing rooms. There will be no rough-housing in buildings.*
(5) Friends may not be brought in to watch or sightsee.

During the next three months the artisans worked efficiently to manufacture some 13,000 new characters, and by the end of May they were nearly finished with their task. Copies of the *Gunsho chiyō* were later placed in several archives, and as a result, scholars today are able to peruse a work that otherwise might have been lost to humankind.

The publication came too late for Ieyasu, however. Two days after ordering Sūden and Razan to print the work, he had gone out hawking near Sumpu, and that night shortly after midnight, he suddenly became ill. He felt intense constriction in his chest and coughed up phlegm. One suspects he had a heart attack. By the next day, however, the sickness had passed. He rested for two more days and then returned to Sumpu to recuperate.

News of his sudden illness sped to Edo and Kyoto, and delegates hurried to Sumpu to inquire after his health. A few days later, on February 1, a distraught Hidetada, unable to contain his anxiety any longer, abruptly left Edo in a nonstop thirty-six-hour dash to Sumpu to determine his father's condition.

Rapidly the town filled with visitors and bearers of good wishes. The Court initiated prayers and rituals for Ieyasu's recovery, and his condition did gradually improve. During February he began to handle routine matters again, until another seizure on the twenty-second returned him to bed. Following that he was in considerable pain, feverish, and coughing, and during March his work slowed nearly to a halt. A worried Court awarded him the title of *dajō daijin*, Imperial Prime Minister, and on March twenty-seventh, despite the difficulties involved, he and Hidetada formally received and thanked the delegates who brought the notice of promotion from Kyoto. Two days later Ieyasu thanked courtiers, daimyo, and their representatives for their solicitude, treated them to a banquet, and bade them go home.

It seemed to those in the castle that death was near, and many wept and marked time, awaiting the end. Ieyasu, however, did not have time to consider that. On April 2, with the rituals of state properly attended to, he summoned Sūden and three other advisors. The task he gave them was to make arrangements for settling affairs after his death. He told his weeping advisors that his ashes were to be placed on nearby Mt. Kuno. The funeral service was to be held at Zōjōji, the family Jōdo temple in Edo. A memorial tablet was to be erected at the Daijūji in Okazaki, the Jōdo temple that had been associated with the Matsudaira family for generations. Finally, he ordered that after an appropriate interval, a small shrine be built on Nikkō mountain north of Edo so that his spirit might stand guard as the tutelary god of the Kantō provinces. As behove one attempting to set an example for generations to come, he outlined a simple set of memorial activities, nothing elaborate or expensive. Withal, he showed proper regard for both Shintō and Buddhism, and for both ancestors and future generations. His heart might be failing, but his mind remained clear.

In the following days he felt improved and ate his *kayu*, medicinal rice porridge heartily, to the great joy of those in the castle. He went over some final arrangements with Hidetada, who called on him daily, and he signed a number of administrative documents. He had a bad night on the ninth, vomited some, lost his appetite on the eleventh, and did not eat thereafter.

That day he summoned Razan. He instructed him to arrange all the records of his years at Sumpu and publish them. They would become a record of his rule, and like the *Azuma kagami* of the revered Minamoto Yorimoto and the *Jōgan seiyō* of T'ai Tsung, they would serve as a source of guidance for future generations. People would know what Ieyasu did and what he intended to achieve. There would be no misunderstanding, no confusion, and so the realm would prosper. Razan did as he was instructed, and the result was the publication known today as *Sumpuki, The Annals of Sumpu*, a history of the four years from August 1611 to December 1615, the period during which a regular archival program had been maintained at Sumpu.

In the following days Ieyasu weakened rapidly, and at about ten o'clock in the cloudy morning of April 17, 1616, he died quietly, with Hidetada nearby. His remains were properly cremated, and the next day his ashes were taken to nearby Mt. Kuno for a simple ceremony of interment. On Mt. Kuno, midway between Edo and

Kyoto, and overlooking those hills and fields where he had hawked again and again, his spirit could hover, holding the realm together, steadying Hidetada, Iemitsu, and the twelve others who would succeed them as Tokugawa shogun for the next 252 years.

During the next two years his ideal of simplicity was forgotten. Shrines called Tōshōgū were built at other places, the greatest and most elegant being at Nikkō in the mountains north of Edo. There, even today, a visitor may tour a great labyrinth of Shintō shrines and Buddhist temples that stand amidst towering cryptomeria, awesomely elegant monuments to the chubby little man whose impact on Japanese history was so immense. His enshrinement name, which is both Buddhist and Shintō, is Tōshō Daigongen, "The Light of the East, the Ultimate made Manifest."

IEYASU'S OFFSPRING

	Sex	Name	Dates	Mother*	Marriage or Adoption (Main Fief)
1.	m	Nobuyasu	1559-1579	Tsukiyama	m. Oda Tokuhime (Okazaki)
2.	f	Kamehime	1560-1625	Tsukiyama	m. Okudaira Nobumasa
3.	f	Tokuhime	1565-1615	Udono	m. Hojo Ujinao; Ikeda Terumasa
4.	m	Hideyasu	1574-1607	Nagai	a. by Hideyoshi; Yuki Harutomo (Fukui)
5.	m	Hidetada	1579-1632	Saijo	m. Asai Tatsuko (Edo)
6.	m	Tadayoshi	1580-1607	Saijo	a. by Matsudaira Ietada (Kiyosu)
7.	f	Furuhime	1580-1617	Akiyama	m. Gamo Hideyuki; Asano Nagaakira
8.	m	Nobuyoshi	1583-1603	Akiyama	named Takeda; later Matsudaira (Mito)
9.	m	Tadateru	1592-1683	Kawamura	a. by Matsudaira Yasutada (Takada)
10.	m	Matsuchiyo	1594-1599	Kawamura	died young
11.	m	Senchiyo	1595-1600	Shimizu	died young
12.	f	Matsuhime	1595-1598	Mamiya	died young
13.	m	Yoshinao	1600-1650	Shimizu	kept name Tokugawa (Nagoya)
14.	m	Yorinobu	1602-1671	Masaki	kept name Tokugawa (Wakayama)
15.	m	Yorifusa	1603-1661	Masaki	kept name Tokugawa (Mito)
16.	f	Ichihime	1607-1610	Ota	died young

*Tsukiyama is a given name; the others are all family names. Tsukiyama's original family name was Sekiguchi. The lady Kawamura is sometimes recorded as being from the Yamada family.

IEYASU'S CHINESE REFERENCES

Sinologists may not recognize Chinese scholarly works by their Japanese titles. The Chinese titles are as follows:

Daizō ichiranshū	大蔵一覧集
Gunsho chiyō	群書治要
Jōgan seiyō	貞観政要
Rongo	論語

SOURCE CITATIONS

Quotation
on Page

4   Adriana Boscaro, *101 Letters of Hideyoshi* (Sophia, Tokyo, 1975) p. 31.

6   Kuwata Tadachika, *Tokugawa Ieyasu* (vol. 6 of *Kuwata Tadachika Chosakushū* (Akita Shoten, Tokyo, 1979) p. 239.

7   *Ibid.*, p. 240.

11   *Ibid.*, pp. 248-249.

16   C.R. Boxer, *The Christian Century in Japan, 1549-1650* (U. Cal., Berkeley, 1951) p. 29.

19   Michael Cooper, ed., *They Came to Japan* (U. Cal., Berkeley, 1965) p. 115.

20   Tsuji Tatsuya, *Edo kaifu* (vol. 13 of *Nihon no rekishi*) (Chūō kōronsha, Tokyo, 1974) p. 82.

26   Nakamura Koya, *Ieyasuden* (Kodansha, Tokyo, 1965) p. 66.

27   Tsuji, *op. cit.*, p. 17.

34   *Ibid.*, p. 339.

37   *Ibid.*, p. 35.

37-38   Kuwata, *op. cit.*, p. 160.

44   *Ibid.*, p. 166.

45   *Ibid.*, p. 175.

46   *Ibid.*, pp. 186-187.

54   *Ibid.*, p. 211.

55-56   Boscaro, *op. cit.*, pp. 37-38.

56   A.L. Sadler, *The Maker of Modern Japan* (Allen & Unwin, London, 1937) p. 158.

57   Kuwata, *op. cit.*, pp. 257-258.

58   *Ibid.*, p. 260.

59   *Ibid.*, p. 285.

66   Tsuji, *op. cit.*, p. 52.

67   Kuwata, *op. cit.*, pp. 227-228.

68   Tsuji, *op. cit.*, p. 64.

77   *Ibid.*, p. 39.

Quotation
on Page

77-78	Kuwata, *op. cit.*, p. 297.
82	*Ibid.*, p. 303.
99	Nakamura, *op. cit.*, pp. 416-417.
99	Kuwata, *op. cit.*, p. 310.
99-100	Tsuji, *op. cit.*, p. 143.
105	Cooper, *op. cit.*, p. 10.
121	David Lu, *Sources of Japanese History* (McGraw Hill, New York, 1974) I, p. 236.
123	Kuwata, *op. cit.*, p. 309.
137-138	Boxer, *op. cit.*, p. 313.
138	P.G. Rogers, *The First Englishman in Japan* (Harvill, London, 1956) pp. 62-63.
138-139	Nakamura, *op. cit.*, p. 613.
139-140	*Ibid.*, p. 646.
143	Kuwata, *op. cit.*, pp. 311-312.
149	Nakamura, *op. cit.*, pp. 543-544.
154	Tsuji, *op. cit.*, p. 203.
154	Theodore T. deBary, *Sources of the Japanese Tradition* (Columbia, New York, 1958) p. 329.
157	Nakamura, *op. cit.*, p. 643.
158	Tsuji, *op. cit.*, p. 214.
164-165	*Ibid.*, p. 179.
166	*Ibid.*, pp. 223-224.
171	*Ibid.*, p. 231.
176	*Ibid.*, pp. 236-237.
182	*Ibid.*, p. 361.
185	Kuwata, *op. cit.*, pp. 316-317.
185	*Ibid.*, p. 318.
187	Nakamura, *op. cit.*, p. 670.

ACKNOWLEDGMENTS

This book is not a definitive scholarly study based on exhaustive research. The biographical information about Ieyasu comes almost entirely from one source, *Ieyasuden (The Biography of Ieyasu)* by Nakamura Kōya. Professor Nakamura devoted a lifetime of scholarship to Ieyasu, assembling and publishing volumes of relevant documents and writing major studies of Ieyasu and his times. I can hardly pretend to improve on his knowledge.

My paramount debt, therefore, is to Professor Nakamura, whose works I have consulted repeatedly in my studies during the past two decades. The authors of the other sources cited also taught me a great deal. In a final revision of the text in 1981, I made use of Ieyasu's letters which appear with valuable annotations in the volume, *Tokugawa Ieyasu* by Kuwata Tadachika. I also consulted *Edo kaifu (Formation of the Edo Bakufu)* by Tsuji Tatsuya. Although written for a general readership, this book is authored by a recognized professional historian writing in his area of expertise.

Forged documents remain one problem in the historiography of Ieyasu. Over the centuries a vast array of spurious anecdotes and fake documents have been produced for a variety of reasons. The scarcity and brevity of genuine writings by Ieyasu, apart from the great number of his official orders and decisions, has given forgers and raconteurs much room for creative invention. Thus the incident of October 1612 pertaining to Hidetada's choice of heir, which may be fiction in itself, gave rise to a major forgery purporting to be Ieyasu's instructions to Hidetada's wife on rearing her children. And Ieyasu's renewed interest in religion in 1612 gave rise to an extensive body of forged documents that purport to show his intense devotion to Amida Buddhism. Recently a major facet of the forgery problem has been discussed at length by Tokugawa Yoshinobu, Executive Director of the Tokugawa Reimeikai Foundation in an article, "Ichiren no Tokugawa Ieyasu no gihitsu to nikka nembutsu" (A set of forgeries and daily invocations of Tokugawa Ieyasu) in volume 8 of *Kinko sōsho (Library of the Golden Dolphin)* (Tokugawa Reimeikai, 1981) pp. 627-797. Two new books by Mr. Tokugawa appeared too late for my use. They are *Tokugawa Ieyasu shinsekishū* (A Collection of the Authentic Writings of Tokugawa Ieyasu) and *Shinshū Tokugawa Ieyasu monjō no kenkyū* (The Study of Tokugawa Ieyasu's Records: A New Collection).

I derived much miscellaneous information from *Nihon rekishi daijiten (Encyclopedia of Japanese History).* I owe an immeasurable debt to the many authors of the other books and articles on Japan that I have read over the years. I know of no way to thank adequately my teachers of Japanese history, most particularly Edwin O. Reishauer, whose grand eloquence was always stimulating. I thank Ikeda Ryōshin, chief priest of the Chōrakuji, the Tokugawa family temple in the former Tokugawa village in Gunma Prefecture, for showing me about his temple and the adjacent Tōshōgū, and for providing me materials pertaining to their history. And finally, I thank my wife, Michiko, for typing the final draft of this manuscript.

MAP ACKNOWLEDGMENTS

The maps in this book are based on maps found in the following works:

Nihon annai bunken chizu (Maps of the Japanese Prefectures), a volume in *Nihon hyakka daijiten* (Encyclopedia of Japan) Shogakkan, Tokyo, 1965.

Nihon rekishi chizu (Historical Maps of Japan), a volume in *Nihon rekishi daijiten* (Encyclopedia of Japanese History) Kawade shobō shinsha, Tokyo, 1961.

Shōwa Nihon chizu (Maps of Modern Japan) Tokyo kaiseikan, Tokyo, 1941.

FURTHER READING

(The books listed here discuss twentieth-century Japan only if marked with an asterisk.)

I.   There are several readable and reliable introductory histories of Japan.

> Duus, Peter. *Feudalism in Japan*
> *Duus, Peter. *The Rise of Modern Japan*
> *Hall, John W. *Japan from Prehistory to Modern Times*
> *Hane, Mikiso. *Japan*
> *Reischauer, Edwin O. *Japan, The Story of a Nation*
> Sansom, G.B. *Japan, A Short Cultural History*
> Totman, Conrad. *Japan Before Perry*
> Varley, H. Paul. *Japanese Culture*

II. There is one good detailed narrative history in English.

> Sansom, George. *A History of Japan* (3 vols.)

III. There are several good works dealing with selected aspects of Japanese history.

> *Anesaki, Masaharu. *History of Japanese Religion*
> *deBary, William T. *Sources of the Japanese Tradition*
> Hall, John W. *Government and Local Power in Japan*
> Keene, Donald. *Anthology of Japanese Literature*
> Keene, Donald. *20 Plays of the NO Theatre*
> Lu, David. *Sources of Japanese History*
> Morris, Ivan. *The World of the Shining Prince*
> Murasaki Shikibu. *The Tale of Genji*
> Warner, Langdon. *The Enduring Art of Japan*

IV. Books on Tokugawa Japan are relatively numerous. Those listed here pursue topics touched upon in this book.

Bellah, Robert. *Tokugawa Religion*
Dunn, Charles J. *Everyday Life in Traditional Japan*
Chikamatsu Monzaemon. *The Major Plays of Chikamatsu*
Hibbett, Howard. *The Floating World in Japanese Literature*
Keene, Donald. *World Within Walls*
Lane, Richard. *Images from the Floating World*
Morris, Ivan. *The Amorous Woman and Other Stories*
*Najita, Tetsuo. *Japan*
Smith, Thomas C. *The Agrarian Origins of Modern Japan*
Statler, Oliver. *Japanese Inn*
Totman, Conrad. *Politics in the Tokugawa Bakufu, 1600-1843*
Tsukahira, Toshio. *The Sankin Kotai System of Tokugawa Japan*

V. There are several works dealing with the age of Tokugawa Ieyasu, particularly with the European presence there.

Boscaro, Adriana. *101 Letters of Hideyoshi*
Boxer, C.R. *The Christian Century in Japan, 1549-1650*
Cooper, Michael, ed. *They Came to Japan*
Cooper, Michael, tr. *This Island of Japon: Joao Rodrigues' Account of 16th-Century Japan*
Elison, George and Bardwell L. Smith, eds. *Warlords, Artists, and Commoners: Japan in the Sixteenth Century*
Rogers, P.G. *The First Englishman in Japan: The Story of Will Adams*
Sadler, A.L. *The Maker of Modern Japan: The Life of Tokugawa Ieyasu*

VI. The principal works on Ieyasu by Nakamura Koya are these.

Ieyasuden (The Biography of Ieyasu)
Ieyasu no shinryo (Ieyasu's Officer Corps)
Ieyasu no zokuyo (Ieyasu's Family)
Tokugawa Ieyasu monjo no kenkyu (A Study of the Records of Tokugawa Ieyasu) (4 vols.)

VII. Three general reference works deserve note, two in Japanese and one in English.

> *Dai jinmei jiten* (Biographical Dictionary) (8 vols.)
> *Encyclopedia of Japan* (Forthcoming) (4 vols.)
> *Nihon rekishi daijiten* (Encyclopedia of Japanese History) (22 vols.)

INDEX

Adams, Will, 14, 16, 19, 85, 91,
104-105, 138-139, 183
Arima, 134-137
Asahihime, 49-50, 65
Ashikaga Yoshiaki, 35, 62, 64
Azuma kagami, 93, 97, 122-123,
188
Battles of: Komaki and Nagakute,
47; Mikatagahara, 38-39; Naga-
shino, 42, 44; Odawara, 54-56,
64-65; Osaka, 165-173; Sekiga-
hara, 71-78; Takatenjin, 44, 54
Buddhism, 146-150. *See also*
Ieyasu's politics; Ikkō
Castles: Chiyoda (Edo), 57, 66-67,
93, 113-115; Fushimi, 6, 21;
Nagoya, 164-165; Nijō, 109-111,
161; Osaka, 3, 47, 177; Sumpu,
50, 66, 97, 141-142, 161
Christianity, *see* Ieyasu's politics;
Portuguese; Spaniards
Confucianism, 11, 13, 68-69, 109,
120-122, 183. *See also* Fujiwara
Seika; Hayashi Razan
Daizō ichiranshū, 186
Date Masamune, 21, 54, 59, 67, 82,
115, 158
Dutchmen, 14-16, 19, 85, 104-105,
134, 170
Economy, *see* Foreign Relations;
Ieyasu's politics; Mining; Minting;
Transportation
Emperors: Go Mizunoō, 109, 112,
115-117, 144, 153, 161; Goyōzei,
11, 50, 64, 86, 87, 109, 111-112,
122, 123, 144; Meishō, 144; Ōgi-

machi, 35. *See also* Hideyoshi;
Ieyasu's politics; Imperial Insti-
tution
Englishmen, 138-139, 183. *See also*
Adams, Will
Engi shiki, 145
Foreign Relations, *see* Adams, Will;
Dutchmen; Englishmen;
Hideyoshi; Korea; Okinawa;
Portuguese; Southeast Asia;
Spaniards
Fujiwara Seika, 68-69, 120
Gamō, 57
Gamō Hideyuki, 70, 84
Gamō Ujisato, 67, 70
Gunsho chiyō, 145, 185-187
Hayashi Razan, 88, 120-121, 124,
137, 157, 173, 180, 183, 185-188
Hideyoshi: and China, 3, 4, 6-7;
and Korea, 3-7, 122; and Euro-
peans, 17-18, 85; and his family,
4, 6, 48-49, 62, 65, 81; and Oda,
17, 37, 45; and daimyo, 3, 46-47,
50, 52, 54-56, 64; and Court,
11-12, 48, 50, 62; death of, 7.
See also Ieyasu's politics
Hōjō, 35, 38, 44-46, 48-50, 52,
64-65
Hōjō regents *(shikken),* 63, 81
Hōjō Ujimasa, 54
Hōjō Ujinao, 46, 54-56, 70
Hōjō Ujinori, 28, 30, 46, 54, 56
Hōjō Ujiyasu, 30, 36
Hōkōji, 6, 112, 153-158, 179
Honda Masanobu, 131-132, 137
Honda Masazumi, 81, 131, 136,

137, 145, 155, 157, 166
Honda Tadakatsu, 34, 38, 49, 56,
    57, 67, 71, 75, 81, 106, 113, 118
Ieyasu: his character, 28, 31, 34,
    36, 39, 42, 46, 54, 69, 108;
    his genealogy, 25, 35, 61-62,
    86-87, 124; his children before
    Sekigahara, 32-33, 40-42, 46-48,
    57, 69-70; his children after
    Sekigahara, 85, 97-99, 112, 115,
    130, 141-144, 153, 166,
    182-183; see also Tokugawa
    Hidetada; Tokugawa Hideyasu;
    Tokugawa Nobuyasu; Tokugawa
    Tadateru. His consorts, 40-41,
    69, 83, 136, 143; his education,
    29-30; his scholarly interests, 11,
    13, 68-69, 84, 97-98, 120-125,
    183, 185-188; his leisure inter-
    ests, 97-98; see also No
Ieyasu's life: youth (1543-1560),
    23-32; rise to power (1560-
    1589), 32-39, 40-51, 54; rise to
    power (1590-1599), 54-56,
    64-70; in 1599, 8, 10-13; in
    January-June, 1600, 3, 8, 10-13,
    20-23, 31, 32, 39, 40, 42, 51,
    52; in June-September, 1600,
    56-60, 61, 64, 70; at Sekigahara,
    71-78; after the battle, 79-82;
    becomes shogun, 86-88, 93; as
    retired shogun, 93-94, 97; in
    retirement, 91-92, 98-100, 129,
    184, 185; dies, 108, 187-188
Ieyasu's politics: general categories:
    civil policies before 1600, 11, 34,
    42, 47, 50-51, 72; civil policies
    after 1600, 82-84, 115, 117, 123,
    144-145, 172, 179-181; eco-
    nomic policies, 50, 66, 94,
    103-108, 112-113, 118-119,
    133-134; foreign policy, see
    Foreign Relations; military
    policy, see Battles
Ieyasu's politics: particular topics:
    and Hideyoshi, 6-8, 12, 45-50,
    54-55, 64-69; and Hideyori, 3,
    12, 13, 130, 151-158, 161,
    165-173, 174-178; and the Court
    before Sekigahara, 11-12, 21,
    35-37, 62; and the Court after

Sekigahara, 80, 82-83; and the
    shogun title, 86-88, 91, 92; and
    the Court when retired, 100,
    109-112, 115-116, 124, 130,
    152; and the Court in his final
    years, 143-145, 161-162, 167,
    172-173, 180-181, 184, 187-188;
    and Buddhism, 25, 30, 31, 33-34,
    130, 146-150, 179-181, 183,
    186; and Europeans, 14, 19, 85,
    103-105, 130, 133-135, 137-140,
    170; and Christianity, 132-140,
    151, 157
Ii Naomasa, 67, 68, 71, 75, 79, 81,
    118
Ikeda Terumasa, 32, 58, 59, 70, 72,
    115, 165
Ikkō, 17, 33-34, 38, 52, 136
Imagawa family, 32-36
Imagawa Yoshimoto, 25-31
Imperial Institution, 61-64, 112,
    181. See also Emperors; Ieyasu's
    politics
Ishida Mitsunari, 6, 8, 10-12, 20,
    31, 40, 58, 71-79
Ishikawa Kazumasa, 28, 29, 32-34,
    37, 46, 47-48
Ishin Sūden, 137-140, 144-145,
    148, 155-157, 170, 173, 174,
    180, 185-188
Japanese names, i, 23, 62, 162
Japanese calendar, i-ii, 23, 25,
    162-163, 179
Jōgan seiyō, 13, 69, 88, 145, 188
Kabuki, 116-117
Kanshitsu Genkitsu, 13, 84, 120,
    122, 123, 137
Katagiri Katsumoto, 155, 157, 158
Katō Kiyomasa, 4, 153-154, 165
Keyōin, 29
Kobayakawa Hideaki, 75-77, 79
Kōdaiin, 55-56, 112, 152, 153
Konishi Yukinaga, 4, 6, 75-77, 79
Korea: Hideyoshi and, 3-7, 68;
    Ieyasu and, 68, 94-95
Lady Tsukiyama, 32, 37, 40, 41
Lady Yodo, 55-56, 65, 124,
    152-154, 157-158, 172, 175,
    177
Maeda Toshiie, 8, 10, 11
Maeda Toshinaga, 11, 21, 59, 74,

83, 153, 165
Matsudaira Hirotada, 25-27, 29
Matsudaira Kiyoyasu, 25, 26, 28, 29
Minamoto Yoritomo, 63, 80, 93,
115
Mining, 105-108
Minting, 107
Missionaries, *see* Ieyasu's politics;
Portuguese; Spaniards
Mizuno family, 25-27, 29, 32
Mogami lord, 21, 50, 57-59, 83
Mōri Terumoto, 71-72, 74, 80-82,
105
Natsuka Masaie, 6, 21, 23, 58,
75-77, 79
Nō, 13, 68, 83, 88, 98, 116, 117,
154, 180
Oda Nobuhide, 25, 26
Oda Nobunaga, 17, 30-33, 35-38,
41, 44, 45, 64, 107, 164
Odai no Kata (Dentsuin), 25-27,
29-31, 85-86
Okinawa, 95, 97, 101
Ōkubo Nagayasu, 105-107, 118-119,
131-132, 136
Ōkubo Tadachika, 37, 66-67, 81,
106, 130-133, 139, 140, 151
Portuguese: trade, 16, 44, 134-135,
138; missionaries, 7, 16-18, 137,
157
Religion, *see* Buddhism; Confucian-
ism; Ieyasu's politics; Portuguese;
Shinto; Spaniards
Rongo, 183
Ronin, 157, 169, 171-172, 175-177,
179, 180
Ryukyus, *see* Okinawa
Saishō Shōda, 13, 84, 120, 122-123,
137
Sakakibara Yasumasa, 36, 44, 49,
54, 57, 66, 68, 81, 118
Satake lord, 21, 58, 59, 86
Senhime, 152, 175, 177, 184-185
Shimazu lord, 74, 77, 80, 81, 83,
86, 95, 97
Shintō, 137, 181, 188, 189

Shogun, 63-64, 87-88, 91, 93
Shoku Nihongi, 145
Southeast Asia, 101-103, 129, 183
Spaniards: trade, 18, 133-135, 137;
missionaries, 18, 85, 133-134,
137
Statler, Oliver, 119
Suminokura Ryōi, 98, 112, 119
Sumpuki, 188
Taigen Sūfu, 29, 31, 88
Taikō, *see* Hideyoshi
Takeda Shingen, 35-39, 42, 44, 54
Tokugawa Hidetada: character of,
34, 99-100; before Sekigahara, 8,
21, 41, 42, 57, 59, 68, 69; at
Sekigahara, 60, 73, 74, 78,
80-81, 83; as shogun, 91-92,
98-99, 115, 121, 124-125, 143;
and Ieyasu's last years, 139,
167-171, 174-177, 180, 183,
187-189
Tokugawa (Yūki) Hideyasu, 40, 41,
65, 84, 99, 141-142
Tokugawa Iemitsu, 124-125, 175,
184
Tokugawa Ieyasu, *see* Ieyasu
Tokugawa Nobuyasu, 32, 33, 37,
41-42, 69, 77, 141
Tokugawa Tadateru, 69, 133,
141-142, 153, 182-183
Torii Mototada, 21, 28-31, 44, 56,
58, 67, 72, 118
Torii Tadayoshi, 30, 31, 34
Toyotomi Hidetsugu, 6, 65, 68
Toyotomi Hideyori, 3, 6-8, 11, 13,
72, 81, 91, 112, 140, 151-158,
166-173, 175-177, 179, 181
Toyotomi Hideyoshi, *see* Hideyoshi
Transportation, 112-113, 118-119,
184
Uesugi Kagekatsu, 12, 20, 21, 35,
40, 42, 52, 57-59, 74, 77, 83,
84, 105
Uesugi Kenshin, 35, 37, 38
Ukita Hideie, 75-77, 80
Will Adams, *see* Adams, Will